CORRECTNESS
AND EFFECTIVENESS
OF EXPRESSION

COWLES/REGNERY GED PROGRAM

CORRECTNESS AND EFFECTIVENESS OF EXPRESSION

Preparation for the High School Equivalency Examination

REVISED AND ENLARGED EDITION

by John A. Beyrer, M.A.

GED Instructor in English, Bryant Evening High School, New York City
Department of English, Lynbrook High School, Lynbrook, N. Y.

COWLES BOOK COMPANY, INC.
A Subsidiary of Henry Regnery Company

Some of the material in this edition was written by Donald S. Sale and Priscilla S. Johnson and appeared in previous editions.

SBN 402-26160-7
Library of Congress Catalog Card Number 70-106212

Cowles Book Company, Inc.
A subsidiary of Henry Regnery Company
114 W. Illinois St., Chicago, Ill. 60610

Published simultaneously in Canada by
General Publishing Company, Ltd.
30 Lesmill Road
Don Mills, Toronto, Ontario

Manufactured in the United States of America

Revised Edition

PREFACE

Correctness and Effectiveness of Expression has one purpose: to help you pass the "Correctness and Effectiveness of Expression" section of the General Educational Development (GED) Test, commonly called the High School Equivalency Examination.

This book is not just another question-and-answer book. It has been written with one examination in mind: the "Correctness and Effectiveness of Expression" section of the GED Test. It is a carefully structured combination of instructional material and drill in grammar and usage, spelling, punctuation, and other essential topics in English. Everything in this volume reflects the latest developments in the GED English examination. Instructional material and questions are designed to teach you the special skills necessary for understanding the difference between correct and incorrect English usage. All practice exercises contain the same kinds of questions that appear on the actual GED "Correctness and Effectiveness of Expression" test. A special feature is the complete two-hour Simulated English Usage Examination, a test which closely follows the content, form, and level of difficulty of the official test.

The author of *Correctness and Effectiveness of Expression* is an expert in both his subject and the GED Test. He has kept in mind at all times the special needs of GED students in order to help you to acquire the knowledge and skills you need for passing the GED "Correctness and Effectiveness of Expression" test. Supplementing the author's own knowledge of the High School Equivalency Examination are the numerous critical evaluations and suggestions which have been gathered by Cowles from the best-qualified GED authorities in the country and from classroom teachers and students.

In order for you to be equally well prepared for the other four sections of the High School Equivalency Examination, you will want to study the other books in the Cowles GED Program. Each reflects the latest developments in the official GED Examination and provides thorough, in-depth instruction in each specific subject area of the test:

Interpretation of Literary Materials. This specialized text provides a carefully planned program of instruction and practice covering the interpretation of prose, poetry, and drama. It also includes synopses of difficult reading selections, a glossary of literary terms, vocabulary study, and a two-hour Simulated GED Literature Examination.

Interpretation of Reading Materials in the Social Studies. This volume presents a structured combination of instruction and drill in United States and world history, economics, and other important social studies areas. Included are glossaries, highlights of United States Presidential administrations, a special section on interpreting maps and graphs, and a two-hour Simulated GED Social Studies Examination.

Interpretation of Reading Materials in the Natural Sciences. This book contains a carefully prepared series of reading exercises in biology, chemistry, physics, and earth science. It also includes a glossary of important scientific terms and a two-hour Simulated Science Examination.

General Mathematical Ability. This specialized text provides you with comprehensive instruction and numerous practice exercises in many areas of mathematics, including fractions, algebra, geometry, and modern mathematics. It also includes a two-hour Simulated GED Mathematics Examination.

You may wish to supplement your study with an additional volume that treats all five subject areas of the test with new and different material. Although it does not contain the more detailed coverage and explanations included in the five individual books described above, it will be especially useful for extra practice.

Preparation for the High School Equivalency Examination. This volume reflects the latest developments in the GED Test and provides instruction and drill in all five subject areas of the examination: English Usage, Social Studies, Science, Literature, and Mathematics. It contains a full ten-hour Simulated GED Test.

Many special features make each volume a unique study tool for the examination. Each of the books contains a Diagnostic Test designed to pinpoint those areas in which you need further study. In addition, each volume contains instructional material and practice exercises, with explanatory answers, prepared to meet your specific needs and educational level. Another feature is the hundreds of examples and exercises which give you the practice that is essential for doing well on the examination. And finally, each book, as described above, concludes with the unique Cowles "Simulated GED Test." This test—patterned as closely as possible on the official examination or the section of it covered in that book—is designed to give you additional review and a "feel" for the real thing. It is a tool that can be of major assistance to you in raising your score on the official examination.

For information on where to take the GED Test, check with your local high school or your county or state department of education. A complete listing of state policies and addresses is included in the Appendix of *Preparation for the High School Equivalency Examination (GED)*.

The Editors

CONTENTS

INTRODUCTION

The main purpose of this book is to help you pass the "Correctness and Effectiveness of Expression" section of the High School Equivalency Examination (the GED Test). It provides you with intensive instruction and drill in grammar, spelling, and all the other topics covered on the official test. There is nothing irrelevant in this book—both the instructional material and the exercises have been specially prepared to meet your specific needs as a GED candidate. Study it thoroughly. The results will be evident on examination day. However, before you begin, let us look at the examination you will be taking.

THE TEST YOU WILL TAKE

Correctness and Effectiveness of Expression is one of the five tests comprising the High School Equivalency Examination. It is designed to measure your ability to recognize *errors* in the following areas: grammatical usage, sentence structure, spelling, diction, punctuation, capitalization, and pronunciation. As you can see, these are topics normally covered in high school English courses.

Although there are several different forms of the official test presently in use, they all share certain important features. It is in a booklet about the size of the page you are now reading, and it is distributed to the candidate by the examiner. The five tests of the High School Equivalency Examination are not given in any particular sequence; hence, you may take the Correctness examination at any time during the testing period. The test can usually be completed in two hours. You may request a reasonable amount of additional time from the examiner, but it is not always practical for him to grant it.

The official Correctness and Effectiveness of Expression test usually consists of about 120 questions covering all of the topics in English listed above. Furthermore, each topic is clearly labeled and followed by a specific number of questions. For instance, twenty questions may be devoted to spelling and five questions to capitalization.

All the questions on the test are of the multiple-choice type. In other words, you are *not* required to write down your responses. Instead, you indicate your answer by blackening a space in pencil on the answer sheet provided by the examiner. Most of the directions ask you to choose an *error* among four numbered choices. You must then blacken the space under the number of that error on the answer sheet. However, if there are no errors, you must blacken the fifth space. To understand the answering process more clearly, look at the following example:

DIRECTIONS: Each of the following groups consists of four words, one of which may be misspelled. On the answer sheet, blacken the space under the number corresponding to the number of the misspelled word. If no word is misspelled, blacken the fifth space.

1. (1) classified (2) conjunction (3) cansel (4) defy
2. (1) dual (2) authentic (3) mechanism (4) periodic

In the first question above, the third word should be spelled *cancel*. You would therefore blacken the space under number 3 next to question 1 on the answer sheet. Since there are no misspellings in the second question, you would blacken the fifth space next to question 2 on the answer sheet. Below is a reproduction of a portion of an answer sheet, with the appropriate spaces marked.

	1	2	3	4	5			1	2	3	4	5			1	2	3	4	5
1.	‖	‖	■	‖	‖		7.	‖	‖	‖	‖	‖		13.	‖	‖	‖	‖	‖
2.	‖	‖	‖	‖	■		8.	‖	‖	‖	‖	‖		14.	‖	‖	‖	‖	‖
3.	‖	‖	‖	‖	‖		9.	‖	‖	‖	‖	‖		15.	‖	‖	‖	‖	‖
4.	‖	‖	‖	‖	‖		10.	‖	‖	‖	‖	‖		16.	‖	‖	‖	‖	‖
5.	‖	‖	‖	‖	‖		11.	‖	‖	‖	‖	‖		17.	‖	‖	‖	‖	‖
6.	‖	‖	‖	‖	‖		12.	‖	‖	‖	‖	‖		18.	‖	‖	‖	‖	‖

An important note: Answer all questions, even if you have to guess. Some of your guesses are sure to be correct, and you will gain valuable points, which you would lose if you leave any questions unanswered.

WHAT THIS BOOK CAN DO FOR YOU

This book is a valuable tool which can help you do well on the official test. However, like all tools, it must be used properly in order to obtain the best results. If you just skim through the book with a "hit-or-miss" approach, you will probably not do as well as the student who studies it carefully from cover to cover. It is wise, then, to give the book a chance, since it can prove to be a very good friend on examination day.

The book begins with a general Diagnostic Test. This test and the specialized diagnostic tests found at the beginning of most chapters are designed to pinpoint those areas of English in which you need further study. Take all of these tests. They will give you a good idea of where you stand before you begin any further studies.

The second chapter, "Spelling," covers the important spelling rules and those "demons" that give students most trouble. The numerous exercises in this section give you valuable practice in preparing for the test.

The next four chapters deal with grammar and usage. Among the topics treated are the parts of a sentence, fragments and run-on sentences, verb tenses, and agreement of subject with verb. Many examples and exercises serve to strengthen your skills in these subjects.

The chapter on style and clarity deals with unclear and awkward sentences. It will help you to understand why some sentences, although grammatically correct, may not be acceptable as good English.

The chapter "Choosing the Right Word" provides you with a guide to over fifty sets of words that often cause confusion. These words, which include *lie-lay* and *principal-principle*, frequently appear on the official test.

The chapter on punctuation covers the chief uses of the period, comma, semicolon, and the other marks used to set off words and phrases. The explanations and examples serve to clarify any points that may be confusing.

The chapter on capitalization contains all the rules you need to know for the test about using and not using capital letters. Again, a number of practice exercises are provided to reinforce the skills learned.

The chapter on pronunciation introduces you to the method of phonetic spelling (spelling words the way they sound) used on the actual test. The numerous examples and exercises serve to sharpen your skill in spotting faulty pronunciation.

Correct answers and explanations for all exercises within a chapter appear at the end of the chapter. This has been done to help you avoid the temptation to "peek" at answers before you have finished a problem —a practice which diminishes learning and self-reliance.

At the end of the book is a simulated version of the "Correctness and Effectiveness of Expression" section of the GED Test. This unique test reflects the content, format, and level of difficulty of the official examination. Take it after you have completed studying all the material in the book. Allow yourself about two hours (the approximate time limit of the actual test) to complete it; then check your answers. If you have not done well, review those areas which gave you the most trouble. If your score was high, you can expect similar results on examination day.

TEST-TAKING TIPS
FOR ENGLISH USAGE

DO read directions carefully. Check to see that you are following the correct procedure for each part of the test.

DO note that each question in the test contains either *one error* or *no errors.* Two marks on the answer sheet will make your entire answer wrong.

DO be conscious that you must always choose the BEST answer to a given question. Very often students try to think of other correct ways to express the same thought in a sentence. Just limit yourself to the choices given for that particular question.

DO judge the sentence as a whole before you decide on your answer. Some students rely on a specific word or phrase to determine their answer. You must consider the whole sentence.

DO check your answers before you place a mark on the answer sheet. Make sure that you match the correct answer with the correct question.

DO answer the easier questions first and come back to the more difficult ones if you have time.

DON'T skip the directions given throughout the test. Changes in directions will affect your answering procedure.

DON'T rush carelessly through the test. If you finish early, you may go back and recheck your answers and fill in any spaces that you left empty.

DON'T try to "find" errors in a sentence when they aren't there. Follow the directions in choosing the kind of error called for.

DON'T read answers into the questions. Select the BEST answer from the choices presented in the test, even if you can think of a better way to express the same thought.

DON'T mark the spaces on the answer sheet in any pattern form. Each question is independent of the questions before and after it. Read each question carefully and answer it according to the directions. You won't outsmart the tester by making a pattern of your answers. The only pattern you will find will be incorrect answers.

DON'T forget to answer *every* question on the examination. On the High School Equivalency Examination **blank answer spaces are marked wrong. Guess rather than leave an answer blank.**

THE DIAGNOSTIC TEST

The test which follows is a diagnostic test—a test that pinpoints your specific strengths and weaknesses in your knowledge and usage of English. When you take this test, you will be able to see which areas of the subject you should stress in your preparation for the High School Equivalency Examination.

This diagnostic test is approximately half as long as the "Correctness and Effectiveness of Expression" section of the official High School Equivalency Examination. However, the form of the questions, the topics tested, the proportion allotted for each topic, and the level of difficulty of the questions are similar to the official test.

Read the directions to the diagnostic test carefully before you start. Give yourself about one hour to do the test. (Experience indicates that about two hours is adequate time to complete the official test, although additional time may be permitted.) Since there are 60 questions on this diagnostic test, you should allow yourself about one minute for each question. *An important note:* On this test, as on the official examination, blank answers are marked wrong. Guess rather than leave an answer blank.

DIRECTIONS: (1–45) Each of the following sentences has four underlined sections. Choose the number of the section that is incorrect. Then blacken the space under that number in the answer column. If there are no incorrect sections, blacken the fifth space.

ANSWERS AND EXPLANATIONS APPEAR AT THE END OF THE TEST

Sentence Structure

1. There were three items to be discussed, we only dealt with two of them.
   $\quad\quad$ 1 $\qquad\qquad\qquad$ 2 $\quad$ 3 $\quad$ 4

   1. 1 2 3 4 5

2. At the end of our street stands an old house. Its windows broken and badly
   $\quad\quad\quad\quad$ 1 $\qquad\qquad\qquad\qquad$ 2 $\quad\quad$ 3 $\quad$ 4
   in need of a paint job.

   2. 1 2 3 4 5

3. The choice was difficult to make, there were red, yellow, and blue.
   $\quad\quad\quad$ 1 $\quad\quad\quad$ 2 $\quad$ 3 $\qquad$ 4

   3. 1 2 3 4 5

4. Each student was asked to write down his favorite program. As far as
   $\quad\quad\quad\quad$ 1 $\qquad\qquad\qquad\qquad$ 2 $\qquad$ 3
   television shows were concerned.
   $\quad\quad\quad\quad\quad$ 4

   4. 1 2 3 4 5

5. We were confident as we left. Although the weather had been threatening.
   $\quad\quad\quad\quad\quad\quad$ 1 $\qquad\quad$ 2 $\quad$ 3 $\quad$ 4

   5. 1 2 3 4 5

6. 1 2 3 4 5

6. After we <u>had gone</u> to the <u>museum. There</u> were still several points of interest
            1   2   3

<u>remaining</u>.
  4

7. 1 2 3 4 5

7. My brother John and his friend Roger <u>had planned</u> on a picnic, <u>however</u>,
                                             1   2

<u>their</u> hopes <u>were washed</u> away by a sudden shower.
  3   4

Style and Clarity

8. 1 2 3 4 5

8. The <u>diamond</u> salesman attempted to make <u>us</u> boys believe <u>they</u> were all <u>real</u>.
       1   2   3   4

9. 1 2 3 4 5

9. The <u>committee</u> studied all <u>aspects</u> of the <u>problem</u>—humane, political,
        1   2   3

and <u>cost</u>.
   4

10. 1 2 3 4 5

10. At one time he <u>tried</u> pitching, but later <u>turning</u> to <u>playing</u> the <u>outfield</u>.
             1   2   3   4

11. 1 2 3 4 5

11. When we boarded the bus for <u>Mississippi</u>, we <u>learned</u> <u>that</u> <u>it</u> would take
                           1   2   3 4

fifteen hours.

12. 1 2 3 4 5

12. He <u>had</u> finally <u>chosen</u> his college <u>and on</u> a <u>career</u>.
    1   2   3   4

Grammar and Usage

13. 1 2 3 4 5

13. Each of the boys <u>wanted</u> <u>to do</u> <u>their</u> best <u>to win</u> the big game.
                1   2   3   4

14. 1 2 3 4 5

14. Either Tom or one of the boys who <u>help</u> him <u>are</u> <u>certainly</u> capable <u>of</u> doing
                                     1   2   3   4

this job.

15. 1 2 3 4 5

15. <u>Was</u> it Ralph <u>to whom</u> you <u>spoke</u> when the phone <u>rang</u> last night?
   1   2   3   4

16. 1 2 3 4 5

16. If you <u>would have</u> tried a <u>bit</u> more, you <u>would have</u> done <u>better</u>.
          1   2   3   4

17. 1 2 3 4 5

17. <u>Her</u> and <u>I</u> have always been good <u>friends</u>, and we <u>intend</u> to keep it that way.
   1   2   3   4

18. 1 2 3 4 5

18. It looked to us <u>as if</u> Harry could complete the job <u>soonest</u> <u>than</u> Fred.
      1   2   3   4

19. 1 2 3 4 5

19. Tom, Mary, and Sue, <u>have</u> <u>already</u> <u>been</u> <u>there</u> before you came.
                     1   2   3   4

20. This movie is really worse than the one I seen last night.
             1   2   3 4

    20. 1 2 3 4 5

21. Ten dollars are really a great deal to pay for one of these contraptions.
                 1 2   3   4

    21. 1 2 3 4 5

22. Many a person have tried to find the secret treasure and all have failed.
                   1 2   3 4

    22. 1 2 3 4 5

23. We had known them for many years before we found out who their previous
            1   2   3   4
employers had been.

    23. 1 2 3 4 5

Word Choice

24. They're sure to be here any minute now.
    1   2   3   4

    24. 1 2 3 4 5

25. Are you familiar with the principal affects of this new medicine?
             1   2   3   4

    25. 1 2 3 4 5

26. He had heard that it would be alright if we were to come along too.
          1   2 3   4

    26. 1 2 3 4 5

27. If the principal doesn't hurry he's liable to be late.
       1   2   3 4

    27. 1 2 3 4 5

28. It's altogether two late to invite him here now.
  1   2   3   4

    28. 1 2 3 4 5

29. When the teacher gave the signal, the class knew that it was time for them
          1   2 3
to precede to the auditorium.
    4

    29. 1 2 3 4 5

Capitalization

30. Who was it who said, "give me liberty or give me death"?
                 1   2   3   4

    30. 1 2 3 4 5

31. Next term, I'll be taking American history, science, and math.
                   1   2   3   4

    31. 1 2 3 4 5

32. People in the East were reluctant to vote for a man from the south.
       1 2   3 4

    32. 1 2 3 4 5

33. The President of the United States has called for greater cooperation among
       1   2   3
Governments everywhere.
    4

    33. 1 2 3 4 5

34. Is Africa really the largest continent in the World?
  1 2   3   4

    34. 1 2 3 4 5

Punctuation

35. $\overset{1\;2\;3\;4\;5}{||\;||\;||\;||\;||}$ 35. It was almost $\underset{1}{4;30}$ $\underset{2}{\text{P.M.}}$ when $\underset{3}{\text{Tom and}}$ his brother $\underset{4}{\text{arrived}}$.

36. $\overset{1\;2\;3\;4\;5}{||\;||\;||\;||\;||}$ 36. When the whistle finally $\underset{1}{\text{blew, at}}$ the end of the $\underset{2}{\text{shift,}}$ all the $\underset{3}{\text{men began}}$ to

pack up their $\underset{4}{\text{hammers and saws}}$.

37. $\overset{1\;2\;3\;4\;5}{||\;||\;||\;||\;||}$ 37. Of course if you would like to $\underset{1}{\text{go, I'm}}$ sure we can work $\underset{2}{\text{something}}$ $\underset{3}{\text{out; as a}}$

matter of $\underset{4}{\text{fact, I'd}}$ be happy to try.

38. $\overset{1\;2\;3\;4\;5}{||\;||\;||\;||\;||}$ 38. I should like to order the $\underset{1}{\text{following; three books,}}$ $\underset{2}{\text{two pencils,}}$ $\underset{3}{\text{a ruler,}}$ $\underset{4}{\text{and a}}$

schoolbag.

39. $\overset{1\;2\;3\;4\;5}{||\;||\;||\;||\;||}$ 39. "When $\underset{1}{\text{you're finished}},$" $\underset{2}{\text{said}}$ the teacher, $\underset{3}{\text{"come}}$ up to the desk and hand in

your $\underset{4}{\text{work}}$."

40. $\overset{1\;2\;3\;4\;5}{||\;||\;||\;||\;||}$ 40. We have read the following short stories: $\underset{1}{\text{"Wash,"}}$ "The Tell-Tale $\underset{2}{\text{Heart,"}}$

and $\underset{3}{\text{"Over}}$ the River and Through the $\underset{4}{\text{Woods"}}$.

41. $\overset{1\;2\;3\;4\;5}{||\;||\;||\;||\;||}$ 41. "The $\underset{1}{\text{man, who}}$ told you $\underset{2}{\text{that must}}$ have been $\underset{3}{\text{mistaken,"}}$ said $\underset{4}{\text{Joe}}$.

42. $\overset{1\;2\;3\;4\;5}{||\;||\;||\;||\;||}$ 42. *Moby Dick* is one of the great American $\underset{1}{\text{novels a}}$ $\underset{2}{\text{book that}}$ will $\underset{3}{\text{be around}}$

for a $\underset{4}{\text{long, long}}$ time.

43. $\overset{1\;2\;3\;4\;5}{||\;||\;||\;||\;||}$ 43. $\underset{1}{\text{John, and}}$ his brother have visited $\underset{2}{\text{Paris,}}$ $\underset{3}{\text{Rome,}}$ and $\underset{4}{\text{Madrid}}$.

44. $\overset{1\;2\;3\;4\;5}{||\;||\;||\;||\;||}$ 44. I was $\underset{1}{\text{sure that}}$ $\underset{2}{\text{the}}$ boys were $\underset{3}{\text{coming; and}}$ that they would soon join in the

$\underset{4}{\text{dancing and}}$ singing.

45. $\overset{1\;2\;3\;4\;5}{||\;||\;||\;||\;||}$ 45. My mother $\underset{1}{\text{asked, "whether}}$ I wanted to $\underset{2}{\text{come along}}$ with $\underset{3}{\text{Dad}}$ and the rest

of the $\underset{4}{\text{family}}$.

Spelling

DIRECTIONS: (46–55) In each of the following groups of words there may be one misspelled word. In the answer column, blacken the space under the number that corresponds to the number of the misspelled word. If there are no misspellings, blacken the fifth space.

46. Atheletics is one of the most important parts of our educational program.
    1   2   3   4

    46. 1 2 3 4 5

47. During our brief sojourn through Paris, we found time to tour the
             1   2   3

    concervatory.
    4

    47. 1 2 3 4 5

48. I cannot say with certainty that three hours will be an adaquate amount of
      1   2   3   4

    time.

    48. 1 2 3 4 5

49. On the Fourth of July, we celebrate America's independance.
           1   2   3   4

    49. 1 2 3 4 5

50. It's a shame there aren't more college courses in psycology.
    1   2   3   4

    50. 1 2 3 4 5

51. An ocassional drink may be good for you, but, like all things, it should be
       1   2

    taken in moderation.
    3   4

    51. 1 2 3 4 5

52. Before we proceed, does anyone in the audience have a question to ask the
             1   2   3

    moderator?
    4

    52. 1 2 3 4 5

53. The principal spoke to the seniors about their responsibilities and then ex-
                                                  1

    tended his congradulations on their imminent graduation.
               2   3   4

    53. 1 2 3 4 5

54. The lawyer was constantly checking the secretary's work for misspellings.
        1   2   3   4

    54. 1 2 3 4 5

55. Freedom of speech and freedom of the press are two of the most importent
                                                                     1

    values of our contemporary society.
    2   3   4

    55. 1 2 3 4 5

Pronunciation

DIRECTIONS: (56–60) Each of the following groups consists of four words. Each word appears as it is normally spelled, followed by a phonetic spelling of the word (spelled as it is pronounced). In the answer column, blacken the space under the number corresponding to the number of the word that is pronounced (phonetically spelled) incorrectly. If all the words in a group are pronounced correctly, blacken the fifth space.

56. (1) quiet—KWI-et   (3) combustible—com-BUS-ti-bl
    (2) athlete—ATH-e-leet (4) diction—DIK-shun

    56. 1 2 3 4 5

57. (1) theater—the-A-ter   (3) dictate—DIK-tat
    (2) structure—STRUK-sher (4) quicken—KWIK-en

    57. 1 2 3 4 5

58. 1 2 3 4 5

59. 1 2 3 4 5

60. 1 2 3 4 5

58. (1) going—go-ING
(2) apologize—a-POL-o-jiz

(3) completely—com-PLEET-lee
(4) hesitate—HEZ-i-tat

59. (1) February—FEB-u-a-ree
(2) wandering—WAN-der-ing

(3) friendly—FREND-lee
(4) reform—re-FORM

60. (1) permit—per-MIT
(2) perspiration—
PER-spi-RA-shun

(3) surrender—sur-REND-er
(4) gentle—JENT-l

ANSWERS AND EXPLANATIONS: THE DIAGNOSTIC TEST

The explanation for an answer follows the asterisk (*). In each case, you are given either a brief explanation of the rule or a reference to the appropriate section and CHAPTER of this book.

SENTENCE STRUCTURE

1. **(2)** Use period (and change *we* to *We*) or semicolon.   *Two independent clauses should be connected by a period or semicolon.

2. **(2)** Change period to comma and *Its* to *its*.   *The second sentence is a fragment and must be made part of the first sentence, which expresses a complete thought.

3. **(2)** Change comma to a period or semicolon.   *Two independent clauses must be connected by a period or semicolon.

4. **(2)** Omit period and change *As* to *as*.   *The second sentence is a fragment and must be made part of the first sentence, which expresses a complete thought.

5. **(1)** Omit period and change *Although* to *although*.   *The second sentence is a dependent clause and must be connected to the first sentence, which is an independent clause.

6. **(2)** Change period to comma and *There* to *there*.   *The first sentence—a dependent clause—must be connected to the second sentence, which is an independent clause.

7. **(2)** , *however* should be ; *however,* or . *However,* *Two independent clauses must be connected by a semicolon or a period.

STYLE AND CLARITY

8. **(3)** Change the vague word *they* to the more specific word *diamonds*. *See "Unclear Reference" in STYLE AND CLARITY.

9. **(4)** Change *cost* to *financial* to make the construction parellel.   *See "Lack of Parallel Construction" in COMMON ERRORS IN SENTENCE STRUCTURE.

10. (2) Change *turning* to *turned* to keep the tense consistent.   *See "Sentence Shifts" in STYLE AND CLARITY.

11. (4) Change the vague word *it* to the more specific words *trip* or *ride*.   *See "Unclear Reference" in STYLE AND CLARITY.

12. (3) Omit *on* to make the construction parallel.   *See "Lack of Parallel Construction" in COMMON ERRORS IN SENTENCE STRUCTURE.

GRAMMAR AND USAGE

13. (3) Change *their* to *his*.   *A pronoun (*their*) must agree in number with its antecedent (*Each*). Since *Each* is singular, *their* (plural) must be made singular (*his*).

14. (2) Change *are* to *is*.   *See Rule 5 under "Agreement of Subject and Verb" in USAGE.

15. (5)

16. (1) Change *would have* to *had*.   *Use the past perfect tense (*had*) when referring to the first of two actions completed in the past.

17. (1) Change *Her* to *She*.   *See "Pronoun Usage" in USAGE.

18. (3) Change *soonest* to *sooner*.   *See Rule 3 under "Modification" in USAGE.

19. (1) Change *have* to *had*.   *Use the past perfect tense (*had*) when referring to the first of two actions completed in the past.

20. (3) Change *seen* to *saw*.   *See "Tenses of Verbs" in USAGE.

21. (1) Change *are* to *is*.   *See Rule 8 under "Agreement of Subject and Verb" in USAGE.

22. (1) Change *have* to *has*.   *The verb must agree in number with its subject (*person*). Since *person* is singular, *have* (plural) must be made singular (*has*).

23. (5)

WORD CHOICE

24. (5)

25. (3) Change *affects* to *effects*.   *See list in CHOOSING THE RIGHT WORD.

26. (2) Change *alright* to *all right*.   *See list in CHOOSING THE RIGHT WORD.

27. (4) Change *liable* to *likely*.   *See list in CHOOSING THE RIGHT WORD.

28. (3) Change *two* to *too*.   *See list in CHOOSING THE RIGHT WORD.

29. (4) Change *precede* to *proceed*.   *See list in CHOOSING THE RIGHT WORD.

CAPITALIZATION

30. (**1**) Give.   *See Rule 1 in CAPITALIZATION.

31. (**5**)

32. (**4**) South.   *See Rule 6 in CAPITALIZATION.

33. (**4**) governments.   *See Rule 2 in CAPITALIZATION.

34. (**4**) world.   *See Rule 2 in CAPITALIZATION.

PUNCTUATION

35. (**1**) 4:30.   *Use a colon between the hour and minutes when writing the time.

36. (**1**) Omit comma.   *There is neither a pause nor a break between clauses, both of which would require using a comma.

37. (**1**) Add comma after *Of course*.   *Use comma after introductory phrase.

38. (**1**) Use a colon (:) instead.   *See Rule 14 in PUNCTUATION.

39. (**5**)

40. (**4**) Period should be placed before closing quotation marks.   *See Rule 20 in PUNCTUATION.

41. (**1**) Omit comma. *Do not use a comma to set off a word or phrase that is necessary to make the meaning clear.

42. (**1**) Add a comma.   *Use a comma to set off a word (*novels*) from a phrase that explains the word (*a book that will be around for a long, long time*).

43. (**1**) Omit comma.   *No comma needed in a compound subject.

44. (**3**) Omit semicolon.   *See Rule 7 in PUNCTUATION.

45. (**1**) Omit comma and quotation marks.   *The correct way of using quotation marks in setting off the exact words of a speaker is explained in Rule 20 in PUNCTUATION.

SPELLING

46. (**1**) *Atheletics* should be *Athletics*

47. (**4**) *concervatory* should be *conservatory*

48. (**4**) *adaquate* should be *adequate*

49. (**4**) *independance* should be *independence*

50. (**4**) *psycology* should be *psychology*

51. (**1**) *ocassional* should be *occasional*

52. (**4**) *modorator* should be *moderator*

53. (2) *congradulations* should be *congratulations*

54. (5)

55. (1) *importent* should be *important*

PRONUNCIATION

56. (2) *ATH-leet*
57. (1) *THEE-ter*
58. (1) *GO-ing*

59. (1) *FEB-roo-a-ree*
60. (5)

Now that you have checked your answers, you should have some idea of where you stand and what areas need your greatest concentration in preparing for the official test. If there are items on this diagnostic test that are unclear, read the corresponding section of this book carefully.

NOW TURN THE PAGE FOR INSTRUCTIONS ON MARKING YOUR SELF-EVALUATION PROFILE.

SELF-EVALUATION PROFILE

1. In the chart below, enter the scores you achieved on the diagnostic test. Note that you are to indicate the number of right answers in each section ("Sentence Structure," "Style and Clarity," etc.), as well as the total score.

2. Compare your scores with the number in the QUESTION TOTAL column. This will give you an indication of which areas you should study the most.

It is impossible to predict with statistical accuracy how well you would do on an actual High School Equivalency Examination. For one thing, you will be given one of several current forms of the test, some of which will seem harder to one person than to another. Therefore, consider the Self-Evaluation Profile as a guide, not a guarantee. And remember, if you study the material in this book, your score is bound to improve.

SECTION	Question Total	Your Score
1. Sentence Structure	7	
2. Style and Clarity	5	
3. Grammar and Usage	11	
4. Word Choice	6	
5. Capitalization	5	
6. Punctuation	11	
7. Spelling	10	
8. Pronunciation	5	
TOTAL	60	

SPELLING

On the official test, you will be given several groups of words and be asked to select the misspelled word in each group. A typical question might look like this:

5. (1) illuminated (2) partial (3) rythm (4) healthy

The correct answer to the question above is (3), since the word should be spelled *rhythm*.

To help prepare you for these questions, we have provided you with the important spelling rules, as well as a list of "spelling demons." Study them carefully. Then take the exercises that follow. The result of your efforts should be a high score on the spelling part of the test.

There are various ways of learning to spell. Some people learn the spelling of a word best by seeing it written; others, by hearing it spelled; still others, by repeatedly writing the word. One or another of these methods may be best for you. Indeed, it may be that all three together would be most effective.

In attacking the lists of commonly misspelled words that begin a few pages ahead, you should take one group of 25 at a time, deciding which ones you do not know how to spell.

Have a dictionary at hand. If you are not sure how a word is sounded, use the dictionary. Each dictionary has its own sound symbols, which you will find explained in the front and at the bottom of certain pages. In learning to spell a word, pronounce it precisely. Sometimes this will be enough to make you remember the differences between words that sound somewhat alike and therefore may cause confusion in spelling. For example, pronounce *accept* and *except*. If you say them correctly, you can hear the difference and so spell them correctly.

SPELLING DIAGNOSTIC TEST

DIRECTIONS: In each of the following groups of words, there may be one misspelled word. In the answer column, blacken the space under the number that corresponds to the number of the misspelled word. If there are no misspellings, blacken the fifth space.

ANSWERS APPEAR AT THE END OF THE TEST

1. (1) inadaquate (2) indebtedness (3) interests (4) intelligent

2. (1) illuminate (2) inganuity (3) logical (4) jurisdiction

3. (1) mercury (2) magnificent (3) manetain (4) merely

	1	2	3	4	5
1.	‖	‖	‖	‖	‖
2.	‖	‖	‖	‖	‖
3.	‖	‖	‖	‖	‖

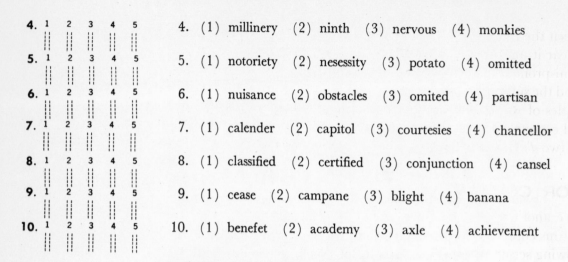

4. (1) millinery   (2) ninth   (3) nervous   (4) monkies

5. (1) notoriety   (2) nesessity   (3) potato   (4) omitted

6. (1) nuisance   (2) obstacles   (3) omited   (4) partisan

7. (1) calender   (2) capitol   (3) courtesies   (4) chancellor

8. (1) classified   (2) certified   (3) conjunction   (4) cansel

9. (1) cease   (2) campane   (3) blight   (4) banana

10. (1) benefet   (2) academy   (3) axle   (4) achievement

ANSWERS: DIAGNOSTIC TEST

1. (1) inadequate
2. (2) ingenuity
3. (3) maintain
4. (4) monkeys

5. (2) necessity
6. (3) omitted
7. (1) calendar

8. (4) counsel or cancel
9. (2) campaign
10. (1) benefit

SPELLING HINTS AND RULES

Following are some hints and rules that will help you in learning to spell the words with which you have trouble.

FIND THE ERROR

Look at a word you often spell wrong. Which part of it are you spelling wrong? Does one of the spelling rules in the following pages apply? Is the spelling of the word an exception to such a rule? Did you pronounce the word incorrectly? Did you fail to recognize the root word from which the word is formed? Did you add the suffix incorrectly?

SYLLABLES

If the spelling of a word gives you trouble, try breaking the word into syllables. The part of the word that is said the loudest, or stressed, is usually the easiest to spell. The parts of the word that are unstressed, or said the softest, are frequently difficult because the sound of the vowel tends to resemble that of other vowels; for example, the *i* in *beautiful* sounds almost the same as the *e* in *marvelous* and the *eau* in *bureaucrat*. This being so, it is frequently helpful deliberately to misprounce the word you are learning to spell in order to stress the tricky vowel sound. For example, you might normally pronounce *preference* either of two ways: pruhFURence or PREFerence. In either case, it is difficult to hear the *e* between the *f* and the *r*. By dividing the word into syllables, however, you hear it and see it this way: pref er ence. You might even deliberately mispronounce the word so as to emphasize its root, *prefer*, and then add the suffix, *ence*.

Examples of words that are often misspelled because they are *not* pronounced correctly are *government* (*govern*—with an *n*—and *ment*), *candidate* (two *d*'s), *library* (two *r*'s), and *recognize* (with a *g*).

ROOT, OR CORE, WORDS

Is there another word within the word you are trying to learn to spell? Does this core, or root, word change in the spelling of your word? In the following sets of words, the first word is the root word for the two words that follow it:

> accompany, accompanied, accompaniment
> beauty, beautiful, beauteous
> occur, occurred, occurring
> benefit, benefited, beneficial

THE I-E RULE

When the letters *e* and *i* come in succession in a word, *i* usually precedes *e*. The reverse is true, however—*e* precedes *i*—when (1) the combination immediately follows the letter *c* (as in *receive*) or (2) the combination is pronounced like the *ay* in *hay* (as in *neigh*).

Remember the rule: *i* before *e,* except after *c* or when pronounced like *ay* as in *neighbor* and *weigh*.

i before *e:*   belief, achieve, yield, piece, relieve
e before *i:*   deceive, receive, conceive, weigh, eighth

PLURALS

Most words form their plurals by adding *s*. Add *es,* though, when the word ends in *s, z, x, sh,* or *ch* sounded as in *church*. Words ending in *y* preceded by a consonant form their plurals by dropping the *y* and adding *ies*. Letters and numbers form their plurals by adding *s* preceded by an apostrophe.

boy, boys	church, churches
rose, roses	watch, watches
boss, bosses	country, countries
buzz, buzzes	posy, posies
fish, fishes	7, 7's
box, boxes	a, a's

A few words, mostly the names of animals, have the same form in the plural as in the singular. *Deer* is an example. Some words have two plurals with slightly different meaning. In the list above, for example, *fishes* is given as the plural of *fish*. That plural suggests *varieties:* "The aquarium had stingrays and other dangerous fishes." But the normal plural of *fish,* when varieties are not meant, is *fish:* "She caught three fish the first hour out."

Finally, a very few words form their plurals in still different ways: *ox, oxen; child, children; goose, geese.*

WORD ENDINGS (SUFFIXES)

Words derived from words ending in *e* often trip up the speller. In such words, if the new word ending (suffix) begins with a vowel (including *y*), drop the *e* from the original word before adding the ending.

> blame, blaming, blamed, blamable (*blameable* is acceptable)
> case, casing, cased
> propose, proposing, proposed, proposable

If the suffix begins with a consonant (that is, any letter except *a, e, i, o, u,* and, in this case, *y*), the *e* of the original word remains.

> shape, shapely   hate, hateful
> amuse, amusement   meddle, meddlesome

But watch for exceptions such as *noticeable, changeable, ninth, wisdom, mileage,* and *judgment.*

DOUBLING THE FINAL CONSONANT

When (1) a consonant (except *w* or *y*) is the last letter of the word, (2) that consonant is preceded by a single vowel, and (3) the word either has only one syllable or is accented on the last syllable, the final consonant is doubled before adding the ending. It makes no difference here what the first letter of the ending is.

> patrol, patrolled   prefer, preferred
> run, running   equip, equipped

If the last syllable is *not* accented or if the final consonant is *not* preceded by a *single* vowel, the consonant is not doubled before the ending is added.

> develop, developing   differ, differed, difference
> devour (last consonant preceded by two vowels), devoured, devouring

If the accent shifts when a suffix is added, do not double the final consonant.

> prefer, preference   refer, reference

SPELLING LISTS

On the following pages are 575 frequently misspelled words, arranged in groups of 25. After you have studied several of these groups, you will be given a spelling test. When you have completed all of the groups, take the six spelling tests at the end of this section.

Group 1

assigned	alcohol	athletic	abutting	apparently
ambassador	adage	anticipate	assessment	adjournment
awkward	adieu	antique	acknowledge	attendance
achievement	affirmative	academy	abandoned	axle
adequate	appropriation	absurd	acquired	architecture

Group 2

attendants	attach	agitation	all right	annum
adopted	appetite	amendment	accommodate	across
aggregate	attorneys	apricot	allies	amplify
ascertain	acquisition	aisle	article	artificial
accent	assassination	advising	acutely	absence

Group 3

authentic	attempt	agreeable	business	bulletin
agreement	arguing	appreciation	brief	bachelor
advisable	aspirations	barely	border	bacteria
assurance	arrest	bored	burglaries	beaker
arduous	accusation	bigamy	bungalow	breeding

Group 4

bimonthly	consequently	carnage	control	caucus
balance	charitable	crochet	competitors	coronation
benefit	competition	courtesies	conclusively	corset
banana	conservatory	cooperate	cavalry	commenced
blight	clothe	congenial	chancellor	colonel

Group 5

countenance	conquer	chauffeur	continually	contagious
chef	candidacy	campaign	canon	cronies
cafeteria	Christian	condemned	(clergyman)	cancel
consistent	capitol	conjunction	cease	chagrined
calendar	(a building)	certified	correspondent	contemptible
	cannon		classified	

EXERCISE 1

DIRECTIONS: In each of the following sentences, there are four underlined words. In the answer column, blacken the space under the number that corresponds to the number of the misspelled word. If there are no misspelled words, blacken the fifth space.

ANSWERS APPEAR AT THE END OF THE CHAPTER

1. The ambassader condemned the amendment to the proposal he had made for controlling the production of atomic weapons.

2. The cafateria attendants were more than willing to cooperate with the manager in an attempt to improve business.

3. The candidate campaigned continually accross the country.

4. You may think it's all right to try to control the market, but I don't think your competetors will be so agreeable.

5. The colonel told the correspondent that the strength of the calvary division was classified information.

6. Apparently, it was the poor attendance that prompted the early adjournment of the bimonthly meeting.

7. As the atorneys walked down the aisle of the courtroom, they seemed cooperative and congenial.

8. During the commencement ceremony, there was an awkward moment when several atheletes decided to show how bored they were.

9. It is adviseable when buying antiques to seek assurances of their authenticity.

10. The chef and the chauffeur were engaged in an arguement over the newspaper article.

Group 6

ceiling	chisel	crowded	committing	declaration
changeable	cavalier	comparative	cameos	dispatch
cauldron	corral	carriage	disgust	deferred
convenient	(enclosure)	comedian	delinquent	democrat
conscript	certain	congestion	deliberate	discretion
	candle			

Group 7

discipline	dissatisfy	delegate	destruction	duchess
dormitory	dining room	distributor	decision	deodorize
duly	disappear	dizzy	dyeing	distillery
dirigible	development	dissatisfied	(coloring)	digestible
diseases	desirable	dessert	definite	doctor
		(food)	delicious	

Group 8

dual (double)	despair	error	economical	enormous
dissolution	elaborate	exhibition	economy	enlargement
dungarees	efficient	embassies	extravagant	extradite
disapprove	everlasting	existence	equipped	emergency
drastically	enthusiastic	emphasize	excel	endurance

Group 9

forcible	fireman	falsity	finely	frostbitten
filial	foreign	falsify	frightfully	financial
fundamental	fragrance	foliage	furl	flexible
fatal	faculties	freshman	forfeit	finally
forty	fraternally	foggy	foretell	fortissimo

Group 10

guardian	gallery	guitar	hence	handicapped
guaranteed	glimpse	grieve	hysterics	hideous
galvanized	grapevines	hosiery	height	itemized
gout	grease	humorists	holly	ignoramus
guild	grammar	herald	hybrid	ignorant

EXERCISE 2

DIRECTIONS: In each of the following sentences, there are four underlined words. In the answer column, blacken the space under the number that corresponds to the number of the misspelled word. If there are no misspelled words, blacken the fifth space.

ANSWERS APPEAR AT THE END OF THE CHAPTER

1.
```
 1    2    3    4    5
||   ||   ||   ||   ||
```
1. The firemen finally broke through the cieling in the dining room.
         1   2   3   4

2.
```
 1    2    3    4    5
||   ||   ||   ||   ||
```
2. Dungarees may be economical, but many people disaprove of them outside
        1   2   3
the dormitory.
        4

3.
```
 1    2.   3    4    5
||   ||   ||   ||   ||
```
3. The enthusiastic distributer took us on a tour of the best equipped
        1   2   3
distillery I had ever seen.
    4

4.
```
 1    2    3    4    5
||   ||   ||   ||   ||
```
4. Forty freshmen were crowded into the comparitively small gallery.
     1   2   3   4

5.
```
 1    2    3    4    5
||   ||   ||   ||   ||
```
5. The fundamental errer in tax rates resulted in an economic emergency.
         1   2   3   4

6.
```
 1    2    3    4    5
||   ||   ||   ||   ||
```
6. Many people are dissatisfied with the existance of so many extravagant
                        1   2   3
embassies in that section of the city.
     4

7.
```
 1    2    3    4    5
||   ||   ||   ||   ||
```
7. The development of even more deseases during the flu season seemed to
            1   2
dissatisfy the doctor.
     3   4

8.
```
 1    2    3    4    5
||   ||   ||   ||   ||
```
8. The fragrence of the hybrid flowers and the lush foliage in the yard seemed
        1   2   3
everlasting to me.
     4

9.
```
 1    2    3    4    5
||   ||   ||   ||   ||
```
9. At the height of the business season, the bachelor was arrested for bigamy.
         1   2   3   4

10.
```
 1    2    3    4    5
||   ||   ||   ||   ||
```
10. A knowledge of grammer can be of enormous benefit in writing news
                      1   2   3
bulletins.
     4

Group 11

inadequate	indebtedness	interests	intelligent	inevitable
institute	immensely	I'd	issuing	incurred
intimate	independence	inconvenience	inasmuch	interrupt
inherent	initiate	immediately	icicle	incessant
infamy	illness	important	intensive	imagine

Group 12

illuminate	ingenuity	jurisdiction	logical	leased
insulation	innocent	judgment	literally	lieutenant
indecent	insurance	kinsman	legitimate	lynch
illustrative	jealous	kindergarten	loot	lovable
idiomatic	jovial	loyalty	luxury	loveliness

Group 13

ladies	larceny	libel	mechanical	mislaid
lose	label	laceration	mortgage	malice
losing	lightning	latter	merely	medal
legend	likeness	likewise	mercantile	misdemeanor
leggings	ligament	leisure	morale	melancholy

Group 14

mercury	museum	marmalade	maturity	mayonnaise
monarchical	misanthrope	matrimony	misstep	millionaire
magnificent	maintain	muscle	mattress	massacre
medicine	millinery	manual	midget	midriff
military	monkeys	mania	mackerel	macaroni

Group 15

ninth	nowadays	obedient	operated	option
nervous	negotiate	occasionally	obliged	preceding
nuisance	niece	opportunity	odyssey	partisan
notary	ninety	obstacles	overwhelming	physician
notoriety	necessity	omissions	omitted	potato

EXERCISE 3

DIRECTIONS: In each of the following sentences, there are four underlined words. In the answer column, blacken the space under the number that corresponds to the number of the misspelled word. If there are no misspelled words, blacken the fifth space.

ANSWERS APPEAR AT THE END OF THE CHAPTER

1. One candle is inadequate to illuminate a large dinning room.
       1   2   3   4

    1. 1 2 3 4 5

2. Inasmuch as I had been inconvenienced, the logical thing to do was to seek
       1   2   3

   a guarantee that it wouldn't happen again.
       4

    2. 1 2 3 4 5

3. In my judgment, all kindergarten children are both lovable and innocent.
       1   2   3   4

    3. 1 2 3 4 5

4. ¹ ² ³ ⁴ ⁵

4. Larceny and libel seem to be inevitable, even in a democratic society.
   1   2   3   4

5. ¹ ² ³ ⁴ ⁵

5. Matrimony can be a serious misstep for those without sufficient maturity and
   1   2   3
   independance.
   4

6. ¹ ² ³ ⁴ ⁵

6. The lieutenant's midriff reminded me more of macaroni than mussle.
   1   2   3   4

7. ¹ ² ³ ⁴ ⁵

7. I merely leased the house to them so that I could help maintain my morgage
   1 2   3   4
   payments.

8. ¹ ² ³ ⁴ ⁵

8. Nowadays, it seems that only ocassionally are negotiations instituted in time
   1   2   3   4
   to prevent strikes.

9. ¹ ² ³ ⁴ ⁵

9. The museum directors imediately sought insurance for their new acquisition.
   1 2   3   4

10. ¹ ² ³ ⁴ ⁵

10. Although my niece is usually obediant, I am obliged to discipline her now
    1   2   3   4
    and then.

Group 16

pattern	principalship	paradoxical	prestige	primarily
plague	people's	portiere	penitentiary	pageant
poultry	parachute	premises	possession	propaganda
prairie	physical	preparation	parliament	prisoner
probably	proprietor	politician	profit	pitiful

Group 17

playwright	postpone	publicly	promptness	partner
primitive	precious	possibilities	papal	proffer
perilous	portend	permanent	parasite	panel
persevere	presume	preference	phrenologist	pervade
perjury	planned	parole	post office	privilege

Group 18

quartet	ridiculous	refrigerator	rhubarb	rheumatism
quantities	resources	receipted	raisin	response
queue	restaurant	remodel	recompense	rabid
quinine	regretted	roommate	renaissance	rickety
questionnaire	recruit	religious	requisition	reconcile

Group 19

righteous	responsible	suburb	statutes	suffrage
reservoir	receipts	salaries	sandwiches	spiritualist
routine	receptacle	sieges	successor	Sabbath
relieve	squirrels	standard	subsidy	similar
recommend	superb	sitting	screech	statistics

Group 20

series	steak (meat)	strenuous	stationary	sophomore
staid	squalor	systematic	(fixed)	saucy
soliciting	soporific	silhouette	sincerely	Saturn
seize	studying	society	strengthen	scrutiny
solemn	specific	speech	scenes	significant
			session	

EXERCISE 4

DIRECTIONS: In each of the following sentences, there are four underlined words. In the answer column, blacken the space under the number that corresponds to the number of the misspelled word. If there are no misspelled words, blacken the fifth space.

ANSWERS APPEAR AT THE END OF THE CHAPTER

1. May I recommend that we publically proclaim our preference?
1   2   3   4

    1. 1 2 3 4 5

2. The posibilities of becoming his political successor bring with them a great
1   2   3

deal of prestige.
4

    2. 1 2 3 4 5

3. Are salries higher in the suburbs or do they just seem that way to people
1   2

in the crowded cities?
3   4

    3. 1 2 3 4 5

4. We sincerely believe that attracting more famous guest stars will significantly
1   2

strenthen the television series.
3   4

    4. 1 2 3 4 5

5. In most countries, routine propaganda is looked upon as a rather mechanical
1   2   3

operation.
4

    5. 1 2 3 4 5

6. The crowd queued up for coffee and sandwiches after filling out the
1   2

standard questionairres.
3   4

    6. 1 2 3 4 5

7. 1 2 3 4 5

7. <u>Freshmen</u> and <u>sophmores</u> undergo a <u>strenuous</u> <u>existence</u> in most modern
    1   2   3   4
universities.

8. 1 2 3 4 5

8. There must have been <u>ninty</u> <u>squirrels</u> <u>sitting</u> on the <u>statue</u> of General Grant.
                       1   2   3   4

9. 1 2 3 4 5

9. As a <u>playwright</u>, Bob has a <u>primative</u> style that seems to <u>pervade</u> his work
       1   2   3
and <u>guarantee</u> his future.
      4

10. 1 2 3 4 5

10. The <u>staid</u> and <u>solem</u> <u>canon</u> spoke of the necessity of observing the <u>Sabbath</u>.
     1   2   3   4

Group 21

serenity	thermometer	tableaux (or	technical	twelfth
surgeon	tragedy	tableaus)	temporarily	tuition
sympathy	troupe	talcum	thought	taciturn
typhoid	(theatrical	triumph	temperature	twins
turkeys	group)	thesis	tournament	treachery
	typewriting	tariff	tyranny	

Group 22

tennis	unfortunately	unnecessary	universe	undecided
traitor	tantalizing	undoubtedly	unauthorized	unanimous
truce	tremendous	taunt	uniform	unconscious
unify	together	terse	transparent	undulate
unbearable	utilize	tetanus	tenet	vacancy

Group 23

voluntary	woman's	worlds	wholly	wiring
verbal	vivisection	witnesses	wretched	warranted
visible	vegetable	vague	welfare	we're
wrapped	vengeance	velvet	voucher	yoke
women's	width	villain	valuing	zephyr

Now test yourself by doing all the exercises that follow. Remember to look at **ALL** the words in each group even if you think you've found the misspelling in the first word or two.

EXERCISE 5

DIRECTIONS: In each of the following groups of words, there may be one misspelled word. In the answer column, blacken the space under the number that corresponds to the number of the misspelled word. If there are no misspellings, blacken the fifth space.

ANSWERS APPEAR AT THE END OF THE CHAPTER

1. (1) negotiate   (2) publicly   (3) twine   (4) trechery   1. 1 2 3 4 5
2. (1) squalor   (2) duley   (3) discretion   (4) development   2. 1 2 3 4 5
3. (1) squirrels   (2) wirring   (3) delinquent   (4) efficient   3. 1 2 3 4 5
4. (1) joviel   (2) occasionally   (3) resources   (4) voluntary   4. 1 2 3 4 5
5. (1) everlasting   (2) distruction   (3) physician   (4) queue   5. 1 2 3 4 5
6. (1) suburb   (2) wholy   (3) appetite   (4) fatal   6. 1 2 3 4 5
7. (1) comitting   (2) official   (3) necessity   (4) penitentiary   7. 1 2 3 4 5
8. (1) fraternally   (2) tremendous   (3) transperant   (4) zephyr   8. 1 2 3 4 5
9. (1) ascertain   (2) forcible   (3) kinsman   (4) preceding   9. 1 2 3 4 5
10. (1) accent   (2) voucher   (3) recruit   (4) hysterics   10. 1 2 3 4 5
11. (1) primitive   (2) stationary   (3) legitamate   (4) brief   11. 1 2 3 4 5
12. (1) matress   (2) partisan   (3) prairie   (4) decision   12. 1 2 3 4 5

EXERCISE 6

DIRECTIONS: In each of the following groups of words, there may be one misspelled word. In the answer column, blacken the space under the number that corresponds to the number of the misspelled word. If there are no misspellings, blacken the fifth space.

ANSWERS APPEAR AT THE END OF THE CHAPTER

1. (1) mislade   (2) negotiate   (3) obliged   (4) poultry   1. 1 2 3 4 5
2. (1) parasite   (2) refridgerator   (3) standard   (4) typewriting   2. 1 2 3 4 5
3. (1) unauthorized   (2) verbal   (3) worlds   (4) adige   3. 1 2 3 4 5
4. (1) crochet   (2) democrat   (3) assassination   (4) congenial   4. 1 2 3 4 5
5. (1) embassies   (2) foreign   (3) glimpse   (4) holly   5. 1 2 3 4 5
6. (1) leased   (2) malise   (3) niece   (4) odyssey   6. 1 2 3 4 5
7. (1) perjury   (2) frenologist   (3) receipted   (4) sitting   7. 1 2 3 4 5
8. (1) scenes   (2) unconscious   (3) vegtable   (4) wretched   8. 1 2 3 4 5
9. (1) assigned   (2) barely   (3) consiquently   (4) disgust   9. 1 2 3 4 5

10. 1 2 3 4 5

11. 1 2 3 4 5

12. 1 2 3 4 5

10. (1) bulletin   (2) Christian   (3) delegate   (4) elaboret

11. (1) gaurdian   (2) itemized   (3) hosiery   (4) jealous

12. (1) loyalty   (2) mechanical   (3) nineth   (4) obedient

EXERCISE 7

DIRECTIONS: In each of the following groups of words, there may be one misspelled word. In the answer column, blacken the space under the number that corresponds to the number of the misspelled word. If there are no misspellings, blacken the fifth space.

ANSWERS APPEAR AT THE END OF THE CHAPTER

1. 1 2 3 4 5

2. 1 2 3 4 5

3. 1 2 3 4 5

4. 1 2 3 4 5

5. 1 2 3 4 5

6. 1 2 3 4 5

7. 1 2 3 4 5

8. 1 2 3 4 5

9. 1 2 3 4 5

10. 1 2 3 4 5

11. 1 2 3 4 5

12. 1 2 3 4 5

1. (1) gout   (2) hence   (3) inadequate   (4) judgment

2. (1) mercantile   (2) notwithstanding   (3) obsticles   (4) potato

3. (1) promptness   (2) quinine   (3) salaries   (4) tragidy

4. (1) unbareable   (2) vague   (3) warranted   (4) adequate

5. (1) clothe   (2) dispach   (3) attorneys   (4) banana

6. (1) dessert   (2) error   (3) fourty   (4) guild

7. (1) institute   (2) loot   (3) morale   (4) nowadays

8. (1) plague   (2) perilous   (3) pappal   (4) questionnaire

9. (1) seiges   (2) troupe   (3) sincerely   (4) unnecessary

10. (1) women's   (2) alcohol   (3) border   (4) carnage

11. (1) acquisition   (2) blight   (3) condemmed   (4) destruction

12. (1) fireman   (2) gallery   (3) hieght   (4) intimate

EXERCISE 8

DIRECTIONS: In each of the following groups of words, there may be one misspelled word. In the answer column, blacken the space under the number that corresponds to the number of the misspelled word. If there are no misspellings, blacken the fifth space.

ANSWERS APPEAR AT THE END OF THE CHAPTER

1. 1 2 3 4 5

2. 1 2 3 4 5

1. (1) prisoner   (2) permanent   (3) quartet   (4) rediculous

2. (1) typhoid   (2) silouette   (3) undecided   (4) vacancy

3. (1) yoke   (2) ambassader   (3) bored   (4) charitable

4. (1) accent   (2) bimonthly   (3) capitol   (4) distribution

5. (1) fillial   (2) guaranteed   (3) humorists   (4) ignoramus

6. (1) kindergarden   (2) logical   (3) mortgage   (4) nervous

7. (1) partisan   (2) pitaful   (3) preference   (4) quantities

8. (1) superb   (2) turkeys   (3) society   (4) utilise

9. (1) wrapped   (2) awkwerd   (3) bigamy   (4) competition

10. (1) attach   (2) balance   (3) exausted   (4) dizzy

11. (1) fundamental   (2) galvenized   (3) herald   (4) ignorant

12. (1) literaly   (2) merely   (3) nuisance   (4) opportunity

EXERCISE 9

DIRECTIONS: In each of the following groups of words, there may be one misspelled word. In the answer column, blacken the space under the number that corresponds to the number of the misspelled word. If there are no misspellings, blacken the fifth space.

ANSWERS APPEAR AT THE END OF THE CHAPTER

1. (1) playright   (2) parole   (3) queue   (4) restaurant

2. (1) thermometer   (2) speech   (3) unanimous   (4) vivisection

3. (1) acheivement   (2) business   (3) conservatory   (4) declaration

4. (1) benefit   (2) chauffer   (3) dissatisfied   (4) enthusiastic

5. (1) agregate   (2) candidacy   (3) arguing   (4) candle

6. (1) endurance   (2) forfit   (3) guitar   (4) hideous

7. (1) incurred   (2) kinsman   (3) liesure   (4) judgment

8. (1) mattress   (2) ninety   (3) option   (4) parachute

9. (1) privelege   (2) persevere   (3) reservoir   (4) soliciting

10. (1) receptacle   (2) together   (3) series   (4) solemm

11. (1) saucy   (2) sergeon   (3) valuing   (4) welfare

12. (1) abandoned   (2) bungalow   (3) competetors   (4) diseases

EXERCISE 10

DIRECTIONS: In each of the following groups of words, there may be one misspelled word. In the answer column, blacken the space under the number that corresponds to the number of the misspelled word. If there are no misspellings, blacken the fifth space.

ANSWERS APPEAR AT THE END OF THE CHAPTER

1. (1) cauldron   (2) amplify   (3) agreeable   (4) cavlier

2. (1) congestion   (2) fortell   (3) hideous   (4) faculties

3. (1) icycle   (2) idiomatic   (3) lieutenant   (4) likeness

4. (1) monkies   (2) notoriety   (3) obliged   (4) prairie

5. (1) maturity   (2) propaganda   (3) parliment   (4) omitted

6. (1) perjury   (2) proffer   (3) planned   (4) predjudice

7. (1) questionnaire (2) religious   (3) staid   (4) seance

8. (1) statutes   (2) successor   (3) tiranny   (4) twelfth

9. (1) rabid   (2) relieve   (3) studying   (4) tantalizing

10. (1) sophmore   (2) session   (3) serenity   (4) significant

11. (1) undulate   (2) vague   (3) abutting   (4) bulliten

12. (1) acquired   (2) aknowledge   (3) cavalry   (4) dissatisfy

ANSWERS: SPELLING EXERCISES

EXERCISE 1

1. (1) ambassador
2. (1) cafeteria
3. (4) across
4. (3) competitors
5. (3) cavalry
6. (1) Apparently
7. (1) attorneys
8. (3) athletes
9. (1) advisable
10. (3) argument

EXERCISE 2

1. (3) ceiling
2. (3) disapprove
3. (2) distributor
4. (3) comparatively
5. (2) error
6. (2) existence
7. (2) diseases
8. (1) fragrance
9. (5)
10. (1) grammar

EXERCISE 3

1. (4) dining
2. (5)
3. (5)
4. (5)

5. (4) independence
6. (4) muscle
7. (4) mortgage

8. (2) occasionally
9. (3) immediately
10. (2) obedient

EXERCISE 4

1. (2) publicly
2. (1) possibilities
3. (1) salaries
4. (3) strengthen

5. (5)
6. (4) questionnaires
7. (2) sophomores

8. (1) ninety
9. (2) primitive
10. (2) solemn

EXERCISE 5

1. (4) treachery
2. (2) duly
3. (2) wiring
4. (1) jovial

5. (2) destruction
6. (2) wholly
7. (1) committing
8. (3) transparent

9. (5)
10. (5)
11. (3) legitimate
12. (1) mattress

EXERCISE 6

1. (1) mislaid
2. (2) refrigerator
3. (4) adage
4. (5)

5. (3) glimpse
6. (2) malice
7. (2) phrenologist
8. (3) vegetable

9. (3) consequently
10. (4) elaborate
11. (1) guardian
12. (3) ninth

EXERCISE 7

1. (5)
2. (3) obstacles
3. (4) tragedy
4. (1) unbearable

5. (2) dispatch
6. (3) forty
7. (5)
8. (3) papal

9. (1) sieges
10. (5)
11. (3) condemned
12. (3) height

EXERCISE 8

1. (4) ridiculous
2. (2) silhouette
3. (2) ambassador
4. (5)

5. (1) filial
6. (1) kindergarten
7. (2) pitiful
8. (4) utilize

9. (2) awkward
10. (3) exhausted
11. (2) galvanized
12. (1) literally

EXERCISE 9

1. (1) playwright
2. (5)
3. (1) achievement
4. (2) chauffeur

5. (1) aggregate
6. (2) forfeit
7. (3) leisure
8. (5)

9. (1) privilege
10. (4) solemn
11. (2) surgeon
12. (3) competitors

EXERCISE 10

1. (4) cavalier
2. (2) foretell
3. (1) icicle
4. (1) monkeys

5. (3) parliament
6. (4) prejudice
7. (5)
8. (3) tyranny

9. (5)
10. (1) sophomore
11. (4) bulletin
12. (2) acknowledge

VOCABULARY SKILLS

We think in words. We use words to formulate ideas. Obviously, the more words we know, the more varied and the more vivid our thoughts can be. A good vocabulary enables us to express our own ideas clearly, and to interpret someone else's ideas correctly. Consequently, a good understanding of vocabulary is essential for interpreting any kind of written material.

If your vocabulary is weak, you may think that it is impossible to make a significant improvement in your knowledge of words in the short time you have left before you take the High School Equivalency Examination. However, the truth is that you would be very unwise to give up. You *can* improve if you apply yourself and if you follow the proper method. No one, not even a writer of dictionaries, is expected to know all the words in a dictionary. What every reader should know, however, and what he can learn in a relatively short time, is certain basic information about how words are constructed and how they are used.

The vocabulary section of this book has been designed specifically with the High School Equivalency Examination in mind. Here you will study the basic parts of words—prefixes, roots, and suffixes. A knowledge of these commonly used word parts will enable you to figure out the meanings of many unfamiliar words.

English words are constructed of word parts, called *prefixes, roots,* and *suffixes.* Different combinations of these word parts produce different words. The *root* is the basic part of any word, the part that gives the word its essential meaning. The essential meaning may be altered or changed completely by adding another word part to the beginning or the end of the root. The word part that is attached to the beginning of the root is known as a *prefix.* The word part that is attached at the end of the root is known as a *suffix.* By knowing the meanings of these basic word parts that appear over and over again in different English words, you will be able to make a good guess as to the meanings of many words that are now totally unfamiliar to you.

To get an idea of how this system of word construction works, look at the following list of words. These ten words are only some of the different words that can be constructed by adding different prefixes and suffixes to the same root *port,* which means "to carry."

report	reporter
deport	deporting
import	imported
export	portage
transport	portable

Another way of constructing words is by combining several roots. For example, in the word *manufacture*, the root *manu* comes from the Latin word *manus,* meaning "hand." The root *facture* comes from the Latin word *facere* meaning "to make." Originally, the English word *manufacture* meant "making by hand." Over the years the word's meaning has become broader, and now it means merely "make"; and, as the commonest form of making is now by machinery, the word has also assumed that meaning.

Knowing the meaning of every part of a word will not necessarily give you the exact meaning of that word as it is used today. The English language is a living language and so is constantly changing. Some words have become broader and more general than the original meaning, while other words have become narrower and more specialized. However, knowledge of the word parts will usually put you on the right track to a word's meaning. This, together with the context of the word in the reading passage, will help you to decide the actual meaning of the word as it is being used.

PREFIXES

A prefix is a letter or sequence of letters attached to the beginning of a word, which usually changes the meaning of the word. For example, the prefix *re* means "back," "anew," or "again"; therefore, the word *rebuild* means "build again." Also, the prefix *trans* means "across," "beyond," or "through"; thus, the word *transatlantic* means "extending across the Atlantic Ocean" or "situated beyond the Atlantic Ocean." (In the second example, the context in which the word is used in a reading passage would indicate which of the two meanings is applicable.)

A knowledge of prefixes is extremely useful in figuring out the meanings of many words that seem difficult at first sight. This knowledge will help you a great deal on the High School Equivalency Examination. Therefore, you should work very hard at learning the prefixes presented in this book. Following is a list of commonly used prefixes in our language.

COMMONLY USED PREFIXES

Prefix	Meaning	Example
ante	before	anteroom
anti	against	antislavery
circum	around	circumnavigate
contra	against	contradict

de	down, from	depose
fore	before, in front of	foresee
i, im, in, ir	not	illegal
inter	between	interstate
intra	within, into, between	intravenous
non	not, reverse of, absence of	nonstandard
per	by, through, throughout, thoroughly	perennial
post	after	postwar
pre	before	predict
pro	forward, before	proclaim
trans	across	transcontinental
un	not	unnecessary

When you think you know all the prefixes in the list of "Commonly Used Prefixes," complete the following exercises. Refer to the above list as you work through the exercises.

EXERCISE 1

DIRECTIONS: Complete each of the following sentences with an appropriate word from the list of "Commonly Used Prefixes." You will find the words you need in the "Example" column.

ANSWERS APPEAR AT THE END OF THE CHAPTER

1. He made a _____ trip in less than 6 hours.
   (across a continent)

2. The army will _____ the king.
   (put down)

3. His lengthy words of warning were _____ because everyone was fully aware of the danger.

4. Magellan was the first to _____ the globe.
   (sail around)

5. The king will _____ this historic day a public holiday.

6. _____ laws were passed after the Civil War.
   (opposed to slavery)

7. Many of the veterans were anxious to make up for lost time during the

   _____ years.

8. The weatherman could not _____ next Tuesday's
   weather.   (say what will happen before it happens)

9. He was asked to wait in the _____ before being
   admitted into the old duke's study.

10. It is considered impolite for a child to _____ his
    parents.

11. The dandelion, like many weeds, is a _____ plant.

12. It is _____ to print your own money.

13. The doctor said that _____ feeding of the patient
    would be discontinued and that he was well enough to take liquid nourish-
    ment by mouth.

14. His intentions were good, but he could not _____
    the harmful effects his scolding would have on the boy.

15. The great network of railroads built in the nineteenth century in this country

    made large-scale _____ commerce a reality.

Following is a list of additional prefixes that will be helpful in preparing for the High School Equivalency Examination.

Prefix	Meaning	Example
ab	away, from	absolve
ac, ad, af, ag	to, toward	accredit, adequate
ambi	both	ambidextrous
amphi, amph	around, on both sides, both	amphibious
auto	self	autobiography
by	secondary	bypath
co, com, con, cor	together, with	coexist
di, dis	apart from	dissociate
e, ex	out, out of, from	exhale
hyper	excessive, excessively, above, beyond	hypersensitive

mal	bad, badly, inadequate	maladjusted
mis	wrong, bad, wrongly, badly, unfavorably, lack of, not	mistreat
mis, miso	hatred	misanthrope
omni	all	omnipresent
pan	all	Pan-American
poly	many	polygon
re	back, again	renew
se	apart	seduce
sub	under	submarine
super	above, on, over	superimpose
vice	in place of	vice president
with	against, from	withstand

ROOTS

The *root* of a word (also known as the *stem*) is the basic part of the word to which a prefix or a suffix may be added.

One root can produce many new words when it is combined with different prefixes and suffixes, or with other roots. In a previous section you saw a list of ten words, all of which grew from the same root *port,* which means "to carry." Below is another example of words that contain the same root: *spec* or *spect,* meaning "to look."

respect	spectacle
inspect	spectacular
suspect	spectator
circumspect	specimen
introspect	perspective
retrospect	respective
prospect	respectable

The above list obviously could be extended much further. You can see, therefore, how important it is for you to learn as many roots as you can. Each new root you learn will help clarify the meanings of dozens of different words.

Following is a list of commonly used roots in our language. You will note that the meanings of the example words are not given in the following table. Try to figure out the meanings from your knowledge of the word parts. If you cannot figure out the meaning of a word, look it up in the dictionary.

COMMONLY USED ROOTS

Root	Meaning	Example
ag, act, ig	act, do	agitate, reaction
anthrop	man	anthropology
bi, bio	life	biography
cede, ceed, cess	go, yield	exceed, process
cred	believe	incredible
cur, course	run	current, concourse
dic, dict	say	dictate
duce, duct	lead	induce, conduct
fact, fict, feit, fect	make, do	factory, perfect
fer	carry	transfer
fort	strong	fortitude
ject	throw	eject
junct	join	junction
loqu, loc	speak	loquacious, elocution
mit, mis, mise	send	remit, mission
pone, pose	place, put	postpone, impose
port	carry	report
scrib, scrip	write	describe, postscript
sequ, secu, sue	follow	sequel, consecutive
spec, spect, spic	look	spectacle
vene, vent	come	convene
vert, vers	turn	convert, reverse
voc, voke	call	vocal

When you think you know all the roots in the list of "Commonly Used Roots," complete the following exercise. Refer to the above list as you work through the exercise.

EXERCISE 2

DIRECTIONS: Complete each of the following sentences with an appropriate word from the list of "Commonly Used Roots." You will find the words you need in the "Example" column.

ANSWERS APPEAR AT THE END OF THE CHAPTER

1. The police will be called to _____ the unruly mob if it does not leave the premises at once.

2. A _____ is a message written below the main body of a letter.

3. The meeting will _____ in the library at 6:00 P.M. and end at 8:30 P.M.

4. When he reached the _____ of the two roads, he knew that he had come too far west.

5. He thought it _____ that her beautiful house had cost so little.

6. The _____ child never stopped talking during the entire trip.

7. His _____ in Africa was to photograph rare species of birds.

8. The young schoolgirls in their Easter finery made a gay and charming

_____.

9. The _____ to the adventure was that Tom abandoned his plans to spend the summer at his family's lakeside cottage and decided to work with Dr. Jasper at the laboratory.

10. No one could _____ him to taste the strange food.

11. The judge could not _____ the verdict of the jury, although he pitied the young criminal.

12. The information booth was located in the main _____ of the bus terminal.

13. They will _____ their trip until Paul is well enough to join them.

14. He said that he did not want to _____ the crowd of unsatisfied customers, but he had orders to close the store.

15. If you want to drive safely, you must not _____ the speed limit.

Following is a list of additional roots that will be helpful in preparing for the High School Equivalency Examination.

Root	Meaning	Example
biblio	book	bibliography
ceive, cept, cip, cap	take	accept
clud, clus	shut	exclude, exclusion
dynam	power	dynamic
gen, geno	birth, race, kind	genetics
ge, geo	earth	geography
graph, gram	write	photograph, program
lat	bear, carry	relate
leg, lect	read	lectern
log	word, study	catalog, psychology
man, mani, manu	hand	manipulate, manufacture
mega, meg	great	megalopolis
meter, metre	measure	thermometer
micro	small	microscope
mot, mov, mob	move	motor, move, mob
nomy	law	astronomy
nov, novus	new	novel
ped	foot	pedal
pend, pens	hang, weigh	pendant, pensive
phil, phile, philo	love	philosopher
phon, phone, phono	sound	phonetics, dictaphone, phonograph
polis	city	metropolis
psych, psycho	mind, spirit	psychology
scop	see	microscope
sent, sens	feel	sentiment, sensitive
soph	wise, wisdom	philosopher
spir, spirit	breathe	inspire, spiritual
sta, sti(t), sist	stand	stationary
tact, tang, teg	touch	tactile, tangible

tele	far off, distant, at a distance	telegraph
ten, tain	hold	retain
tend, tens	stretch	intend, tension
tra, tract	draw	retract
the, theo	god	theology
ver	true	verify
vid, vis	see	evident, vision
vit, viv	live	vitality, vivacity

SUFFIXES

A suffix is a group of letters attached at the end of a word or root. When a suffix is added to a word or root, or when the suffix of a word is changed, a new word is formed. For example, when the suffix *or* is added to the word *act,* the new word *actor* is formed. The suffix *or* means "one who," and the word *actor* means "one who acts."

Following is a list of commonly used suffixes in our language. Study each suffix very carefully, and try to figure out the meanings of the example words.

COMMONLY USED SUFFIXES

Suffix	Meaning	Example
able, ible	able to	livable, possible
acious, cious	having the quality of	tenacious, spacious
ance, ancy	state or quality of being	recognizance, truancy
ar, ary	connected with or concerning	ocular, rudimentary
en	made of or indicating smallness	golden, weaken
ent, er, or	one who	student, teacher, sailor
ion	act or condition of	correction
ism	philosophy, act, or practice of	Americanism, communism
ive	containing the nature of, giving or leaning toward	selective, corrective
less	not having or beyond	limitless, hopeless

ly	like in manner	quickly, hopefully
ory	pertaining to	laudatory
ose, ous	full of, state or quality of being	verbose, conspicuous
ship	art or skill of, state or quality of being	leadership
try, tude	art or profession of, state or quality of	chemistry, servitude

When you think you know all the suffixes in the list of "Commonly Used Suffixes," complete the following exercises. Refer to the above list as you work through the exercises.

EXERCISE 3

DIRECTIONS: Complete each of the following sentences with an appropriate word from the list of "Commonly Used Suffixes." You will find the words you need in the "Example" column.

ANSWERS APPEAR AT THE END OF THE CHAPTER

1. In praise of the performance, he called it most _____.

2. Because he spoke so much, they said that he was _____.

3. He was tired of his condition of _____ and vowed to become his own master.

4. His excellent _____ guided the team to victory.

5. He was very _____ in choosing the personnel.

6. After their unexpected victory, they spoke more _____ about the future.

7. He responded _____ to the emergency.

8. The opportunities are _____ for a man of ability and determination.

9. Some people equate democracy with _____.

10. He was _____ as a fighter.

Below is a list of additional suffixes that will be helpful in preparing for the High School Equivalency Examination.

Suffix	Meaning	Example
acy, cy, age, al	state or quality of being, pertaining to	legacy, courage, nominal
an, ian	pertaining or belonging to, designated as	Jamaican, guardian
eer, ier	one who	auctioneer, furrier
ard, art	one characterized by performing some action or possessing some quality excessively	coward, braggart
esque	manner of, like	picturesque
ette	little one, group	kitchenette, octette
ful, hood	full of, condition or quality of	cheerful, neighborhood
fy	to make	fortify
ic, ical	of, pertaining to, similar or like	historic, historical
ice, ile, il	act, quality, or state of, pertaining to	justice, servile, civil
ish	acting like, in the nature of, similar to	foolish, selfish
ist	one who	pacifist
ity, ty	state or quality of being	gratuity, plenty
lent, ulent	abounding in	violent, fraudulent
ment	state, quality, or act of	entanglement
ness	state or quality of being	fairness
ster (masculine), stress (feminine)	one who does, handles, operates, makes, or uses; one who is	teamster, songstress, youngster
ure	act, process, being, office, function	exposure, tenure

ANSWERS: VOCABULARY EXERCISES

EXERCISE 1

1. transcontinental
2. depose
3. unnecessary
4. circumnavigate
5. proclaim

6. Antislavery
7. postwar
8. predict
9. anteroom
10. contradict

11. perennial
12. illegal
13. intravenous
14. foresee
15. interstate

EXERCISE 2

1. eject
2. postscript
3. convene
4. junction
5. incredible

6. loquacious
7. mission
8. spectacle
9. sequel
10. induce

11. reverse
12. concourse
13. postpone
14. agitate
15. exceed

EXERCISE 3

1. laudatory
2. verbose
3. servitude
4. leadership

5. selective
6. hopefully
7. quickly

8. limitless
9. Americanism
10. tenacious

THE PARTS OF A SENTENCE

On the official test, you will be asked to spot errors in the way sentences are put together. For instance, you may be given the sentence, "The boys gone to the store," and be asked to select the number of the under-
$$\underset{1}{\text{boys}} \ \underset{2}{\text{gone}} \ \text{to} \ \underset{3}{\text{the}} \ \underset{4}{\text{store}}$$
lined part that is incorrect. Of course, the answer is 2 (*gone* should be *went*).

Questions of this sort are found throughout the examination. To do well on them, you have to be able to recognize the difference between a well-constructed sentence and a faulty sentence. In the next three chapters, we have provided you with simple, easy-to-study guides that will help you in this area. Study them carefully. They are important keys to passing on examination day.

What is a sentence? Simply put, it is a construction of words that always expresses a *complete thought*. "Fred is going to the park" expresses a complete thought—it is a sentence. On the other hand, "Fred is going to" does not express a complete thought—it is not a sentence.

Look at the five examples below. Are they sentences? Does each express a complete thought?

1. The ship docked at noon
2. After he finished lunch
3. My trousers are too long
4. To do well on any test
5. Sarah traveled to Spain and Portugal

Examples 1, 3, and 5 express complete thoughts—they are sentences. However, examples 2 and 4 do not express complete thoughts—they are not sentences. Example 2 should either begin or finish a complete thought: "After he finished lunch, he helped his wife with the dishes" or "He helped his wife with the dishes after he finished lunch." Similarly, example 4 cannot stand by itself, but must be made part of a complete thought: "To do well on any test, you must study hard."

EXERCISE 1

DIRECTIONS: Complete the following fragments to make real sentences. Make sure each one expresses a complete thought—is truly a sentence.

ANSWERS AND EXPLANATIONS APPEAR AT THE END OF THE CHAPTER

1. When I can come _____.

2. At night, just before the last hour strikes _____

_____.

3. _____ every time I turn around.

4. _____, if he is elected, _____.

5. I wish every star in the sky _____.

EXERCISE 2

DIRECTIONS: In each group below there are four constructions. In the answer column, blacken the space under the number corresponding to the number of the construction that is NOT a sentence (that does not express a complete thought). If all the constructions are complete sentences, blacken the fifth space.

ANSWERS APPEAR AT THE END OF THE CHAPTER

1. (1) John and I are good friends.   (3) In a minute.
    (2) We did that yesterday.   (4) He told me his name.

    1. 1 2 3 4 5

2. (1) I am still busy.   (3) When I have finished lunch.
    (2) Uncle Harry came to din-   (4) One of the men has returned.
        ner.

    2. 1 2 3 4 5

3. (1) Thirty people came to the   (3) The Mets are my favorite team.
        dance.   (4) One day in the early part of
    (2) Do you enjoy watching tele-   December.
        vision?

    3. 1 2 3 4 5

4. (1) I had forgotten my umbrella.   (3) Coming quickly down the block.
    (2) There were three trees in   (4) We saw the first signs of Spring.
        our yard.

    4. 1 2 3 4 5

5. (1) Do you know his name?   (3) My mother works hard.
    (2) We saw John yesterday.   (4) I enjoy reading good books.

    5. 1 2 3 4 5

SUBJECT AND PREDICATE

A sentence, as you have learned, must always express a complete thought. A sentence does this because it contains two basic parts: a *subject* and a *predicate*.

THE SUBJECT

The subject of a sentence is the person or thing that is either doing something or being spoken about. In the sentence, "Marie is studying engineering," *Marie* is the subject—the person who is doing the action. Sometimes, there are two or more subjects. For example, in the sentence, "Milk, butter, and eggs are on the kitchen table," there are three subjects—*milk, butter,* and *eggs.*

Note: A subject is usually a *noun* or a *pronoun.*

EXERCISE 3

DIRECTIONS: What is the subject or subjects in the following sentences?

ANSWERS AND EXPLANATIONS APPEAR AT THE END OF THE CHAPTER

1. The girls run around the field.
2. The boys play ball.
3. They are tired after an hour's exercise.
4. He is a hero.
5. Ann cries at night.
6. Planning ahead saves time.
7. Evelyn and Tom went to the movies.
8. The pitcher, the catcher, and the manager met at the pitcher's mound.
9. Cake and candy are not good for your teeth.
10. "Necessity is the mother of invention."

All of the subjects in the exercise above were either *simple* or *compound*. A simple subject is a noun or pronoun. ("*Tom* works after school.") A compound subject is two or more simple subjects connected by *and* or *or* ("*Tom* and *Joe* work after school."). Notice that both simple and compound subjects are not surrounded by *modifiers*—words like *red* and *lazy*, which describe or modify another word. However, there are times when a simple or compound subject is accompanied by modifiers. In such cases, the subject is called a complete subject. In the sentence, "The young man with the long hair was playing on a guitar," the complete subject is *The young man with the long hair*. In the next example, the complete subject is everything that precedes the verb *danced:* "The boy in the brown sweater and the girl in the pink dress danced."

THE PREDICATE

The predicate of a sentence is the word or words which tell you something about the subject. A predicate, like a subject, may be *simple, compound,* or *complete*. A simple predicate is a verb without any modifiers. Two examples are *inspected* in "The customs official inspected Mr. Gordon's luggage," and *jumped* in "Harry jumped into the pool from the high diving board."

A compound predicate is two or more simple predicates (verbs) connected by *and* or *or*. In the following examples, the compound predicates are in *italics:*

Sue *washed* and *dried* the dishes after supper.
I *come* or *go* whenever I want.
The pilot *entered* the cabin, *switched on* the controls, and then *waited* for a signal from the control tower.

The complete predicate is made up of a simple predicate (single verb) or a compound predicate (two or more verbs) *with all of its modifiers*. The complete predicate, then, is everything outside the complete subject. Note the complete predicates (in italics) in the following examples:

Emanuel *stood near the car.*
Nancy and Fred *went to the movies.*
Gary *walked up to the door, knocked, then waited for it to open.*

Remember, no matter how long a sentence is, it can always be divided into its subject and its predicate. The following examples show you how this is done (the subject is in *italics* and the predicate is in **boldface**):

SIMPLE SUBJECT—SIMPLE PREDICATE: *Bob* **danced.**

COMPOUND SUBJECT—SIMPLE PREDICATE: *Bob* and *Jane* **danced.**

COMPLETE SUBJECT—SIMPLE PREDICATE: *Bob* and *Jane, who were very much in love,* **danced.**

SIMPLE SUBJECT—COMPOUND PREDICATE: *Bob* **danced** and **laughed.**

SIMPLE SUBJECT—COMPLETE PREDICATE: *Bob* **danced and laughed the whole evening.**

COMPOUND SUBJECT—COMPOUND PREDICATE: *Bob* and *Jane* **danced and laughed.**

COMPLETE SUBJECT—COMPLETE PREDICATE: *Bob and Jane, who were very much in love,* **danced and laughed the whole evening.**

Now test your ability to recognize subjects and predicates by doing the exercises below.

EXERCISE 4

DIRECTIONS: In each of the following sentences, there are five underlined words. Choose the number of the word that is the simple subject of the sentence. Then blacken the space under that number in the answer column.

ANSWERS AND EXPLANATIONS APPEAR AT THE END OF THE CHAPTER

1. The boy ran quickly down the street.
   1   2   3   4   5

2. Six men were standing on the corner.
   1   2   3   4   5

3. The old man smiled and walked away.
   1   2   3   4   5

4. We lived there many years ago.
   1   2   3   4   5

5. 1 2 3 4 5   5. The team has won another game.
‖ ‖ ‖ ‖ ‖   1 2 3 4   5

6. 1 2 3 4 5   6. Tom went to the movies last night.
‖ ‖ ‖ ‖ ‖   1   2   3   4   5

7. 1 2 3 4 5   7. My parents helped me with my homework.
‖ ‖ ‖ ‖ ‖   1   2   3   4   5

8. 1 2 3 4 5   8. Have you seen that show before?
‖ ‖ ‖ ‖ ‖   1   2   3   4   5

9. 1 2 3 4 5   9. Two men were in the car.
‖ ‖ ‖ ‖ ‖   1   2   3   4   5

10. 1 2 3 4 5   10. I am really tired tonight.
‖ ‖ ‖ ‖ ‖   1 2   3   4   5

EXERCISE 5

DIRECTIONS: In each of the following sentences, there are five underlined words. Choose the number of the word that is the simple predicate of the sentence. Then blacken the space under that number in the answer column.

ANSWERS AND EXPLANATIONS APPEAR AT THE END OF THE CHAPTER

1. 1 2 3 4 5   1. Last night, Tom and Jane saw a good television program.
‖ ‖ ‖ ‖ ‖   1   2   3   4   5

2. 1 2 3 4 5   2. We like coffee very much.
‖ ‖ ‖ ‖ ‖   1   2   3   4   5

3. 1 2 3 4 5   3. He certainly goes to work early.
‖ ‖ ‖ ‖ ‖   1   2   3   4   5

4. 1 2 3 4 5   4. Harry told me an amusing story.
‖ ‖ ‖ ‖ ‖   1   2   3   4   5

5. 1 2 3 4 5   5. We did our work quickly.
‖ ‖ ‖ ‖ ‖   1   2   3   4   5

6. 1 2 3 4 5   6. Mr. Peters is an old friend of the family.
‖ ‖ ‖ ‖ ‖   1   2 3   4   5

7. 1 2 3 4 5   7. Tom, Sue, and Jean came to the party.
‖ ‖ ‖ ‖ ‖   1   2   3   4   5

8. 1 2 3 4 5   8. I saw only three people in the room.
‖ ‖ ‖ ‖ ‖   1 2   3   4   5

9. 1 2 3 4 5   9. He gave me his name and address.
‖ ‖ ‖ ‖ ‖   1   2   3   4   5

10. 1 2 3 4 5   10. Ralph was pleased about his new job.
‖ ‖ ‖ ‖ ‖   1   2   3   4   5

EXERCISE 6

DIRECTIONS: For each of the following sentences, choose the simple subject and the simple predicate.

ANSWERS AND EXPLANATIONS APPEAR AT THE END OF THE CHAPTER

1. Before breakfast, the boys took a twelve-mile hike.

2. The new teacher, more ambitious than competent, nervously met his class.

3. During the summer, we frequently take long rides in the country.

4. I have never met a more reliable fellow.

5. Everything was arranged in just the right fashion.

6. Joe emerged from the room at ten o'clock.

7. The conference had been a complete success by any standard.

8. We eagerly awaited the results of the examination.

9. Three of the girls had arrived early.

10. I had seen the movie before.

11. After lunch, we chatted over coffee.

12. Our friends had been waiting for three hours.

13. We left early in the evening.

14. There were two boys present.

15. Around the corner chugged an old truck.

EXERCISE 7

DIRECTIONS: For each of the following sentences, underline the complete subject once and the complete predicate twice.

ANSWERS AND EXPLANATIONS APPEAR AT THE END OF THE CHAPTER

1. John and I are going to the movies tonight.

2. I used to live in Nebraska.

3. The girl in the red dress is my sister.

4. The boys did their best in the big game.

5. We could barely see the picture.

6. The old man was eighty-seven last month.

7. Mom and Dad celebrated their twenty-fifth anniversary.

8. Have you known them very long?

9. This car costs four thousand dollars.

10. Martha and I will be going to college in the fall.

11. We won't be going with you tomorrow.

12. Tom Reynolds, the tallest boy in the school, is the starting center on the basketball team.

13. His attitude seems to have changed in recent weeks.

14. We always go there on Saturday.

15. A new car pulled into the driveway.

16. I have been waiting for hours.

17. The box in the corner was left here this morning.

18. Next year, we intend to take a trip to California.

19. John's new suit looks very expensive.

20. Haste makes waste.

COMPLEMENTS OF A VERB

In many sentences, the complete predicate often contains a word or words used to complete the action of a verb, identify the subject, or describe the subject. Such words are called *complements*. One type of complement is the *direct object*. A direct object is a noun or pronoun that acts as the direct receiver of an action verb. For example, in the sentence, "She kicked the table," *table* is the direct object of the action verb *kicked*. In "Mary ate a hamburger," *hamburger* is the direct object of the action verb *ate*.

To determine whether a sentence has a direct object, you must first find the action verb. When you have done this, ask the questions WHAT? or WHOM? after the verb. If the answer is a noun or pronoun in the sentence, then that word is the direct object. In the sentence "I offered him a ticket to the show," *ticket* is the direct object since it answers the question: "WHAT was offered?"

EXERCISE 8

DIRECTIONS: Each of the following sentences has four underlined words. Choose the number of the word that is the direct object. Then blacken the space under that number in the answer column. If there is no direct object, blacken the fifth space.

ANSWERS AND EXPLANATIONS APPEAR AT THE END OF THE CHAPTER

1. Mary cuts the cake.
   1   2   3   4

2. I like the book very much.
   1 2   3   4

3. Jay takes his lunch to school.
   1   2   3   4

4. A baby puts anything in its mouth.
   1   2   3   4

5. The students grow vegetables for their science class.
   1   2   3   4

1. 1   2   3   4   5

2. 1   2   3   4   5

3. 1   2   3   4   5

4. 1   2   3   4   5

5. 1   2   3   4   5

A second type of complement is the *indirect object*. An indirect object is a noun or a pronoun that acts as the indirect receiver of an action verb. For example, in the sentence, "Tony threw him the basketball," *basketball* is the direct receiver of the action verb *threw*. But what does *him* do? It receives the action—indirectly. Tony threw the basketball to *him*. The word *him,* then, is the indirect object of the verb *threw*.

To determine whether a sentence has an indirect object, you must first find the action verb. When you have done this, ask the questions TO WHAT? TO WHOM? FOR WHAT? FOR WHOM? after the verb. If the answer is a noun or pronoun in the sentence, then that word is the indirect object. In the sentence, "Fred told us a secret," *us* is the indirect object since it answers the question: TO WHOM was the secret told?

EXERCISE 9

DIRECTIONS: In each of the following sentences, there are four underlined words. In the answer column, blacken the space under the number that corresponds to the number of the indirect object. If there is no indirect object, blacken the fifth space.

ANSWERS AND EXPLANATIONS APPEAR AT THE END OF THE CHAPTER

1. We gave Mary a new jacket for her birthday.
   1   2   3   4

1. 1   2   3   4   5

2. 1   2   3   4   5
        || || || || ||

3. 1   2   3   4   5
        || || || || ||

4. 1   2   3   4   5
        || || || || ||

5. 1   2   3   4   5
        || || || || ||

2. The teacher asked us several questions before the test.
         1   2   3   4

3. My library has brought me great comfort through the years.
      1   2   3   4

4. I told him your name and address.
     1   2   3   4

5. Did you give them the directions this morning?
       1   2   3   4

EXERCISE 10

DIRECTIONS: In each of the following sentences, underline the direct object once and the indirect object twice.

ANSWERS AND EXPLANATIONS APPEAR AT THE END OF THE CHAPTER

1. We gave him the tickets for the ball game.

2. Mother told me the good news.

3. They asked us many questions.

4. Can you lend me five dollars?

5. Tom gave his brother a new shirt for Christmas.

6. I'll give you five minutes more.

7. The teacher read the girls a letter from the principal.

8. He did us a great favor.

9. My brother has written me a letter.

10. Please tell me a story.

A third type of complement, called the *predicate nominative*, is a noun or a pronoun that follows a linking verb and renames the subject. In the sentence, "Nick is a truck driver," *truck driver* is such a complement. Note that it follows the linking verb *is* and renames the subject *Nick*. Other examples of the predicate nominative are *baseball player*, in "Mickey Mantle was a great baseball player" and *he* in "I am he."

EXERCISE 11

DIRECTIONS: In each of the following sentences, there are four underlined words. In the answer column, blacken the space under the number that corresponds to the number of the predicate nominative. If none of the words is a predicate nominative, blacken the fifth space.

ANSWERS AND EXPLANATIONS APPEAR AT THE END OF THE CHAPTER

1. We <u>were</u> sure it <u>was</u> <u>John</u>.
     1   2 3   4

                                                         1. 1 2 3 4 5

2. <u>It</u> <u>was</u> <u>I</u> <u>who</u> told them.
   1 2 3 4

                                                         2. 1 2 3 4 5

3. Could <u>it</u> <u>really</u> have <u>been</u> your <u>brother</u>?
        1 2   3   4

                                                         3. 1 2 3 4 5

4. <u>Was it Mary who</u> called?
   1 2 3   4

                                                         4. 1 2 3 4 5

5. <u>John</u> and <u>Tom</u> <u>are</u> the <u>co-captains</u>.
   1   2 3   4

                                                         5. 1 2 3 4 5

There is one important thing to know about the *pronoun* when used as a complement. If the noun it replaces is a direct or indirect object, the pronoun has an objective form. If the noun it replaces is a predicate nominative, the pronoun has a subjective form. For example, in the sentence, "Nancy lent Sue a beautiful sweater," *Sue* is the indirect object of the action verb *lent*. The pronoun, then, that you would use to replace *Sue* is *her:* "Nancy lent her a beautiful sweater." Other objective forms of pronouns are *me, him, us,* and *them*.

In "I am a doctor," *doctor* is the predicate nominative. Thus, the pronoun used to replace doctor would be *he:* "I am he." Other subjective forms of pronouns are *I, she, we,* and *they*.

It and *you* may be either objective or subjective:

> I gave the *machine* a kick.—I gave *it* a kick.
> It is a *machine*.—It is *it*.
> I told *Ed* the story.—I told *you* the story.
> It is *Ed*.—It is *you*.

The fourth—and last—type of complement, the *predicate adjective*, is an adjective that follows a linking verb and describes the subject. In the sentence, "The boy is tall," *tall* is such a complement. Note that it follows the linking verb *is* and describes the subject *boy*. Other examples of the predicate adjective are *well* in "Mary appears well" and *sweet* in "The flowers smell sweet."

EXERCISE 12

DIRECTIONS: In each of the following sentences, there are four underlined words. In the answer column, blacken the space under the number that corresponds to the number of the predicate adjective. If none of the words is a predicate adjective, blacken the fifth space.

ANSWERS AND EXPLANATIONS APPEAR AT THE END OF THE CHAPTER

1. He was lucky that we came.
       1   2   3   4

2. I am very tired today.
    1 2   3   4

3. The setting sun looks beautiful.
          1   2   3   4

4. The old man seems rather sad today.
            1   2   3   4

5. Those two boys are completely reliable.
          1   2   3   4

EXERCISE 13

DIRECTIONS: In each of the following sentences, there is one underlined word. Blacken the answer column as follows: 1—direct object; 2—indirect object; 3—noun used as predicate nominative; 4—pronoun used as predicate nominative; 5—predicate adjective.

ANSWERS AND EXPLANATIONS APPEAR AT THE END OF THE CHAPTER

1. They gave us their names and addresses.

2. I haven't seen him around here before.

3. They seem to be rather happy today.

4. The sentry alerted the captain to the impending danger.

5. He couldn't see his hand in front of his face.

6. Will you give Joe another chance?

7. We were sure it was she.

8. The soup was delicious.

9. Mary and her sister were enthralled by the music.

10. John turned on the television and settled back in his chair.

11. We gave <u>it</u> to them yesterday.

11. 1 2 3 4 5

12. I have finally reached a <u>decision</u>.

12. 1 2 3 4 5

13. The band played a rousing <u>march</u>.

13. 1 2 3 4 5

14. It was <u>music</u> to my ears.

14. 1 2 3 4 5

15. This will teach <u>Tom</u> a lesson.

15. 1 2 3 4 5

16. They were tired and <u>thirsty</u>.

16. 1 2 3 4 5

17. The stranger told <u>you</u> his name.

17. 1 2 3 4 5

18. Life is a <u>bowl of cherries</u>.

18. 1 2 3 4 5

19. We were <u>happy</u> to see them.

19. 1 2 3 4 5

20. The bat cracked, the ball sailed over the fence, and the fans were <u>delighted</u>.

20. 1 2 3 4 5

INDEPENDENT AND DEPENDENT CLAUSES

As you recall, a sentence is a group of words made up of a subject and a predicate *and* expressing a complete thought. Some sentences, however, express more than one idea. Such sentences are made up of *clauses*. A clause is a group of words containing a subject and a predicate. Unlike all sentences, however, a clause may or may not express a complete thought. If it does, it is called an *independent clause*. In the last sentence, all the words after the comma make up an independent clause. If a clause does not express a complete thought, it is called a *dependent clause*. All the words preceding the comma in the last sentence make up a dependent clause.

Words that connect clauses are called *conjunctions*. If the connected clauses are independent, the conjunction is called a *coordinating conjunction*. In the sentence, "I remember the town, and I remember the street," *and* acts as the coordinating conjunction. Other examples are *for*, *nor*, and *or*.

A conjunction connecting an independent clause to a dependent clause is called a *subordinating conjunction*. In the sentence, "I will go out after it stops raining," *after* acts as the subordinating conjunction. Other examples are *if, now that, what, when, before, as* and *because*.

EXERCISE 14

DIRECTIONS: Indicate whether each of the clauses below is independent or dependent.

ANSWERS AND EXPLANATIONS APPEAR AT THE END OF THE CHAPTER

1. Tommy ran out into the snow

2. Although I love you

3. He is the nicest man I know

4. A bird in the hand is worth two in the bush

5. If winter is here

PREPOSITIONAL PHRASES

A *modifier* is a word that modifies, describes, or limits another word. There are two types of modifiers: *adjectives* and *adverbs*. *Adjectives* modify nouns and pronouns, while *adverbs* modify verbs, adjectives and other adverbs. In the sentence, "The green snake moved quietly through the grass," *green* is an adjective modifying the noun *snake*, and *quietly* is an adverb modifying the verb *moved*.

Adjectives and adverbs are *one-word* modifiers. However, there are *groups* of words which act like adjectives and adverbs. These groups of words are called *prepositional phrases*, because they begin with prepositions (*to, in, at, by, under*, etc.). In the sentence, "The lighthouse on the hill warns ships," *on the hill* is a prepositional phrase that works like an adjective by modifying the noun *lighthouse*. And in "He swam across the stream," *across the stream* is a prepositional phrase that works like an adverb by modifying the verb *swam*. How does the prepositional phrase *in the ocean* work in the sentence "The natural resources in the ocean are beyond calculation"?

Now notice how the prepositional phrases work like modifiers in the following sentences:

> We walked *across the street*.
> The boy *with red hair* walked *along the road*.
> He stood *behind me*.

In the first sentence, *across the street* works like an adverb by modifying the verb *walked*. In the second sentence, there are two prepositional phrases. *With red hair* works like an adjective because it modifies the noun *boy*. *Along the road* functions like an adverb because it modifies the verb *walked*. In the third sentence, *behind me* works like an adverb because it modifies the verb *stood*.

EXERCISE 15

DIRECTIONS: In each of the following sentences, underline the prepositional phrases and tell whether they work like adverbs or adjectives.

ANSWERS AND EXPLANATIONS APPEAR AT THE END OF THE CHAPTER

1. After dinner, we went for a walk.

2. He sits behind me in school.

3. The man from New York came into the room.

4. He leaned against the side of the building.

5. The girl with blonde hair left her glasses on the desk.

EXERCISE 16

DIRECTIONS: In each of the following sentences, there is one underlined section. Blacken the spaces in the answer column
as follows: 1—prepositional phrase used as adverb;
2—prepositional phrase used as adjective; 3—independent clause; 4—dependent clause.

ANSWERS AND EXPLANATIONS APPEAR AT THE END OF THE CHAPTER

1. <u>After lunch</u>, Charles returned to his homework.

2. The man <u>in the black coat</u> seemed very mysterious.

3. When dinner is finished, <u>I will wash the dishes</u>.

4. <u>When I graduate</u>, I hope to go to college.

5. He did the job <u>with great accuracy</u>.

6. When the play ended, <u>the audience cheered</u>.

7. He has lived <u>in this city</u> for three years.

8. It was John who stood <u>in the rain</u>.

9. <u>He waved to me</u> as he drove by.

10. <u>Around the corner</u> came an old sedan.

11. <u>After he left</u>, the telephone rang.

12. The girl <u>in the car</u> is John's date.

13. I'll know the man <u>when I see him</u>.

14. The boy <u>from Brooklyn</u> passed the test.

15. <u>When duty calls</u>, I must answer.

16. After we had left the room, <u>the teacher found the missing paper</u>.

17. 1 2 3 4

17. If you see <u>John</u>, tell him I miss him.

18. 1 2 3 4

18. I will meet you <u>at six o'clock</u>.

19. 1 2 3 4

19. Just leave the package <u>on the table</u>.

20. 1 2 3 4

20. <u>Things began to change</u> when George joined the team.

ANSWERS AND EXPLANATIONS: PARTS-OF-SENTENCE EXERCISES

EXERCISE 1

Some ways in which the sentences might have been completed are:

1. When I can come, I will.
2. At night, just before the last hour strikes, I am sleepy.
3. There you are every time I turn around.
4. Willy promises, if he is elected, to keep taxes down.
5. I wish every star in the sky would blink at the same time.

Remember, each of these examples is a sentence because it expresses a complete thought.

EXERCISE 2

1. (3) In a minute *what?*
2. (3) *What will happen? What will you do?*
3. (4) *What happened on that day?*
4. (3) *What did you do? What did you see?*
5. (5) All of these constructions express complete thoughts—they are sentences.

EXERCISE 3

1. girls   *Who is running?*
2. boys   *Who is playing ball?*
3. They   *Who are tired?*
4. He   *Who is the hero?*
5. Ann   *Ann is the person doing the action—crying.
6. Planning ahead   *What saves time?*
7. Evelyn and Tom   *It is Evelyn and Tom who did the going.*
8. Pitcher, catcher, manager   *Who "met"?*
9. Cake and candy   *What is not good for your teeth?*
10. Necessity   *What is being spoken about?*

EXERCISE 4

1. (1) *It is the boy who ran quickly.*
2. (2) *Who were standing on the corner?*
3. (2) *Who smiled and walked away?*
4. (1) *Who lived there?*
5. (2) *The team did the winning.*
6. (1) *It is Tom who went.*
7. (2) *Who helped me?*
8. (2) *If you reverse the question to make a sentence ("You have seen that show before"), you see that* you *is the actor or subject.*
9. (2) *It is the men who were in the car.*
10. (1) *Who is tired?*

EXERCISE 5

(Note that the simple predicate in each of the ten sentences is a verb.)

1. 5	3. 3	5. 2	7. 2	9. 2
2. 2	4. 2	6. 2	8. 2	10. 2

EXERCISE 6

(In each of the sentences, the simple subject is the person or thing doing the action or being spoken about, while the simple predicate is the verb.)

Subject	Predicate
1. boys	took
2. teacher	met
3. we	take
4. I	have met
	(*never* is an adverb)
5. Everything	was arranged
6. Joe	emerged
7. conference	had been
8. We	awaited
9. Three	had arrived
10. I	had seen
11. we	chatted
12. friends	had been waiting
13. We	left
14. boys	were
(*There* is never a subject.)	
15. truck	chugged

EXERCISE 7

(Remember, a complete subject may be one or more actors, with all of its modifiers. Likewise, a complete predicate may be a simple verb, or two or more verbs, with all of its modifiers.)

1. John and I are going to the movies tonight.

2. I used to live in Nebraska.

3. The girl in the red dress is my sister.

4. The boys did their best in the big game.

5. We could barely see the picture.

6. The old man was eighty-seven last month.

7. Mom and Dad celebrated their twenty-fifth anniversary.

8. Have you known them very long?

9. This car costs four thousand dollars.

10. Martha and I will be going to college in the fall.

11. We won't be going with you tomorrow.

12. Tom Reynolds, the tallest boy in the school, is the starting center on the basketball team.

13. His attitude seems to have changed in recent weeks.

14. We always go there on Saturday.

15. A new car pulled into the driveway.

16. I have been waiting for hours.

17. The box in the corner was left here this morning.

18. Next year, we intend to take a trip to California.

19. John's new suit looks very expensive.

20. Haste makes waste.

EXERCISE 8

1. (4) *What is being cut?*
2. (3) *What do you like?*
3. (3) *What does Jay take to school?*
4. (3) *What does baby put in its mouth?*
5. (3) *What do the students grow?*

EXERCISE 9

1. (2) *To whom was the jacket given?*
2. (2) *Of whom were the questions asked?*
3. (3) *My library has brought great comfort to whom?*
4. (2) *To whom did I tell your name and address?*
5. (2) *To whom did you give the directions?*

EXERCISE 10

(The direct object can be spotted easily by asking the questions WHAT? or WHOM? after the verb. To pick out the indirect object, ask TO WHAT? TO WHOM? FOR WHAT? FOR WHOM? after the verb.)

1. We gave him the tickets for the ball game.

2. Mother told me the good news.

3. They asked us many questions.

4. Can you lend me five dollars?

5. Tom gave his brother a new shirt for Christmas.

6. I'll give you five minutes more.

7. The teacher read the girls a letter from the principal.

8. He did us a great favor.

9. My brother has written me a letter.

10. Please tell me a story.

EXERCISE 11

1. (4) *John* follows the linking verb *was* and renames the subject *it*.
2. (3) The pronoun *I* is the same as the subject *It*.
3. (4) *Brother* is the same as the subject *It*.
4. (3) *Mary* equals the subject *it*.
5. (4) *Co-captains* follows the linking verb *are* and renames the compound subject *John and Tom*.

EXERCISE 12

1. (3) *Lucky* follows the linking verb *was* and modifies the subject *He*.
2. (4) *tired* follows the linking verb *am* and modifies the subject *I*.
3. (4) *beautiful* follows the linking verb *looks* and modifies the subject *sun*.
4. (4) *sad* follows the linking verb *seems* and modifies the subject *man*.
5. (4) *reliable* follows the linking verb *are* and modifies the subject *boys*.

EXERCISE 13

1. (2) *To whom did they give their names and addresses?*
2. (1) *Whom haven't you seen?*
3. (5) Happy *follows a linking verb* seem *and modifies the subject* they.
4. (1) *Who was alerted?*

5. (1) *What couldn't he see?*
6. (2) *Give another chance to whom?*
7. (4) She *is the same as* it.
8. (5) Delicious *follows a linking verb* was *and describes the subject* soup.
9. (5) Enthralled *follows a linking verb* were *and describes how the subjects* Mary and her sister *felt about the music.*
10. (1) *What was turned on?*
11. (1) *What was given?*
12. (1) *What was reached?*
13. (1) *What was the band playing?*
14. (3) Music *equals* it.
15. (2) *To whom will the lesson be taught?*
16. (5) Thirsty *follows a linking verb* were *and describes the subject* they.
17. (2) *To whom did the stranger tell his name?*
18. (3) Bowl of cherries *is the same as* life.
19. (5) Happy *follows a linking verb* were *and describes the subject* we.
20. (5) Delighted *follows a linking verb* were *and describes the subject* fans.

EXERCISE 14

(Remember, an independent clause expresses a complete thought, while a dependent clause leaves the thought unfinished.)

1. independent
2. dependent
3. independent

4. independent
5. dependent

EXERCISE 15

1. *after dinner* and *for a walk* both modify *went;* work like adverbs
2. *behind me* and *in school* both modify the verb *sits;* work like adverbs
3. *from New York* tells more about the noun *man;* works like an adjective
4. *against the side* modifies the verb *leaned;* works like an adverb; *of the building* modifies the noun *side;* works like a noun
5. *with blonde hair* tells more about the noun *girl;* works like an adjective; *on the dark* tells more about the verb *left;* works like an adverb

EXERCISE 16

1. (1) It modifies the verb *returned* by answering the question WHEN?
2. (2) It modifies the noun *man* by describing how he was dressed.
3. (3) It expresses a complete thought.
4. (4) It is dependent on the following independent clause.
5. (1) It modifies the verb *did* by answering the question HOW?
6. (3) It expresses a complete thought.
7. (1) It modifies the verb *has lived* by answering the question WHERE?
8. (1) It modifies the verb *stood* by answering the question WHERE?
9. (3) It expresses a complete thought.

10. **(1)** It modifies the verb *came* by answering the question FROM WHERE?
11. **(1)** It modifies the verb *rang* by answering the question WHEN?
12. **(2)** It modifies the noun *girl* by telling more about her.
13. **(4)** It is dependent on the previous independent clause.
14. **(2)** It modifies the noun *boy* by telling you more about him.
15. **(4)** It is dependent on the following independent clause.
16. **(3)** It expresses a complete thought.
17. **(4)** It is dependent on the following independent clause.
18. **(1)** It modifies the verb *will meet* by answering the question WHEN?
19. **(1)** It modifies the verb *leave* by answering the question WHERE?
20. **(3)** It expresses a complete thought.

COMMON ERRORS IN SENTENCE STRUCTURE

On the official test, you are often asked to detect errors in sentence structure. For instance, you may be given a group of four sentences and asked to spot the faulty sentence. One of the sentences might look like this: "I asked Sally to come with me to the movies she said that she would love to." Of course, this is a troublemaker. (A period should follow *movies* and *she* should be capitalized to begin a new sentence.)

There are four types of errors related to faulty sentence structure: (1) the sentence fragment; (2) the run-on sentence; (3) lack of parallel construction; and (4) faulty modification. In the next few pages, you will study each of them. However, before you begin, take the diagnostic test below.

SENTENCE STRUCTURE DIAGNOSTIC TEST

DIRECTIONS: On a separate sheet of paper, rewrite any of the following sentences that are incorrect.

ANSWERS APPEAR AT THE END OF THE TEST

1. Having ridden all day, the tall dark stranger wearing the mask and carrying the golden gun with the silver bullets.

2. Mary and Tom, weary from their day's efforts. Which had consisted of taking three tests and walking a mile when their car wouldn't start.

3. Sitting in a tree, we saw three elephants.

4. I came home, took off my hat and coat and hung them in the closet, then, because there was still an hour before dinner, I decided to take a short nap.

5. Charlie is a fine student, an outstanding athlete, and, as a person, someone you can always talk to.

6. Woodville is a long walk from here. About three miles, as a matter of fact.

7. We were eager and excited on the day of the big game, however, our spirits waned somewhat when the storm clouds began to gather at about ten o'clock.

8. I like fishing, swimming, and, every now and then, to hunt for small game such as rabbits.

9. Coming home from the dance last week, we met John.

10. Growling ferociously, we encountered a huge, black bear in the woods.

ANSWERS: DIAGNOSTIC TEST

1. Having ridden all day, the tall, dark stranger wearing the mask and carrying the golden gun with the silver bullets *was tired*.

2. Mary and Tom *were* weary from their day's efforts which had consisted of taking three tests and walking a mile when their car wouldn't start.

3. *When we were* sitting in a tree, we saw three elephants.

4. I came home, took off my hat and coat, and hung them in the *closet. Then* (or *closet; then,*) because there was still an hour before dinner, I decided to take a short nap.

5. Charlie is a fine student, an outstanding athlete, *and a sympathetic listener.*

6. Woodville is a long walk from here—about three miles, as a matter of fact.

7. We were eager and excited on the day of the big *game; however,* (or *game, but* . . .) our spirits waned somewhat when the storm clouds began to gather at about ten o'clock.

8. I like to go fishing, swimming, *and hunting.* Or: I like *to fish and swim,* and, every now and then, to hunt for small game such as rabbits.

9. We met John *when we were* (or *when he was*) coming home from the dance last week.

10. *When* we encountered a huge, black bear in the woods, *he growled* ferociously. Or: In the woods, we encountered a huge, black bear *which* was growling ferociously.

Note: These are only suggested revisions. There are other ways in which the sentences might have been correctly rewritten. The important thing is that you realize WHY the original sentences were wrong. The following pages attempt to explain this.

SENTENCE FRAGMENTS

A sentence fragment is exactly what the name implies—part of a sentence that is incorrectly designated as being complete because it begins with a capital letter and is followed by a period. This kind of error usually arises from confusing what is acceptable in spoken English with what is required for written English. When we are speaking to someone, and he says, "Why did you leave early?" it is perfectly clear and very correct to reply, "Because I was tired." Or if someone were to say, "What time did you leave?" it would be acceptable to respond: "When the dance was over" or "At about ten o'clock." But written English differs from spoken English in that every written sentence must be able to stand by itself, even though its meaning may be fairly clear because of the sentences preceding and following it. Look again at the three responses above, and you will see that they are all incomplete. In other words, none fulfills the three qualifications of a complete sentence: (1) a subject, (2) a predicate, and (3) the expression of a complete thought.

"Because I was tired":	This has a subject and a predicate, but it should really be part of another, larger construction: "I went home because I was tired."
"When the dance was over":	This has a subject (*dance*) and a predicate (*was*), but it does not express a complete thought. The reader is left to wonder, "What happened?"
"At about ten o'clock":	This is only a prepositional phrase, containing neither subject nor predicate.

Sentence fragments should be subordinated to (or made part of) a larger sentence that expresses a complete thought: "When the dance was over at about ten o'clock, *I went home* because I was tired."

Note how all three fragments have been combined with the key sentence (or independent clause): "I went home."

RUN-ON SENTENCES

You have seen that a sentence fragment error consists of calling something that is less than a sentence a complete sentence. A run-on sentence may be defined as almost the opposite of this: *putting too much into one construction and calling it a sentence.* Typically, a run-on results from two errors:

1. *Using a comma instead of a period, a semicolon, or a connecting word:* "We were delighted at the prospect of going, we eagerly began to make plans."
This construction actually contains two separate and distinct thoughts, each of which is a complete sentence by itself.

   Any of the following revisions would be acceptable:
   "We were delighted at the prospect of going. We eagerly..."
   "We were delighted at the prospect of going; we eagerly..."
   "We were delighted at the prospect of going, and we eagerly..."

2. *Using too many connecting words in one sentence instead of beginning a new sentence:* "It was dark and we were tired *so* Jane and I decided to call home and ask Dad to pick us up *and* we had a lot of trouble getting through *but* we finally did *and* everything turned out all right."

Notice how the revision is smoother (and easier to say): "It was dark and we were tired, so Jane and I decided to call home and ask Dad to pick us up. After some difficulty, we finally got through, and everything turned out all right."

Important: Be sure to choose the most effective connecting words and to punctuate properly. When the connecting words *and*, *but*, *so*, and *or* are used to connect clauses (complete thoughts), they are usually preceded by a comma. When they merely connect words, no comma is used.

> *Incorrect:* John was tired, *and* thirsty.
> *Correct:* It was extremely hot, *and* I became very thirsty.

Do not use a comma if the clauses are very short:

> *Incorrect:* I will go, *and* he will stay.
> *Correct:* I will go *and* he will stay.

Longer connecting words, such as *therefore* and *however*, are preceded by a semicolon and followed by a comma when they connect clauses.

> *Incorrect:* I should very much like to see him, *however*, there are a few things that must be cleared up first.
> *Correct:* Joe had worked all day perfecting his technique; *therefore*, he was more than prepared by the time the contest began.

LACK OF PARALLEL CONSTRUCTION

A parallel construction is one in which related ideas are expressed in the same grammatical form. Your ear should tell you what is wrong with each of the following sentences.

1. I like hunting, fishing, and to swim.
2. He proved to be not only tall but also a strong man.
3. The report showed that the cost had risen while there was a decrease in value.
4. She wore clothes that were better than the other girls.
5. Ricky is not only a good fielder but also a hitter with power.

Now notice how the following revisions of these faulty sentences increase smoothness and clarity by the use of parallel construction.

1. I like hunt*ing*, fish*ing*, and swimm*ing*.
   I like to *hunt*, *fish*, and *swim*.
2. He proved to be not only *tall* but also *strong*.
   He proved to be *tall* and *strong*.

3. The report showed that the *cost had risen* while the *value had decreased*.
    The report showed *rising cost* and *decreasing value*.
4. She wore *clothes* that were *better than those* worn by the other girls.
    She wore clothes that were *better than* the other girls' clothes.
5. Ricky is a *good fielder* and a *power hitter*.
    Ricky is good *in the field* and *at bat*.
    Ricky is not only *a good fielder* but also a *power hitter*.

Note: When *not only* is used, it is invariably paired with *but also*.

FAULTY MODIFICATION

Always be sure that the reader can tell what the modifier is modifying.

> *Weak:*   Sitting in a chair we saw John. (**Who** was sitting in the chair? We? John?)
>
> *Better:* When we were sitting in the chair, we saw John. **Or:** We saw John, who was sitting in the chair.

It is also important to be sure that your sentence structure is concise. Frequently, two distinct, but related, ideas can be more effectively expressed by putting them in the same sentence.

> *Weak:*   Sally did her best. She just couldn't pass the test.
>
> *Better:* *Although* Sally did her best, she just couldn't pass the test. **Or:** Sally did her best *but* she just couldn't pass the test.

The information presented in the preceding pages, if carefully studied, will provide you with guidelines that will enable you to successfully answer nearly all of the test items on sentence structure on the official examination. Now take the practice tests which follow. Be sure you understand WHY the errors are errors.

EXERCISE 1

DIRECTIONS: In each group of sentences below, there may be one sentence that contains an error in sentence structure. You are to indicate the number of the incorrect sentence and the type of error it shows. If all the sentences are correct, write "All correct."

ANSWERS AND EXPLANATIONS APPEAR AT THE END OF THE CHAPTER

1. (1) You have, however, impressed us with your integrity.
    (2) We looked all over for him; however, he was nowhere to be found.
    (3) We slept and ate most of the day, later on we went for a walk.

    (4) We therefore feel that it would not be advisable to sign the contract at this time.

2. (1) The tan car speeding down the road and looking as if it had come through World War II.
    (2) Jack looked very tired; as a matter of fact, he seemed exhausted.
    (3) As we walked into the room, we were greeted by a most extraordinary sight.
    (4) We spoke to a man who was not only learned but also interesting.

3. (1) This may be the way you are used to doing things, however, our procedures are slightly different.
    (2) Stretching down the road as far as we could see was a double row of giant evergreen trees.
    (3) He has not only exhausted our patience but has also cost us a substantial sum of money.
    (4) As a consequence of the intensive deliberations, the new contract appeared to be equitable for all concerned.

4. (1) I came as Johnson was leaving.
    (2) Come here, please.
    (3) He came to swim.
    (4) He likes singing and to dance.

5. (1) Mary Thomas, who as we all know is a most versatile and talented performer, appeared at the country club last week and simply astounded the audience.
    (2) I was tired and hungry.
    (3) This is the only way to do the job properly; therefore, any alternative methods are not to be followed.
    (4) Bill Dempsey, who everybody thought would win the award because of his past experience and the fact that he had participated in events like this for many years—ever since he had been a child, in fact.

6. (1) If he comes, I go.
    (2) I go if he comes.
    (3) He comes and I go.
    (4) He comes, I go.

7. (1) Walking in the dark, my foot struck something hard and cold.
    (2) When he comes, tell him I've gone home.
    (3) You may be very well prepared in terms of theory, but I think you'll find the realities of actually working on the project rather demanding.
    (4) We heard that the players, coming off the field, were complaining about the way the umpire had called the final play.

8. (1) All babies need sleep and to be fed at regular intervals.
    (2) Our appetites had been whetted by weeks of preparation for the annual banquet, and the rain that fell dampened our spirits as well as the sidewalks.
    (3) Can you remember the name of the clerk to whom you spoke when you made an attempt to exchange the dress last week?

(4) As far as I can determine, the directions indicate that we should place the bolt here; however, I would not want to make a bet on it.

9. (1) We have therefore directed our attorney to take appropriate legal action.
(2) Coming into the room, chaos met our eyes.
(3) *Moby Dick,* one of the classics of American literature, was the topic of the lecture, and, as a result, the hall was filled.
(4) We didn't entirely approve of his going; therefore, we were rather concerned when he hadn't called by ten o'clock.

10. (1) We are, however, very much interested in what you might think.
(2) This is a very fine play indeed.
(3) By midnight, it was ten degrees below zero, and we were freezing.
(4) Good books are like good friends: they're always around when needed.

EXERCISE 2

DIRECTIONS: Each sentence below contains an underlined section followed by four possible revisions. In the answer column, blacken the space under the number that corresponds to the number of the most acceptable revision. If none of the revisions is acceptable, or if the sentence is correct as it stands, blacken the fifth space.

ANSWERS AND EXPLANATIONS APPEAR AT THE END OF THE CHAPTER

1. In everything George Washington undertook, he showed the same charac-teristic. An almost overpowering desire to succeed.
   (1) characteristic an   (3) characteristic, an
   (2) characteristic; An   (4) characteristic, An

2. Although the author resented some of the criticism of his novel, he had to admit that some of the objections were valid.
   (1) novel. He   (3) novel; he
   (2) novel he   (4) novel—he

3. In English this year, we are reading some of the classics, so far we have covered *Huckleberry Finn* and *The Scarlet Letter.*
   (1) classics, so, far   (3) classics so far
   (2) classics; so far   (4) classics and so far

4. Mr. Phipps has urged all the players to continue working out and he knows that when the season is over, some athletes tend to relax a bit too much.
   (1) out; and he   (3) out because he
   (2) out, and he   (4) out because; he

5. To gain entrance, they tried both cajoling and to force their way in.
   (1) cajoling, and force   (3) cajoling, and forcing
   (2) cajoling and forcing   (4) to cajole, and force

6. Daily exercise, a strict sleeping schedule, and <u>eating nutritious foods</u> are all necessary to good health.

   (1) eating foods that are nutritious.
   (2) eating nutritious foods.
   (3) good nutrition.
   (4) you should eat good food

6. 1 2 3 4 5

7. The teacher explained the origin of labor unions and <u>how they affected</u> national commerce.

   (1) about how they affected
   (2) their affecting of
   (3) the way they affected
   (4) their effect upon

7. 1 2 3 4 5

8. The airline is running a special flight for Chicago commuters <u>leaving</u> at six o'clock.

   (1) which leave
   (2) who leaves
   (3) which is leaving
   (4) It leaves

8. 1 2 3 4 5

9. He was <u>not only elected</u> president of his class but also captain of the team.

   (1) only elected
   (2) elected only
   (3) elected not only
   (4) not only electing

9. 1 2 3 4 5

10. The announcement of the tryouts came <u>late, therefore we</u> had to set up a vigorous training schedule.

   (1) late. Therefore, we
   (2) late, therefore, we
   (3) late therefore we
   (4) late; therefore, we

10. 1 2 3 4 5

EXERCISE 3

DIRECTIONS: Each sentence below is followed by four alternatives. In the answer column, blacken the space under the number that corresponds to the number of the correct alternative. If there are no correct alternatives, or if the sentence is correct as is, blacken the fifth space.

ANSWERS AND EXPLANATIONS APPEAR AT THE END OF THE CHAPTER

1. I worked hard, I received a raise.
   (1) I worked hard, so I received a raise.
   (2) I worked hard; and I received a raise.
   (3) I worked hard but I received a raise.
   (4) I worked hard, therefore, I received a raise.

1. 1 2 3 4 5

2. It was a difficult test but we had studied hard because we wanted to do well and when the results were posted and we saw our scores we were more than gratified.
   (1) We had studied hard because we wanted to do well on the difficult test so when we saw our scores when the results were posted we were more than gratified.
   (2) We had studied hard for the difficult test because we wanted to do well. When the results were posted, and we saw our scores, we were more than gratified.

2. 1 2 3 4 5

(3) It was a difficult test therefore we wanted to do well. We therefore studied hard and were consequently greatly gratified when the results were posted and we saw our scores.

(4) It was a difficult test. We studied hard. When the results were posted. We saw our scores. We were greatly gratified.

3.   1   2   3   4   5

3. My father had been getting up very early on these cold mornings. And putting in long, hard hours at the plant.

(1) My father had been getting up very early on these cold mornings; and putting in long, hard hours at the plant.

(2) My father had been getting up very early on these cold mornings and putting in long, hard hours at the plant.

(3) My father had been getting up early, he was working hard.

(4) My father had been working early during these hard hours.

4.   1   2   3   4   5

4. Hungry, thirsty, and generally exhausted, the troop of men nevertheless managed to step smartly as they reentered the gates of Fort Apache.

(1) Hungry, thirsty and generally exhausted; the troop of men nevertheless managed to step smartly. As they reentered the gates of Fort Apache.

(2) The tired, hungry, men were exhausted; nevertheless, they reentered the gates of Fort Apache.

(3) Stepping smartly, the troop of tired, hungry, exhausted men as they reentered the gates of Fort Apache.

(4) The men were tired, hungry and exhausted. And they reentered the gates of Fort Apache, but they stepped smartly.

5.   1   2   3   4   5

5. Good pitching is the key to a winning season but long-ball hitters are also an asset.

(1) Although good pitching is the key to a winning season, long ball hitters are also an asset.

(2) Good pitching and long ball hitters are the asset to a winning season.

(3) Long ball hitters are an asset. Although good pitching is the key.

(4) Good pitching is the key to a successful season, and long ball hitters are an asset too.

6.   1   2   3   4   5

6. Cigarettes have been related to cancer and millions of people continue to smoke.

(1) Although millions of people continue to smoke, cigarettes are related to cancer.

(2) Cigarettes have been related to cancer; therefore many people continue to smoke.

(3) Cigarettes have been related to cancer, however, millions of people continue to smoke.

(4) Although cigarettes have been related to cancer, millions of people continue to smoke.

7.   1   2   3   4   5

7. Melville was one of the great American writers and he was not honored until after his death.

(1) Melville was one of the great American writers, but he was not honored until after his death.

(2) Because Melville was one of the great American writers, he was not honored until after his death.

(3) Melville was one of the great American writers, however, he was not honored until after his death.

(4) Melville was one of the great American writers. He was not honored until after his death.

8. Mary's paper is better-written than any of the boys.

   (1) Mary's paper is better-written than any of the boys are.
   (2) Mary's paper is better-written than that of any of the boys.
   (3) Mary's paper is better-written. Than any of the boys.
   (4) Mary's paper, however, is better than any of the boys.

8. 1 2 3 4 5

EXERCISE 4

DIRECTIONS: Each sentence below is followed by four alternatives. In the answer column, blacken the space under the number that corresponds to the number of the correct alternative. If there are no correct alternatives, or if the sentence is correct as is, blacken the fifth space.

ANSWERS AND EXPLANATIONS APPEAR AT THE END OF THE CHAPTER

1. Wandering along the road one day, I came upon a young deer.

   (1) As I wandered along the road one day, I came upon a young deer.
   (2) Wandering along the road one day. I came upon a young deer.
   (3) Wandering along the road one day; I came upon a young deer.
   (4) I came upon a young deer who was wandering along the road, one day.

1. 1 2 3 4 5

2. He is not only a leader in class but also in the whole school.

   (1) He is a leader in class so he is a leader in school.
   (2) He is a leader not only in class but also in the whole school.
   (3) Not only is he a leader in class, but also in the whole school as well.
   (4) He is a leader in class. But he is also a leader in school too.

2. 1 2 3 4 5

3. I know him better than you.

   (1) I know him better than he knows you.
   (2) I know him better than you know me.
   (3) I know him better than you do.
   (4) He knows me better than you.

3. 1 2 3 4 5

4. He regarded Jane as capable, diligent, and able to be depended upon.

   (1) He regarded Jane as capable, diligent, and you could depend on her.
   (2) He regarded Jane as capable, diligent, and dependable.
   (3) He regarded Jane as capable, diligent and dependent upon.
   (4) He regarded Jane as capable, diligent; and dependable.

4. 1 2 3 4 5

5. The class did extremely well not only on the oral test but also on the written exam.

   (1) The class did extremely well on only the oral exam but not the written test.

5. 1 2 3 4 5

(2) The class did extremely well on not only the written exam but also on the oral test.
(3) The class did extremely well on not only the oral test but also on the written exam.
(4) The class not only did well on the oral test but also on the written exam.

6. 1 2 3 4 5

6. Come to the meeting prepared to take notes and with some questions to ask.
(1) Come to the meeting with some notes to take and some questions to ask.
(2) Come to the meeting not only with some notes but also with some questions.
(3) Come to the meeting prepared to take notes and ask questions.
(4) Come to the meeting. Be prepared to take notes, and ask questions.

7. 1 2 3 4 5

7. George decided when he came home to watch television for an hour.
(1) When he came home, George decided to watch television for an hour.
(2) Coming home, George decided to watch television for an hour.
(3) George decided to watch television for an hour coming home.
(4) When he had been home for an hour, George decided to watch television.

8. 1 2 3 4 5

8. His work was not only interesting but also profitable.
(1) His work was not only interesting, but it was profitable.
(2) His work was interestintg; it was also profitable.
(3) His work was interesting, and profitable.
(4) Not only was his work interesting, but it was also profitable.

9. 1 2 3 4 5

9. To complain about a problem is not as good as doing something about it.
(1) Complaining about a problem is not as good as to do something about it.
(2) Complaining about a problem is not as good as doing something about it.
(3) Complaining about a problem is not good. Do something about it.
(4) Complaining about a problem is as good as doing something about it.

10. 1 2 3 4 5

10. The choice was difficult, the selection was so large.
(1) Because the choice was difficult, the selection was so large.
(2) The choice was difficult because the selection was so large.
(3) The selection was so large and the choice was difficult.
(4) The choice was difficult and this made the selection large.

EXERCISE 5

DIRECTIONS: Read the selection below, paying particular attention to the underlined sections. Following the selection are groups of alternatives for each underlined part. In the answer column, blacken the space under the number that corresponds to the number of the acceptable alternative. If there are no acceptable alternatives, or if the underlined section is correct as is, blacken the fifth space.

ANSWERS AND EXPLANATIONS APPEAR AT THE END OF THE CHAPTER

Improvisation of <u>sketches is a chancy affair whether topical or not</u>. It goes
$\qquad$1
best when practiced like a parlor game <u>among friends, there is</u> more risk in a cafe
$\qquad$2
or <u>night club; but</u> with relaxed, imbibing customers around the <u>performers, it</u>
$\quad$3$\qquad\qquad\qquad\qquad\qquad\qquad\qquad$4
takes on the atmosphere of carnival sport. In a theater with a sober, paying
audience waiting in expectant rows to be entertained <u>swiftly and with efficiency</u>,
$\qquad\qquad\qquad\qquad\qquad\qquad\qquad$5
improvisation is all but impossible.

Indeed, sketches which bear the marks of improvisatory genius seldom hold
up in the formal procedures of a theater <u>review; because</u> they have a tendency
$\qquad\qquad\qquad$6
<u>to stammer and dawdle and seeming coy and amateurish</u>. They make an audi-
$\qquad\qquad\qquad$7
ence <u>restless</u>. <u>For they</u> spread a sense of <u>indecision and ineffectualness and there</u>
$\quad$8$\qquad\qquad\qquad\qquad\qquad\qquad$9
is little that is more disaffecting in the theater than a <u>lack of authority and not</u>
$\qquad\qquad\qquad\qquad\qquad\qquad$10
<u>having control</u> on the stage.

1. (1) sketches whether topical, or not are a chancy affair
   (2) sketches, whether topical or not, is a chancy affair
   (3) sketches is a chancy affair. Whether topical or not
   (4) sketches is a chancy affair; whether topical or not

2. (1) among friends there is   (3) among friends. There is
   (2) among friends; there is   (4) among friends; There is

3. (1) night club; But   (3) night club, but
   (2) night club, and   (4) night club but

4. (1) performers, it   (3) performers and it
   (2) performers; it   (4) performers. It

5. (1) swiftly, and efficiently
   (2) swiftly and efficiently
   (3) swiftly, and with efficiency
   (4) efficiently and with great speed

6. (1) review. Because   (3) review, because
   (2) review; Because   (4) review because

7. (1) to stammer and dawdle seeming coy and amateurish
   (2) to stammer and dawdle and to seem coy and amateurish
   (3) to stammer and dawdle and to seem coy, and amateurish
   (4) to stammer and dawdle; and to seem coy and amateurish

8. (1) restless; for they   (3) restless; For they
   (2) restless for they   (4) restless, for they

9. 1 2 3 4 5

9. (1)   indecision and ineffectiveness; And there
   (2)   indecision, and ineffectiveness. And there
   (3)   indecision, and ineffectiveness, and there
   (4)   indecision and ineffectiveness. And there

10. 1 2 3 4 5

10. (1)   lack of authority, and not having control
    (2)   lack of authority; and not having control
    (3)   lack of authority and control
    (4)   lack of authority, and control

EXERCISE 6

DIRECTIONS: Read the selection below, paying particular attention to the underlined sections. Following the selection are groups of alternatives for each underlined part. In the answer column, blacken the space under the number that corresponds to the number of the acceptable alternative. If there are no acceptable alternatives, or if the underlined section is correct as is, blacken the fifth space.

ANSWERS AND EXPLANATIONS APPEAR AT THE END OF THE CHAPTER

After about an hour, we saw a dilapidated old Model T Ford turn the
_____
        1

corner. Its fenders hanging off, its lights blinking and the doors were wide open.
_____   _____
   2   3

As it drew closer. We could begin to make out the driver. He was an old man.
         _____   _____
              4   5

There was a twinkle in his eye, however, that belied his age; and we wondered
                            _____   _____
                                    6   7

what he would have to say. "Good morning boys," he called, "could you direct

me to the expressway?" We were quite amused, who in his right mind would
                                   _____
                                                    8

want to take an old wreck like that on an expressway? We could tell; though,
                                                                _____
                                                                      9

that there would be no reasoning with this man we gave him the directions. And
____   _____
                                                   10

off he went.

1. 1 2 3 4 5

1. (1)   After about an hour; we   (3)   After about an hour we
   (2)   After about an hour. We   (4)   After about an hour; We

2. 1 2 3 4 5

2. (1)   corner its   (3)   corner, its
   (2)   corner. Its   (4)   corner; its

3. 1 2 3 4 5

3. (1)   blinking, its doors wide open
   (2)   blinking with the doors wide open
   (3)   blinking; its doors were wide open
   (4)   blinking because the doors were wide open

4. (1) closer; we   (3) closer we
   (2) closer; We   (4) closer, we

4. 1 2 3 4 5

5. (1) driver, he   (3) driver who
   (2) driver; he   (4) driver. Who

5. 1 2 3 4 5

6. (1) eye however that   (3) eye; however that
   (2) eye; however, that   (4) eye. However that

6. 1 2 3 4 5

7. (1) age. And   (3) age, and
   (2) age, but   (4) age; And

7. 1 2 3 4 5

8. (1) amused; who   (3) amused. Who
   (2) amused who   (4) amused who,

8. 1 2 3 4 5

9. (1) tell though that   (3) tell, though that
   (2) tell though, that   (4) tell, though, that

9. 1 2 3 4 5

10. (1) man, so   (3) man, therefore
    (2) man, but   (4) man, and

10. 1 2 3 4 5

EXERCISE 7

DIRECTIONS: Look carefully at each construction below. Identify the error in sentence structure. Then, in the answer column, blacken a space under the number as follows: 1—sentence fragment; 2—run-on sentence; 3—lack of parallel structure; 4—faulty modification. If there are no errors, blacken the fifth space.

ANSWERS AND EXPLANATIONS APPEAR AT THE END OF THE CHAPTER

1. The mysterious masked man sitting on the big white horse.

1. 1 2 3 4 5

2. First we did our shopping, we went home to rest.

2. 1 2 3 4 5

3. Coming down the street, we saw the burning building.

3. 1 2 3 4 5

4. I enjoy playing baseball and to play football.

4. 1 2 3 4 5

5. I have decided on a college and what to major in.

5. 1 2 3 4 5

6. Because we had studied all evening and were tired.

6. 1 2 3 4 5

7. During the intermission, the audience discussed the first act.

7. 1 2 3 4 5

8. We were surprised to see him, we hadn't known he was coming.

8. 1 2 3 4 5

9. When you see Toby.

9. 1 2 3 4 5

10. He seemed calm, cool, and had complete relaxation.

10. 1 2 3 4 5

11. If you do your best, you will surely succeed.

11. 1 2 3 4 5

12. I waited for about ten minutes, I got up and went home.

12. 1 2 3 4 5

13. 1 2 3 4 5

13. If you do as I have suggested, being careful not to leave out any important details.

14. 1 2 3 4 5

14. I like to go fishing, hunting, and to swim.

15. 1 2 3 4 5

15. I saw a car parked in the driveway which was shiny and looked new.

16. 1 2 3 4 5

16. Tired and hungry, we saw the old man coming down the mountain.

17. 1 2 3 4 5

17. The man who told me about the problem is no longer here.

18. 1 2 3 4 5

18. Racing down the highway at about seventy miles an hour with a siren shrieking and its lights flashing.

19. 1 2 3 4 5

19. Because you have done a good job in your present position.

20. 1 2 3 4 5

20. He asked for my name, age, and what my address was.

ANSWERS AND EXPLANATIONS: SENTENCE STRUCTURE EXERCISES

EXERCISE 1

1. (3) is a run-on.
2. (1) is a fragment.
3. (1) is a run-on.
4. (4) is not parallel.
5. (4) is a fragment.
6. (4) is a run-on.
7. (1) has faulty modification.
8. (1) is not parallel.
9. (2) has faulty modification.
10. (5)

EXERCISE 2

1. (3) See "Sentence Fragments."
2. (5) See "Run-On Sentences."
3. (2) See "Run-On Sentences."
4. (3) See "Run-On Sentences."
5. (2) See "Lack of Parallel Construction."
6. (3) See "Lack of Parallel Construction."
7. (4) See "Lack of Parallel Construction."
8. (4) See "Faulty Modification."
9. (3) See "Lack of Parallel Construction."
10. (4) See "Run-On Sentences."

EXERCISE 3

1. (1) *So* is the clearest word; (2) and (4) are not properly punctuated.
2. (2) Captures the meaning of the original in the most concise language.
3. (2) The others either change the meaning or are not properly punctuated.
4. (5)
5. (1) Preserves the meaning in the most concise language.
6. (4) Punctuated properly; does not change the meaning.
7. (1) This best maintains the sense of the original.
8. (2) This is the most satisfactory way of expressing the thought in parallel terms. The others seem to compare the paper with the boys themselves.

EXERCISE 4

1. (1) Choices (3), (4), and (5) are punctuated incorrectly.
2. (2) Keeps *not only–but also* close to the related ideas.
3. (3) Completes the parallel construction; the others change the meaning.
4. (2) Completes the parallel structure.
5. (3) Keeps the connecting words as close as possible to what they connect.
6. (3) Completes the parallel structure; does not change the meaning.
7. (1) Makes the reference as clear as possible.
8. (5)
9. (2) Completes the parallel structure without separating the ideas.
10. (2) Uses the most accurate connecting word (*because*).

EXERCISE 5

1. (2) Keep modifiers close to what they modify.
2. (3) This run-on sentence requires a new sentence.
3. (5) Correct as is; semicolon needed to separate very long clauses.
4. (5) Correct as is; comma needed to separate introductory clause.
5. (2) No comma when *and* joins words (*swiftly* and *efficiently*).
6. (4) Punctuation is usually not needed when *because* is used.
7. (2) Parallel construction needed; no punctuation required.
8. (4) Use comma before short connecting words.
9. (4) Begin with *and* for effect.
10. (3) Parallel structure needed; no comma required.

EXERCISE 6

1. (5)
2. (3) See "Sentence Fragments."
3. (1) See "Lack of Parallel Construction."
4. (4) See "Sentence Fragments."
5. (5)
6. (5)
7. (3) Use a comma when two clauses are closely related.
8. (3) See "Run-On Sentences."

9. (4) A comma is used to set off a word or phrase that interrupts the smooth flow of the sentence.
10. (1) See "Run-On Sentences."

EXERCISE 7

1. (1) Finish the description. *What did he do?*
2. (2) If you add *and then* after *shopping,* you can correct this run-on sentence.
3. (4) WHO was coming down the street? *Correct:* As we were coming down the street, we saw the burning building.
4. (3) Change *to play* to *playing.*
5. (3) Change *what to major in* to *a major.*
6. (1) Finish the thought.
7. (5)
8. (2) Place a semicolon between these two independent clauses *or* write them as two separate sentences.
9. (1) Finish the thought.
10. (3) Change *had complete relaxation* to *relaxed.*
11. (5)
12. (2) Place a semicolon and the word *then* between these two independent clauses *or* write them as two separate sentences.
13. (1) Finish the thought.
14. (3) Change *to swim* to *swimming.*
15. (3) Change *looked new* to *new.*
16. (4) WHO was tired and hungry? *Correct:* We were tired and hungry as we saw the old man coming down the mountain.
17. (5)
18. (1) *What happened?*
19. (1) Finish the thought.
20. (3) Change *what my address was* to *address.*

USAGE

Usage is a term used to describe the acceptable use of words and grammatical correctness. One section of the test you will be taking is concerned with usage. In fact, as much as twenty-five percent of the test may deal with this topic. Usage can be broken down into four basic parts: verb tenses, subject-verb agreement, pronoun usage, and modification. In the next few pages, these items will be discussed at length. However, before going on to them, take the diagnostic test which follows.

USAGE DIAGNOSTIC TEST

DIRECTIONS: In each of the following sentences, there are two words in parentheses. Choose the correct word.

ANSWERS AND EXPLANATIONS APPEAR AT THE END OF THE TEST

1. They had (went, gone) before you did.

2. If you (had, would have) come on time, you would have seen her.

3. Tom (have, has) been here several times already.

4. I (have gone, will be going) there tomorrow.

5. This hat (go, goes) well with the dress.

6. I (saw, seen) him when I came in.

7. Then I (stand, stood) up and shouted, "Look out!"

8. We (have done, done) the best we could.

9. They (layed, laid) the book on the desk.

10. After dinner, I generally (lie, lay) down for an hour.

11. The boys (was, were) late coming home last night.

12. One of the pictures (was, were) missing.

13. Everyone should try (his, their) best.

14. Everyone (need, needs) food, clothing, and shelter.

15. Either he or I (are, am) going.

16. There (was, were) three chairs in the room.

17. The class (was, were) asked to give their opinions.

18. Ten dollars (is, are) too much to pay for a shirt.

19. Measles (is, are) a childhood disease.

20. It (doesn't, don't) make any difference to me.

21. (We, Us) boys are excited about going.

22. Tom and (I, me) have been friends for years.

23. I didn't know that John was older than (he, him).

24. Can you do the job as well as (we, us)?

25. Just between you and (I, me), this is a secret.

26. Was it (she, her) who called?

27. Are you positive that it was (he, him)?

28. He is a man (who, whom) I admire.

29. (Who, Whom) do you think will win?

30. To (who, whom) did you speak?

31. Mary sings (beautiful, beautifully).

32. The roast smelled (strange, strangely).

33. I felt (bad, badly) about burning the turkey.

34. He acted (well, good) in the school play.

35. It was really a (well, good) job.

36. I'll take the (bigger, biggest) of the two pieces.

37. John is taller than(anyone, anyone else) in the class.

38. This is better than (any, any other) dress I've seen.

39. This is the (tallest, most tallest) building in the world.

40. Mary was the (more beautiful, most beautiful) of the two.

ANSWERS AND EXPLANATIONS: DIAGNOSTIC TEST

1. gone   *The past perfect tense is formed by *had* plus the past participle *gone* (*went* is the past tense).

2. had   *Use the past perfect tense (*had come*) for the first of two actions completed in the past.

3. has   *A singular subject (*Tom*) must be followed by a singular verb (*has*).

4. will be going   *The word *tomorrow* signals the use of the future tense.

5. goes   *A singular subject (*hat*) must be followed by a singular verb (*goes*).

6. saw   *Use the past participle (*seen*) only when it is preceded by *have, has,* or *had*.

7. stood   *The word *shouted* signals the use of the past tense (*stood*).

8. have done   *The past participle *done* cannot stand alone—it must be preceded by *has, have,* or *had*.

9. laid   *laid* is the past tense of the verb lay, meaning to "place," while *layed* is the past tense of the verb *lie,* meaning to "recline."

10. lie   *See explanation for 9 above.

11. were   *The verb must be plural to agree with plural subject *boys*.

12. was   *The verb must be singular to agree with the singular subject *One* (not *pictures*).
13. his   *The pronoun must be singular to agree with its singular antecedent, *Everyone*.
14. was   *The verb must be singular to agree with the singular subject *Everyone*.
15. am   *The verb must be singular to agree with singular subject *I*.
16. were   *The verb must be plural to agree with plural subject *chairs*.
17. were   *See Rule 8 in "Agreement of Subject and Verb."
18. is   *See Rule 8 in "Agreement of Subject and Verb."
19. is   *See Rule 9 in "Agreement of Subject and Verb."
20. doesn't   *See Rule 10 in "Agreement of Subject and Verb."
21. We   *See "Pronoun Usage." This sentence calls for the subject form of the pronoun.
22. I   *See "Pronoun Usage." This sentence calls for the subject form of the pronoun.
23. he   *See Rule 2 in "Pronoun Usage."
24. we   *See Rule 2 in "Pronoun Usage."
25. me   *See Rule 3 in "Pronoun Usage."
26. she   *See Rule 4 in "Pronoun Usage."
27. he   *See Rule 4 in "Pronoun Usage."
28. whom   *See Rule 5 in "Pronoun Usage."
29. Who   *See Rule 5 in "Pronoun Usage."
30. whom   *See Rule 5 in "Pronoun Usage."
31. beautifully   *Use an adverb to modify a verb.
32. strange   *See Rule 1 in "Modification."
33. bad   *See Rule 2 in "Modification."
34. well   *Use the adverb to modify an action verb. See Rule 2 in "Modification."
35. good   *See Rule 2 in "Modification."
36. bigger   *See Rule 3 in "Modification."
37. anyone else   *See Rule 4 in "Modification."
38. any other   *See Rule 4 in "Modification."
39. tallest   *See Rule 5 in "Modification."
40. more beautiful   *See Rule 3 in "Modification."

TENSES OF VERBS

Verbs are words used to express an action or a state of being. The time at which the action or state of being takes place is called the tense. In English, there are six major tenses, each one expressing a different quality of time.

The **Present Tense** is used to describe an action or state of being that is happening right now or one that is always going on.

> He *speaks* to her.
> She *is laughing*.

The **Past Tense** is used to describe an action that has been completed or is no longer going on.

> He *spoke* to her.
> She *laughed*.

The **Future Tense** is used to describe something that is going to happen.

> He *will speak* to her.
> She *will laugh*.

EXERCISE 1

DIRECTIONS: In each of the following sentences there is an italicized verb. You are to indicate whether the verb is in the present tense, the past tense, or the future tense.

ANSWERS APPEAR AT THE END OF THE CHAPTER

1. I *go* there every day.

2. We *were* at the beach yesterday.

3. I *came* when he called.

4. I *enjoyed* the movie.

5. I *will see* you tomorrow.

6. I was going home when I *saw* John.

7. I *do* it every day.

8. They *will do* it tomorrow.

9. He *did* it yesterday.

10. I *am* happy to see you.

Do not be confused by slight changes in form. For example, "I talk" and "I am talking" are both present tense. "I talked" and "I was talking" are both past tense. "I shall talk" and "I shall be talking" are both future tense.

The **Present Perfect Tense** describes an action or state of being that began in the past and is either still going on or has just ended.

> He *has spoken* to her.
> She *has laughed*.

The **Past Perfect Tense** refers to the first of two actions completed in the past.

> He *had spoken* to her on the telephone before he arrived.
> She *had laughed* before the others did.

The **Future Perfect Tense** refers to the first of two actions that will be completed in the future.

> By the time he arrives, he *shall have spoken* to her on the telephone.
> By tomorrow, she *will have laughed* many times.

It is important to note that all perfect tenses are formed by an *auxiliary verb* plus the *past participle of the main verb:*

Tense	= *Auxiliary*	+ *Past Participle of Main Verb*
Present Perfect	= present tense *have* +	*fallen*
Past Perfect	= past tense *had* +	*fallen*
Future Perfect	= future tense *will have* +	*fallen*

EXERCISE 2

DIRECTIONS: For each of the following sentences, choose the correct tense of the italicized verb. Classify the verb as follows: 1—present tense; 2—past tense; 3—future tense; 4—present perfect tense; 5—past perfect tense. Then blacken the space under the number corresponding to your choice.

ANSWERS APPEAR AT THE END OF THE CHAPTER

1. We *have been* there before.

2. I *had gone* before he came.

3. They *will come* here tomorrow.

4. I *am going* home now.

5. He *does* his best.

6. I *was thinking* of you yesterday.

7. Irene *had called* earlier.

8. I *have lived* here for ten years.

9. Last night, she *watched* a movie on television.

10. I *knew* him right away.

PRINCIPAL PARTS OF VERBS

The principal parts of verbs are the *present tense*, the *past tense*, and the *past participle*. Together with auxiliary verbs (*be, have, shall*, etc.), these three parts form all the tenses. Note the principal parts of the verbs below.

Present	Past	Past Participle
melt	melted	melted
smell	smelled	smelled
sing	sang	sung
run	ran	run

Melt and *smell* are called regular verbs because they form the past and the participle forms by adding *ed* or *d* to the present tense. *Sing* and *run* change in other ways and are called *irregular verbs*.

Note the way the three principal parts form all the tenses:

1. To form the *present tense*, use the present part:

   I dance, you dance, he dances
   I swear, you swear, he swears

2. To form the *past tense*, use the past principal part:

   I danced, you danced, he danced
   I swore, you swore, he swore

3. To form the *future tense*, use *will* with the present part:

   I will dance, you will dance, he will dance
   I will swear, you will swear, he will swear

4. To form the *present perfect tense*, use *have* or *has* with the past participle.

   I have danced, you have danced, he has danced
   I have sworn, you have sworn, he has sworn

5. To form the *past perfect tense*, use *had* with the past participle:

   I had danced, you had danced, he had danced
   I had sworn, you had sworn, he had sworn

6. To form the *future perfect tense*, use *will have* with the past participle.

   I will have danced, you will have danced, he will have danced
   I will have sworn, you will have sworn, he will have sworn

EXERCISE 3

DIRECTIONS: Below are the principal parts of **sing**, **throw**, and **look**. See how these verbs are used in the sentences that follow. For each italicized verb, blacken the space under a number as follows: 1—present tense; 2—past tense; 3—future tense; 4—present perfect tense; 5—past perfect tense.

sing	sang	sung
throw	threw	thrown
look	looked	looked

ANSWERS AND EXPLANATIONS APPEAR AT THE END OF THE CHAPTER

1. We *looked* everywhere for the missing wallet.

2. They *will sing* for us tonight.

3. He *had thrown* the ball out of the park.

4. John *sings* beautifully.

5. We *have looked* at that already.

6. She *threw* down her book in disgust.

7. Please *throw* me the football.

8. *Has* she *sung* yet?

9. They *sang* the national anthem.

10. We *will look* for it tomorrow.

	1	2	3	4	5
1.	‖	‖	‖	‖	‖
2.	‖	‖	‖	‖	‖
3.	‖	‖	‖	‖	‖
4.	‖	‖	‖	‖	‖
5.	‖	‖	‖	‖	‖
6.	‖	‖	‖	‖	‖
7.	‖	‖	‖	‖	‖
8.	‖	‖	‖	‖	‖
9.	‖	‖	‖	‖	‖
10.	‖	‖	‖	‖	‖

When we show all possible forms of a verb, we are showing its *conjugation*. Perhaps the most difficult word to conjugate is the verb *be*. For this reason, all its forms are shown below. The conjugation is followed by a list of the principal parts of irregular verbs. Study them carefully and watch your scores improve on the tests that end this chapter.

THE VERB <u>BE</u>

Present Tense

Singular	*Plural*
1. I *am*	We *are*
2. You *are*	You *are*
3. He (she, it) *is*	They *are*

Past Tense

Singular	*Plural*
1. I *was*	We *were*
2. You *were*	You *were*
3. He (she, it) *was*	They *were*

Future Tense

Singular	*Plural*
1. I *shall be*	We *shall be*
2. You *will be*	You *will be*
3. He (she, it) *will be*	They *will be*

Present Perfect Tense

Singular	*Plural*
1. I *have been*	We *have been*
2. You *have been*	You *have been*
3. He (she, it) *has been*	They *have been*

Past Perfect Tense

Singular	*Plural*
1. I *had been*	We *had been*
2. You *had been*	You *had been*
3. He (she, it) *had been*	They *had been*

Future Prefect Tense

Singular	*Plural*
1. I *will have been*	We *will have been*
2. You *will have been*	You *will have been*
3. He (she, it) *will have been*	They *will have been*

PRINCIPAL PARTS OF IRREGULAR VERBS

Regular verbs add *ed* or *d* to the present tense to form the past tense and the past participle. Verbs that do not do this are called *irregular verbs*. The following list of the present, past, and past participle forms of the most common irregular verbs will help you to use these verbs properly.

Present	*Past*	*Past Participle*
be	was	been
begin	began	begun
blow	blew	blown

Present	*Past*	*Past Participle*
break	broke	broken
bring	brought	brought
build	built	built
burst	burst	burst
choose	chose	chosen
dive	dived *or* dove	dived
do	did	done
draw	drew	drawn
drink	drank	drunk
drive	drove	driven
eat	ate	eaten
fall	fell	fallen
flee	fled	fled
fly	flew	flown
forbid	forbade	forbidden
get	got	gotten *or* got
give	gave	given
go	went	gone
grow	grew	grown
have	had	had
know	knew	known
lay (place)	laid	laid
lead	led	led
leave (depart)	left	left
let (allow)	let	let
lie (recline)	lay	lain
pay	paid	paid
raise (elevate)	raised	raised
ride	rode	ridden
ring	rang	rung
rise (ascend)	rose	risen
run	ran	run
see	saw	seen
set (place)	set	set
shake	shook	shaken
shine	shone, shined	shone, shined
sing	sang	sung
sit	sat	sat
slay	slew	slain
speak	spoke	spoken
spring	sprang	sprung
steal	stole	stolen
sting	stung	stung
swear	swore	sworn
swing	swung	swung
swim	swam	swum
take	took	taken

Present	Past	Past Participle
tear	tore	torn
throw	threw	thrown
wake	waked *or* woke	waked
wear	wore	worn
write	wrote	written

EXERCISE 4

DIRECTIONS: Write the past tense and past participle after each of the following verbs.

ANSWERS AND EXPLANATIONS APPEAR AT THE END OF THE CHAPTER

1. blow

2. burst

3. drink

4. eat

5. fly

6. forbid

7. go

8. lie

9. lay

10. sit

11. rise

12. raise

AGREEMENT OF SUBJECT AND VERB

Nouns and pronouns have one quality in common: they may be either singular (*friend, she*) or plural (*friends, they*). In addition, verbs may be either singular or plural. Now, when you use a singular noun or pronoun as the subject of a sentence, the verb must also be singular (His best *friend* **is** Martin. *She* **is** coming, too). Similarly, when we use a plural subject, the verb must be plural (His best *friends* **are** Joe and Tom. *They* **are coming**, too.).

Look at the following sentences. Do the subjects and verbs agree in each case?

1. This *apple* **is** delicious.
2. *Joyce and Ellen* **were asked** to remain.
3. My *sister* **speak** French.

In the first sentence, the subject, *apple*, and the verb, *is*, are both singular —they agree. In the second sentence, the subject, *Joyce and Ellen*, and the verb, *were*, are both plural—they agree. However, in the last sentence, the subject, *sister*, is singular, while the verb, *speak*, is plural—they do not agree. In order to agree, both the subject and the verb must be either singular (My *sister* **speaks** *French.*) or plural (My *sisters* **speak** French.).

The following rules will provide you with some essential guides for spotting errors in subject-verb agreement. Study them carefully, for they will be of great help on the GED Test.

RULE 1:   A verb agrees with its subject in number.
Singular subjects take singular verbs:

> The *pot* **is** on the stove.
> That *bird* **is flying** south.

Plural subjects take plural verbs:

> The *pots* **are** on the stove.
> Those *birds* **are flying** south.

RULE 2:   The number of the subject (singular or plural) is not changed by words that come between the subject and the verb.

> *One* of our men *is* missing. *Of our men* is a prepositional phrase.
> The subject *one* and the verb *is* are both singular.

RULE 3: The following words are singular: EACH, EITHER, NEITHER, ONE, NO ONE, ANYONE, EVERYONE, SOMEONE, ANYBODY, SOMEBODY, EVERYBODY.

> *Someone* in the game **was** (not **were**) hurt.
> *Neither* of the girls **is** (not **are**) crying.

RULE 4:   The following words may be singular or plural, depending upon their use in a sentence: SOME, ANY, NONE, ALL, MOST.

> *Most* of the news **is** good.   (Singular)
> *Most* of the victims **were** children.   (Plural)

RULE 5:   Subjects joined by AND are plural. Subjects joined by OR or NOR take a verb that agrees with the last subject.

>   *Bob and George* **are** leaving.
>   *Neither Bob nor George* **is** leaving.
>   *Neither Bob nor his friends* **are** leaving.

RULE 6:   THERE and HERE are never subjects. In sentences that begin with these words, the subject is usually found later on in the sentence.

>   There **were** five *books* on the shelf.   (**were** agrees with the subject *books.*)

RULE 7:   Collective nouns may be singular or plural, depending on their use in the sentence. A collective noun is a noun used to name a whole group. Some common examples are:

army	crowd	orchestra
audience	flock	public
class	group	swarm
club	herd	team
committee	jury	troop

The *orchestra* **is playing** a Mozart symphony.   (*Orchestra* is considered as one unit—singular.)
The *orchestra* **were asked** to give their musical backgrounds.   (*Orchestra* is considered as separate individuals—plural).

RULE 8:   Expressions of time, money, measurement, and weight are usually singular when the amount is considered as one unit.

>   Five dollars *is* (not *are*) too much to ask.
>   Ten days *is* (not *are*) not nearly enough time.

On occasion, however, these terms are used in a plural sense:

>   There **were** *thirty minutes* to countdown.

RULE 9:   Some nouns, while plural in form, are actually singular in meaning.

>   Mathematics *is* (not *are*) an easy subject for some people.
>   The United States *was* (not *were*) represented at the conference.

RULE 10:   DON'T and DOESN'T must agree with the subject. Use DOESN'T after HE, SHE, and IT.

>   *Doesn't* he (not *don't*) know how to do it?
>   They *don't* (not *doesn't*) make movies like that anymore.

VERBALS

A *verbal* is a word that comes from a verb but does not act like a verb. There are three types of verbals: the *infinitive*, the *gerund*, and the *participle*.

Infinitive. An infinitive is formed by *to* plus the present tense of the verb. Examples of this verbal are: *to get*, *to give*, and *to lose*. Infinitives function like nouns (*"To lose* is not so bad"; "I like *to win*"), like adjectives ("He showed me a way *to forget*"), or like adverbs ("She is eager *to come*").

Gerund. The gerund is formed by adding *ing* to the present tense of the verb—in some cases after dropping the final *e* (*tame*, *taming*) or doubling the final consonant (*hit*, *hitting*). Gerunds are used as nouns, and like nouns, they may be modified by adjectives (*"Swimming* is good for your health"; "I love salt-water *fishing*").

Participle. A verbal that functions like an adjective is called a participle. There are two kinds of participles: (1) *present participles*, formed by adding *ing* to the present tense of the verb (a *swimming* pool, his *batting* average) and (2) *past participles*, formed by adding *d* or *ed* to the present tense of the verb (a *rested* army, an *informed* person).

EXERCISE 5

DIRECTIONS: In each of the following sentences, there is one italicized section. For each of these sections, blacken the answer column as follows: 1—gerund; 2—infinitive; 3—participle; 4—something else.

ANSWERS AND EXPLANATIONS APPEAR AT THE END OF THE CHAPTER

#	Sentence	1	2	3	4
1.	*Swimming* is fun and it's also good exercise.	‖	‖	‖	‖
2.	*To give* is better than to receive.	‖	‖	‖	‖
3.	Billy raced to the *covered* wagon.	‖	‖	‖	‖
4.	I like *building* sand castles.	‖	‖	‖	‖
5.	He watched the rain *coming* down in torrents.	‖	‖	‖	‖
6.	*To do* this properly, one must have the tools.	‖	‖	‖	‖
7.	My brother and I *are going* to camp this summer.	‖	‖	‖	‖
8.	Careful revision is the key to good *writing*.	‖	‖	‖	‖
9.	Please try *to keep* quiet.	‖	‖	‖	‖

10. 1 2 3 4

10. To be or not *to be*—that is the question.

11. 1 2 3 4

11. *Laughing* and crying—we did both.

12. 1 2 3 4

12. *Hunting* is a popular activity in this state.

13. 1 2 3 4

13. I *saw* the movie last week.

14. 1 2 3 4

14. *Jogging* is becoming a national sport.

15. 1 2 3 4

15. Joe stared at the *waving* flag.

16. 1 2 3 4

16. *Eating* the proper foods is one way to stay healthy.

17. 1 2 3 4

17. I didn't know whether *to go* or stay.

18. 1 2 3 4

18. The man walked *slowly* across the street.

19. 1 2 3 4

19. Good secretaries are concerned about their *grooming*.

20. 1 2 3 4

20. We will be *seeing* you shortly.

EXERCISE 6

DIRECTIONS: Each group of sentences below is based on one of the preceding rules of agreement of subject and verb. In the answer column, blacken the space under the number that corresponds to the number of the incorrect sentence in each group. If all the sentences are correct, blacken the fifth space.

ANSWERS AND EXPLANATIONS APPEAR AT THE END OF THE CHAPTER

1. 1 2 3 4 5

1. (1) My father is a young man.
   (2) Their books were lost.
   (3) Joe are my best friend.
   (4) He came here last week.

2. 1 2 3 4 5

2. (1) John, as well as his brother, was at the party.
   (2) Every single one of the desks were clean.
   (3) One of the men is going to speak.
   (4) One of the students was absent.

3. 1 2 3 4 5

3. (1) Every boy should do the job.
   (2) Somebody cares about you.
   (3) No one speaks to him.
   (4) Everybody are welcome.

4. 1 2 3 4 5

4. (1) Some of the boys are coming.
   (2) Most of the people were sleeping.
   (3) Most of the cake were eaten.
   (4) All of the paint was spilled.

5. (1) Joseph and I are brothers.
   (2) Neither he nor I was interested.
   (3) Either James or his brother are willing to help.
   (4) Either Tommy or Jack is coming tonight.

6. (1) There were two boys in the room.
   (2) There is something on your coat.
   (3) Here are my brother and sister.
   (4) Here is the books from the library.

7. (1) The jury has reached a verdict.
   (2) An army travels on its stomach.
   (3) The audience were on their feet at the end of the play.
   (4) The crowd are growing larger.

8. (1) Forty-five minutes is too long to wait.
   (2) Two-thirds of the membership is present.
   (3) Two miles is too far to walk on a rainy night.
   (4) Half the people was late for work.

9. (1) The news were good tonight.
   (2) Measles is a childhood disease.
   (3) The troops were tired after the long march.
   (4) The boys have gone home.

10. (1) He doesn't like carrots.
    (2) We don't often see them.
    (3) I don't care about it.
    (4) It really don't matter to me.

PRONOUN USAGE

A pronoun is a word used in place of a noun. A pronoun can be used either as a subject or as a complement. The form of a pronoun changes according to the way the word is used in a sentence.

These pronouns are used as subjects and pronoun complements: *I, you, he, she, him, her, it, we, us, they,* and *them.*

> *I* love you.   (subject)
> It was *they.*   (complement)

These pronouns are used as direct and indirect objects: *me, you, him, her, it, us, them.*

> The car struck *him.*   (direct object)
> She showed *him* a precious diamond.   (indirect object)

These pronouns are used to indicate possession: *my, your, his, her, its, our, their.*

> Is that *his* car?
> *Their* word is good enough for me.

Now look at the following rules. They will help to clarify some of the ways in which pronouns are used.

RULE 1:   When you are not sure about the use of a double pronoun, try each pronoun separately in a sentence.

1. (*She* and *I*) (*Her* and *me*) are good friends.
   She is a good friend. *I* am a good friend.
   Her is a good friend. *Me* is a good friend.
   Answer: She and I are good friends.

2. My parents gave the car to (*he and I*) (*him and me*).
   My parents gave the car to *he*. My parents gave the car to *I*.
   My parents gave the car to *him*. My parents gave the car to *me*.
   Answer: My parents gave the car to *him* and *me*.

EXERCISE 7

DIRECTIONS: In the following sentences, choose the correct pronoun or pair of pronouns in parentheses.

ANSWERS APPEAR AT THE END OF THE CHAPTER

1. John and (*I, me*) were invited.

2. We paid a visit to Tom and (*he, him*).

3. (*He and she*) (*Her and him*) went to the movies.

4. Did you see Mary and (*she, her*)?

5. The boys and (*we, us*) are going.

RULE 2:   When THAN and AS introduce an incomplete construction, use the form of the pronoun you would use if the construction were completed.

She is as smart as I. (*as I am.*)
He is much stronger than she. (*than she is.*)
I know Jim better than him. (*than I know him.*)
I like you less than her. (*than I like her.*)

EXERCISE 8

DIRECTIONS: In the following sentences, choose the correct pronoun in parentheses.

ANSWERS AND EXPLANATIONS APPEAR AT THE END OF THE CHAPTER

1. Tom is two years older than (*I, me*).

2. Can Willy run as fast as (*he, him*)?

3. No one looked as pretty as (*she, her*).

4. Martin is a better choice for captain than (*I, me*).

5. Have they lived here as long as (*we, us*)?

RULE 3:   Always use the object form after the preposition BETWEEN.

Share it *between* Bill and *him.*   (**not** *he*)
This is a secret *between* you and *me.*   (**not** *I*)
Joe stood *between* Mary and *her.*   (**not** *she*)

RULE 4:   Pronoun complements take the subject form.

Remember that a pronoun complement answers the question WHAT? or WHO? after a linking verb. Use the same pronoun form you would for a subject:

It was *she.*   (**not** *me*)
It was *he.*   (**not** *him*)

EXERCISE 9

DIRECTIONS: In the following sentences, choose the correct pronoun in parentheses.

ANSWERS APPEAR AT THE END OF THE CHAPTER

1. Was it (*she, her*) who called?

2. It was (*I, me*) who saw it.

3. We were sure that it was (*they, them*) who did it.

4. I don't know if I am (*he, him*).

5. The most intelligent girl in my class is (*her, she*).

RULE 5:   To choose between WHO and WHOM, use HE and HIM as clues.

The *who-whom* choice often confuses people. When you have to make a choice between *who* and *whom*, change the sentence (but not the meaning), so that you choose between *he* and *him*. If you choose *he*, the answer is *who*. If you choose *him*, the answer is *whom*.

Now let us see how this rule works when we apply it to the following examples:

EXAMPLES: 1. He is a man (*who, whom*) I love.
2. (*Who, whom*) do you know?

Step 1:   Change to *he-him*:

1. He is a man. I love (*he, him*).
2. Do you know (*he, him*)?

Step 2:   Make your choice:

1. He is a man. I love *him*.
2. Do you know *him*?

Step 3:   Go back to the original. Remember *he* goes with *who*; *him* goes with *whom*.

1. He is a man WHOM I love.
2. WHO do you know?

EXERCISE 10

DIRECTIONS: In the following sentences, choose the correct pronoun in parentheses.

ANSWERS AND EXPLANATIONS APPEAR AT THE END OF THE CHAPTER

1. (*Who, whom*) was invited to the concert?

2. To (*who, whom*) did you speak?

3. He is a man in (*who, whom*) I have great confidence.

4. Joe was the first one (*who, whom*) came.

5. It was Tony (*who, whom*) shouted.

RULE 6:   Use the possessive form of the pronoun before a gerund (verb forms ending in ING that are used as nouns).

Do you like *our* (**not** *we* or *us*) singing?

He could not take *his* (**not** *he* or *him*) complaining.

EXERCISE 11

DIRECTIONS: In the following sentences, choose the correct pronoun in parentheses.

ANSWERS AND EXPLANATIONS APPEAR AT THE END OF THE CHAPTER

1. Does anyone object to (*my, me*) smoking?

2. The teacher was unhappy about (*our, us*) failing the test.

3. We were undecided about (*their, them*) trying again.

4. Did Tom know about (*you, your*) coming late?

5. We encouraged (*him, his*) going on to college.

MODIFICATION

As you may recall, there are two basic kinds of modifiers: *adverbs* (which modify verbs, adverbs, and adjectives) and *adjectives* (which modify nouns and pronouns).

Some of the questions on the test may ask you to choose between an adverb and an adjective modifier. An example is: "He talks (*soft, softly*)." To answer this question, you need only ask yourself: "Which *part of speech* in the sentence is being modified?" In the example above, *talks*—the word being modified—is a verb. Thus, the modifier must be an adverb—*softly*.

RULE 1: Linking verbs (BE, FEEL, TASTE, LOOK, etc.) are usually followed by an adjective. Action verbs are usually followed by an adverb.

This apple pie *tastes* (linking verb) **delicious** (**not** *deliciously*)

Jerry *ran* (action verb) **swiftly.** (**not** *swift*)

RULE 2: BAD-BADLY. GOOD-WELL. BAD is an adjective. BADLY is an adverb. GOOD is an adjective. WELL may be used as either an adjective or adverb.

The butter smells *bad.* (**not** badly)

He works *badly* with others. (**not** bad)

I just love *good* food.

He writes *well.* (**adverb**)

I feel *well.* (**adjective**)

RULE 3: Comparison of adjectives and adverbs.

Positive Degree (Simple Statement)	*Comparative Degree* (Use for two)	*Superlative Degree* (Use for more than two)
Frank's job is *good*,	but Joe's is *better*,	and Don's is the *best* of all.
Mary sings *well*,	but Alice sings *better*,	and Donna sings *best.*
Henry is *short*,	but Bill is *shorter*,	and Jim is the *tallest.*
Maria is *beautiful*,	but Nancy is *more beautiful*,	and Beth is the *most beautiful.*

Comparisons of adjectives and adverbs are made in one of three ways:

1. Adding *er* and *est*: long—long*er*—long*est*.

2. Changing the word: much—*more*—*most*.

3. Using *more* and *most*: clever—*more* clever—*most* clever.

RULE 4:   Use OTHER or ELSE when comparing someone or something with other members of a group.

Incorrect: He is shorter than any boy in the class.
Correct: He is shorter than any *other* boy in the class.
Incorrect: He has better marks than anyone in the class.
Correct: He has better marks than anyone *else* in the class.

RULE 5:   Avoid double comparisons: use ER-EST or MORE-MOST —not both.

He is the *bravest* person I know.   (**not** He is the most bravest person I know).
She is prettier than Jane.   (**not** She is more prettier than Jane).

EXERCISE 12

DIRECTIONS: In each of the following sentences, underline all adjectives and adverbs and indicate what word or words each modifies.

ANSWERS AND EXPLANATIONS APPEAR AT THE END OF THE CHAPTER

1. The tall man limped painfully into the office.

2. A green car with a vinyl top pulled into the parking lot.

3. After class, we walked quietly down the corridor.

4. Three girls were chatting merrily outside the room.

5. The tall tree swayed gently in the breeze.

6. Joe saw a large, brown dog in his yard last night.

7. "I don't know," he said sadly.

8. "Get out !" he shouted angrily.

9. The boy turned to me and smiled broadly.

10. "This is my favorite dress," said Mary.

ANSWERS AND EXPLANATIONS: USAGE EXERCISES

EXERCISE 1

1. present
2. past
3. past
4. past
5. future
6. past
7. present
8. future
9. past
10. present

EXERCISE 2

1. **(4)** present perfect
2. **(5)** past perfect
3. **(3)** future
4. **(1)** present
5. **(1)** present

6. **(2)** past
7. **(5)** past perfect
8. **(4)** present perfect
9. **(2)** past
10. **(2)** past

EXERCISE 3

1. **(2)** past
2. **(3)** future
3. **(5)** past perfect
4. **(1)** present
5. **(4)** present perfect

6. **(2)** past
7. **(1)** present
8. **(4)** present perfect
9. **(2)** past
10. **(3)** future

EXERCISE 4

1. blow, blew, blown
2. burst, burst, burst
3. drink, drank, drunk
4. eat, ate, eaten
5. fly, flew, flown
6. forbid, forbade, forbidden

7. go, went, gone
8. lie, lay, lain
9. lay, laid, laid
10. sit, sat, sat
11. rise, rose, risen
12. raise, raised, raised

EXERCISE 5

(If the answer is 1—gerund, 2—infinitive, or 3—participle, see the explanation under the section titled "Verbals." If the answer is 4—something else, the explanation is provided below.)

1. **(1)**
2. **(2)**
3. **(3)**
4. **(1)**
5. **(3)**
6. **(2)**
7. **(4)** *are going* is a form of the present tense of the verb *go*. Note, however, that in this sentence it is used to express future time.
8. **(1)**
9. **(2)**
10. **(1)**

11. **(1)**
12. **(1)**
13. **(4)** *saw* is the past tense of the verb *see*.
14. **(1)**
15. **(3)**
16. **(1)**
17. **(2)**
18. **(4)** *slowly* is an adverb modifying the verb *walked*.
19. **(1)**
20. **(4)** *seeing* is part of the whole verb *will be seeing*, which is the future tense of *see*.

EXERCISE 6

(The following references are to rules under "Agreement of Subject and Verb.")

1. **(3)** See Rule 1. Joe *is* my best friend.
2. **(2)** See Rule 2. Every single one of the desks *was* clean.
3. **(4)** See Rule 3. Everybody *is* welcome.
4. **(3)** See Rule 4. Most of the cake *was* eaten.
5. **(3)** See Rule 5. Either James or his brother *is* willing to help.
6. **(4)** See Rule 6. Here *are* the books from the library.
7. **(4)** See Rule 7. The crowd *is* growing larger.
8. **(4)** See Rule 8. Half the people *were* late to work.
9. **(1)** See Rule 9. The news *was* good tonight.
10. **(4)** See Rule 10. It really *doesn't* matter to me.

EXERCISE 7

(See Rule 1 under "Pronoun Usage.")

1. I   2. him   3. He and she   4. her   5. we

EXERCISE 8

(See Rule 2 under "Pronoun Usage.")

1. Tom is two years older than *I* (AM).
2. Can Willy run as fast as *he* (CAN)?
3. No one looked as pretty as *she* (DID).
4. Martin is a better choice for captain than *I* (AM).
5. Have they lived here as long as *we* (HAVE)?

EXERCISE 9

(See Rule 4 under "Pronoun Usage.")

1. she   2. I   3. they   4. he   5. she

EXERCISE 10

1. WHO (Was *he* invited to the concert?)
2. WHOM (Did you speak to *him*?)
3. WHOM (He is a man. I have great confidence in *him*.)
4. WHO (Joe came. *He* was the first one.)
5. WHO (It was Tony. *He* shouted.)

EXERCISE 11

(See Rule 6 under "Pronoun Usage.")

1. my   2. our   3. their   4. your   5. his

EXERCISE 12

1. The adjective *tall* modifies the noun *man*.
   The adverb *painfully* modifies the verb *limped*.

2. The adjective *green* modifies the noun *car*.
   The adjective *vinyl* modifies the noun *top*.
   The adjective *parking* modifies the noun *lot*.

3. The adverb *quietly* modifies the verb *walked*.

4. The adjective *Three* modifies the noun *girls*.
   The adverb *merrily* modifies the verb *chatting*.

5. The adjective *tall* modifies the noun *tree*.
   The adverb *gently* modifies the verb *swayed*.

6. The adjectives *large* and *brown* modify the noun *dog*.
   The adjective *last* modifies the noun *night*.

7. The adverb *sadly* modifies the verb *said*.

8. The adverb *angrily* modifies the verb *shouted*.

9. The adverb *broadly* modifies the verb *smiled*.

10. The adjective *favorite* modifies the noun *dress*.

TEN GRAMMAR
AND USAGE EXERCISES

In the last three chapters, you have studied the kinds of materials that most often appear in the grammar and usage section of the official test. Now you will be given a chance to test yourself on *all* that you have learned. The ten exercises that follow simulate the form, content, and level of difficulty of examination-type questions. In addition, the directions for answering these questions closely follow those given on the actual examination.

After you complete each exercise, check your answers against the correct ones at the end of this chapter. And make sure you understand the reason for an answer being correct. If you are not clear, go back to the appropriate section in the instructional materials.

EXERCISE 1

DIRECTIONS: In each of the following sentences, there are four underlined parts. In the answer column, blacken the space under the number that corresponds to the number of the incorrect part. If there are no errors, blacken the fifth space.

ANSWERS AND EXPLANATIONS APPEAR AT THE END OF THE CHAPTER

1. Either John or I am sure to be there before she.
   1   2   3   4

2. John and I have said that if everyone does their best, there can be no doubt
   1   2   3
   that the project will be a success.
                      4

3. Mary, Tom, and I am concerned that the movie might have begun before
   1   2   3
   we arrive.
   4

4. One of the girls were later in arriving than anyone else in her class.
   1   2   3   4

5. There seem to be several extremely important factors which must be taken
   1   2   3
   into consideration before any meaningful decision can be made.
   4

6. Each witness agreed that the suspect left the building before 9 P.M.
   1   2   3   4

7. If the weather <u>had been</u> <u>fairer</u>, you could <u>have depended</u> on <u>him</u> going to
the game with you.

7. 1 2 3 4 5
‖ ‖ ‖ ‖ ‖

8. If you <u>had been</u> concerned about her welfare, you <u>would</u> have <u>went</u> to
greater lengths to <u>insure</u> her safety.

8. 1 2 3 4 5
‖ ‖ ‖ ‖ ‖

9. The boys and I <u>have</u> every reason to believe that we <u>can do</u> the job faster
<u>than</u> <u>them</u>.

9. 1 2 3 4 5
‖ ‖ ‖ ‖ ‖

10. <u>Either</u> the boys <u>or</u> Sally <u>is</u> pleased by <u>his</u> decision.

10. 1 2 3 4 5
‖ ‖ ‖ ‖ ‖

EXERCISE 2

DIRECTIONS: In each of the following sentences, there are four underlined parts. In the answer column, blacken the space
under the number that corresponds to the number of
the incorrect part. If there are no errors, blacken the
fifth space.

ANSWERS AND EXPLANATIONS APPEAR AT THE END OF THE CHAPTER

1. Each of the people <u>who</u> <u>were</u> involved in the accident <u>has</u> been <u>questioned</u>
by the police.

1. 1 2 3 4 5
‖ ‖ ‖ ‖ ‖

2. John, as well as his brother, <u>is</u> to be considered for the position when each of
the applicants <u>has been</u> interviewed and every judge <u>has</u> made <u>his</u> decision.

2. 1 2 3 4 5
‖ ‖ ‖ ‖ ‖

3. The man <u>who</u> you <u>had spoken</u> to on the phone <u>came</u> to the office today
to <u>confirm</u> the appointment.

3. 1 2 3 4 5
‖ ‖ ‖ ‖ ‖

4. Arthur, together with Leonard and Joan, <u>were</u> walking along the street when
<u>he</u> heard a sound that <u>frightened</u> <u>him</u>.

4. 1 2 3 4 5
‖ ‖ ‖ ‖ ‖

5. <u>Who</u> did you say <u>had called</u> before I <u>came</u> in to <u>lie</u> down?

5. 1 2 3 4 5
‖ ‖ ‖ ‖ ‖

6. Many a man <u>has</u> done the same thing before <u>they</u> <u>was</u> called upon to ac-
count for <u>himself</u>.

6. 1 2 3 4 5
‖ ‖ ‖ ‖ ‖

7. 1 2 3 4 5

7. As soon as the class <u>had been</u> dismissed, the teacher <u>found</u> that someone
                         1   2

<u>had forgotten</u> <u>his</u> lunch.
      3   4

8. 1 2 3 4 5

8. As the results from the outlying precincts <u>were</u> reported, it <u>became</u> clear that
                                               1   2

the winner <u>would be</u> <u>he.</u>
              3   4

9. 1 2 3 4 5

9. After the room <u>had been</u> empty for an hour, we <u>were</u> surprised <u>to find</u> a
                     1   2   3

small bundle <u>laying</u> in the corner.
                4

10. 1 2 3 4 5

10. The class <u>were</u> asked to <u>raise</u> their hands if any of them <u>were</u> interested in
                1   2   3

attending a performance of the play that <u>had been</u> studied.
                                             4

EXERCISE 3

DIRECTIONS: In each of the following sentences, there are four underlined parts. In the answer column, blacken the space
under the number that corresponds to the number of
the incorrect part. If there are no errors, blacken the
fifth space.

ANSWERS AND EXPLANATIONS APPEAR AT THE END OF THE CHAPTER

1. 1 2 3 4 5

1. If you <u>had</u> asked John, he <u>would have told</u> you that by the time Kenny
            1   2

<u>arrives,</u> <u>I shall have been</u> there for two hours.
    3   4

2. 1 2 3 4 5

2. They wanted to know whether it <u>were</u> <u>we</u> <u>who</u> <u>had</u> raised the question.
                                    1   2   3   4

3. 1 2 3 4 5

3. Dick, <u>together with</u> three of his friends, are <u>the</u> ones to <u>whom</u> we
              1   2   3

<u>should express</u> our thanks.
      4

4. 1 2 3 4 5

4. If everyone <u>were</u> as old as <u>he,</u> <u>there</u> would never <u>have been</u> a generation gap.
                 1   2   3   4

5. 1 2 3 4 5

5. Mary is one of the girls <u>who</u> <u>has</u> been selected to participate in the cere-
                             1   2

monies to be held <u>upon</u> our <u>team's</u> return.
                     3   4

6. 1 2 3 4 5

6. I seen the three men <u>mentioned</u> in the newspaper <u>article</u> that Joe <u>had shown</u>
     1   2   3   4

me last week.

7. Mary's maid of honor wore an outfit that was neither tasteful or suitable
    ――   ――   ――――   ――
    1   2   3   4
for an afternoon wedding.

                                                          7 1 2 3 4 5

8. I do not have any faith in John running for office.
   ――――   ――   ―――― ――――
    1   2   3   4

                            8. 1 2 3 4 5

9. After the debate, every one of the judges agreed that the winner
               ――――――――   ――――   ――
                     1   2   3
had presented an excellent argument.
   ――――――
    4

                            9. 1 2 3 4 5

10. To you and him belong the credit.
     ――   ―― ――――   ――――
     1   2   3   4

                          10. 1 2 3 4 5

EXERCISE 4

DIRECTIONS: In each of the following sentences, there are four underlined parts. In the answer column, blacken the space
under the number that corresponds to the number of
the incorrect part. If there are no errors, blacken the
fifth space.

ANSWERS AND EXPLANATIONS APPEAR AT THE END OF THE CHAPTER

1. I'll never forget how badly I felt when he looked at me so coldly and bitterly.
                    ――――   ――――   ――――   ――――――
                      1   2   3   4

                            1. 1 2 3 4 5

2. I had been told of Joe's integrity, but his story still sounded suspiciously to
   ――――――   ――――   ―――――― ――――――――
    1   2   3   4
me.

                            2. 1 2 3 4 5

3. If you had spoken more firmly, I am sure the group would have responded.
        ――――   ――――   ――――   ――――――
         1   2   3   4

                            3. 1 2 3 4 5

4. Passengers sitting in the front car were injured when the train had crashed.
            ――――   ―――― ――――   ――――
             1   2   3   4

                            4. 1 2 3 4 5

5. Two seniors, Allen and him, were called upon to stand after the principal
                     ―――― ――――
                      1   2
had finished his remarks.
――――   ――――
  3   4

                            5. 1 2 3 4 5

6. Tony is the one who has been selected from among the twenty young men
     ――   ―――― ――――
     1   2   3
who applied.
   ――――――
    4

                            6. 1 2 3 4 5

7. The school being open on a holiday came as a great surprise to Helen,
    ――――――   ――――   ――――
     1   2   3
Maria, and me.
      ――――
       4

                            7. 1 2 3 4 5

8. 1 2 3 4 5

8. Mary, Tom, and <u>myself</u> <u>will be</u> delighted to confer with you after we
             1   2

   have <u>planned</u> and <u>decided</u> upon our initial course of action.
        3   4

9. 1 2 3 4 5

9. There are two men <u>who</u> are eminently successful; yet, <u>for</u> all their wealth,
             1   2

   they are individuals <u>who</u> fame and fortune <u>have</u> not made proud.
            3   4

10. 1 2 3 4 5

10. No one <u>knew</u> <u>who</u> <u>won</u> the election until we <u>finished</u> counting the ballots.
          1   2 3   4

EXERCISE 5

DIRECTIONS: In each of the following sentences, there are four under-lined parts. In the answer column, blacken the space under the number that corresponds to the number of the incorrect part. If there are no errors, blacken the fifth space.

ANSWERS AND EXPLANATIONS APPEAR AT THE END OF THE CHAPTER

1. 1 2 3 4 5

1. <u>Have</u> either of the men <u>told</u> you what <u>happened</u> at last night's <u>meeting</u>?
    1   2   3   4

2. 1 2 3 4 5

2. I would have <u>liked</u> <u>to have</u> been there when the senator <u>finished</u> his speech
           1   2   3

   and <u>received</u> a standing ovation.
       4

3. 1 2 3 4 5

3. If I <u>had</u> more time, I <u>would have been</u> able <u>to talk</u> longer when Tom <u>called</u>
       1   2   3   4

   last night.

4. 1 2 3 4 5

4. Mr. Hopkins <u>told</u> me earlier that he <u>would appreciate</u> <u>you</u> coming in a little
            1   2   3

   <u>earlier</u> this evening.
    4

5. 1 2 3 4 5

5. People <u>had been lining</u> up for hours before the box office finally <u>opened</u> and
           1   2

   everyone <u>had</u> a chance to buy <u>their</u> ticket.
        3   4

6. 1 2 3 4 5

6. The captain, <u>along</u> with three carefully selected men, <u>was</u> assigned to
           1   2

   <u>accompany</u> the general on <u>his</u> tour of inspection.
      3   4

7. 1 2 3 4 5

7. Just between you and <u>me</u>, I would <u>like</u> to have <u>seen</u> the look on his face
                  1   2   3

   when he <u>heard</u> the decision.
       4

8. Martin and Marian, who <u>have been</u> engaged for what <u>seem</u> like ten years,
1   2

<u>are</u> finally <u>going</u> to be married next month.
3   4

8. 1 2 3 4 5

9. John, who <u>is</u> three inches taller than <u>me</u>, <u>was chosen</u> as the starting quarter-
1   2   3

back for the big game with Central <u>High School</u>.
4

9. 1 2 3 4 5

10. Whenever Joe and I <u>were</u> able <u>to get</u> some time off from work, we <u>use</u> to <u>go</u>
1   2   3   4

to the ball game.

10. 1 2 3 4 5

EXERCISE 6

DIRECTIONS: Each group below consists of four sentences. In the answer column, blacken the space under the number that corresponds to the number of the incorrect sentence. If there are no errors, blacken the fifth space.

ANSWERS AND EXPLANATIONS APPEAR AT THE END OF THE CHAPTER

1. (1) If you had studied, you might have passed.
   (2) Do you object to me smoking?
   (3) Was it he who called?
   (4) We can do it faster than they.

1. 1 2 3 4 5

2. (1) That coat looks well on you.
   (2) We didn't know if he had gone.
   (3) This cake tastes more sweetly than the other.
   (4) Either Mary or her father is going.

2. 1 2 3 4 5

3. (1) Has someone forgotten their lunch?
   (2) He is a man whose experience has been extensive.
   (3) My father and I enjoyed the game immensely.
   (4) Laura is more competent than her sister.

3. 1 2 3 4 5

4. (1) He was older than she.
   (2) No one knew who the winner was.
   (3) I can't tell her sister and her apart.
   (4) Please wait for Tom and I.

4. 1 2 3 4 5

5. (1) Consult Dr. MacGregor, whom, I am sure, will tell you the same thing.
   (2) Sally, Sue, and I are giving a party next Wednesday.
   (3) He is a man who comes highly recommended.
   (4) We have some members whom I have never met.

5. 1 2 3 4 5

6. (1) will talk with whoever gets the job.
   (2) Get Harry and him to help you with the car.
   (3) Who did he say was the best qualified candidate?
   (4) The people were eager to know who they had elected.

6. 1 2 3 4 5

7. 1 2 3 4 5

7. (1) Somebody, either Harry or he, was certainly able to do it.
    (2) I did not enjoy his playing.
    (3) Matthew and myself were chosen to participate.
    (4) The class's taking the test without additional preparation was a big mistake.

8. 1 2 3 4 5

8. (1) Helen and I stayed after school.
    (2) Have you seen Maurice and him?
    (3) Today I have received letters from both Joseph and him.
    (4) The man whom I saw was not very young.

9. 1 2 3 4 5

9. (1) He refused to let us drive the car.
    (2) Did you know about John's going?
    (3) I do not approve of their habitually talking during class.
    (4) Mary couldn't cook nearly so well as she.

10. 1 2 3 4 5

10. (1) His brother and himself were held responsible.
    (2) Harry and I took turns at the wheel.
    (3) Herman is a man whom I have long admired.
    (4) No one could be sure that it was they.

EXERCISE 7

DIRECTIONS: Each group below consists of four sentences. In the answer column, blacken the space under the number that corresponds to the number of the incorrect sentence. If there are no errors, blacken the fifth space.

ANSWERS AND EXPLANATIONS APPEAR AT THE END OF THE CHAPTER

1. 1 2 3 4 5

1. (1) The cost of his explorations was paid for by the museum.
    (2) Neither the President nor his assistant was willing to give us any information.
    (3) Everyone of those boys has been successful.
    (4) This is one of those books that are difficult to put down.

2. 1 2 3 4 5

2. (1) The question of taxes doesn't belong in this discussion.
    (2) Neither our idea nor the ones suggested by our competitors was accepted.
    (3) Bacon and eggs is my favorite breakfast.
    (4) Everyone, including the teacher, has seen the play.

3. 1 2 3 4 5

3. (1) "The Three Strangers" is worth reading.
    (2) Most of the Truman papers have been made available to the public.
    (3) There seems to be good arguments both pro and con.
    (4) The mayor of New York and the governor of Nebraska have been in conference for several hours now.

4. 1 2 3 4 5

4. (1) High school and college standards are vastly different.
    (2) It doesn't make any difference to me whether he goes.
    (3) One of the apples was spoiled.
    (4) The news is not too good this evening.

5. (1) Two weeks is really not enough time.
   (2) Just between you and I, Mary has been here already.
   (3) He had finished the task before I came.
   (4) There were three of us in the back of the car.

5. 1 2 3 4 5

6. (1) Both Joe and Bob are capable students.
   (2) Each of the wines was sampled by the chef.
   (3) The fruit on the sidewalk stands look tempting.
   (4) Neither his grades nor his experience is enough to qualify him.

6. 1 2 3 4 5

7. (1) Many a student fails to work up to his ability.
   (2) It was he who had started the rumor.
   (3) This is one of those pens that writes under water.
   (4) The rivers have reached the flood stage.

7. 1 2 3 4 5

8. (1) All of the stories in this book are wonderful.
   (2) Only one of the ideas make sense.
   (3) He is a man I have known for many years.
   (4) He looked as if he had been drinking.

8. 1 2 3 4 5

9. (1) He is an individual who makes the best of everything.
   (2) He couldn't plan his strategy until he knew who his opponents would be.
   (3) Many of the men who were on strike wanted to go back to work.
   (4) Give this job to someone who we can trust.

9. 1 2 3 4 5

10. (1) Mildred was older than she.
    (2) This book was much more longer than the other.
    (3) They gave the assignment to us trusted assistants.
    (4) Scotch and soda makes a fine end to a long day.

10. 1 2 3 4 5

EXERCISE 8

DIRECTIONS: Each group below consists of four sentences. In the answer column, blacken the space under the number that corresponds to the number of the incorrect sentence. If there are no errors, blacken the fifth space.

ANSWERS AND EXPLANATIONS APPEAR AT THE END OF THE CHAPTER

1. (1) The glass dish was broken beyond repair.
   (2) The letter had been torn to bits.
   (3) The water had froze overnight.
   (4) Someone had stolen the plans.

1. 1 2 3 4 5

2. (1) The students drunk a toast to their Alma Mater.
   (2) The package lay on the floor near the window.
   (3) He had lain there all morning.
   (4) We laid the new rug before leaving.

2. 1 2 3 4 5

3. (1) Father lies down every afternoon when he comes home from work.
   (2) Set the box on the table for now.
   (3) He came in as we were finishing the job.
   (4) The Atlantic cable was lain in 1858.

3. 1 2 3 4 5

4. 1 2 3 4 5

4. (1) Mr. Thomas is the man to whom we spoke.
(2) Was it he whom you saw last night?
(3) Give the medal to whomever you want.
(4) Whom do you suppose will be elected?

5. 1 2 3 4 5

5. (1) The fish defrosted and began to smell bad.
(2) Herb handled the ball carefully during the first period.
(3) I like these kind of apples.
(4) The directions were not clearly written.

6. 1 2 3 4 5

6. (1) Richard was really excited about the party.
(2) We'll surely be glad when the test is over.
(3) When no one is looking, he acts different.
(4) This kind is my favorite.

7. 1 2 3 4 5

7. (1) Our team has scored more points than any team in the league.
(2) The car runs well now that it has a new transmission.
(3) Those kinds of rumors should be stopped as soon as they begin.
(4) It was the brightest light I had ever seen.

8. 1 2 3 4 5

8. (1) We enjoyed their performance of *Twelfth Night*.
(2) Which of the players were faster, the shortstop or the second baseman?
(3) Fewer people attended this meeting than the last one.
(4) Either you or I am to represent the school in the oratorical contest.

9. 1 2 3 4 5

9. (1) We read the *Star* and the *Press,* but we like the *Star* best.
(2) Joe laid his hat and coat on the bed when he came in.
(3) Three of our neighbors had called in the morning.
(4) Pumpkin tastes good if it's put in a pie.

10. 1 2 3 4 5

10. (1) There is no real disagreement between you and me.
(2) Mary is older than anyone in the class.
(3) Did you hear the news about her and her sister?
(4) Why don't you wait for Floyd and me in the lobby?

EXERCISE 9

DIRECTIONS: Each group below consists of four sentences. In the answer column, blacken the space under the number that corresponds to the number of the incorrect sentence. If there are no errors, blacken the fifth space.

ANSWERS AND EXPLANATIONS APPEAR AT THE END OF THE CHAPTER

1. 1 2 3 4 5

1. (1) Everyone must have a medical file on record before being permitted to get on the bus.
(2) A box of tomatoes were left lying in the corner.
(3) Ten hours is a long time to wait for anyone.
(4) The game over, the players hurried from the field.

2. 1 2 3 4 5

2. (1) Yesterday, The Old Flash hung up his spikes for the last time.
(2) I just laid there all morning, basking in the sun.
(3) The house looked as if a bomb had hit it.

(4) Politics is a dangerous way to live for a man not used to being in the public eye.

3. (1) *Hamlet,* as well as *Macbeth* and *King Lear,* are favorites of mine.
   (2) Five dollars is not too much to pay for this kind of picture.
   (3) A series of original Beatle records is being made available to our listeners.
   (4) If you like Mary, you'll love Sally.

3. 1 2 3 4 5

4. (1) Not one in ten students spot this error.
   (2) He who tries succeeds.
   (3) Set the basin on the table standing in the corner.
   (4) Both women hurried along the street as if they had seen a ghost.

4. 1 2 3 4 5

5. (1) It is he whom I spoke about at the party last night.
   (2) Everyone came on time except him.
   (3) Neither the critics nor the author were right in their prediction of public reaction.
   (4) Anyone who wants to come is welcome.

5. 1 2 3 4 5

6. (1) I feel bad about you having to do double work.
   (2) Run for your life! The dam has burst!
   (3) Mary and the twins, Harry and Fred, are coming this evening.
   (4) Half a loaf is better than none.

6. 1 2 3 4 5

7. (1) The people will approve of whoever I choose.
   (2) The man to whom you spoke is at the door, and he wants his money.
   (3) The job had been done well and I felt good about it.
   (4) Actually the better of the two resorts is the less well known.

7. 1 2 3 4 5

8. (1) John McCarthy or Tom O'Leary are the ones to see in connection with your problem.
   (2) Two-thirds of the people are here already.
   (3) Two-thirds of the work is now completed.
   (4) Where are Tony and Sal?

8. 1 2 3 4 5

9. (1) The class were eager to begin their oral reports.
   (2) The committee has come to their decision.
   (3) The team was excited about the big game.
   (4) The Mets are about to take the field.

9. 1 2 3 4 5

10. (1) One or the other of the mechanics has damaged my car.
    (2) Whom does he think he is?
    (3) Mary's wearing miniskirts to school leaves something to be desired.
    (4) Neither the accountant nor the chief teller has explained the shortage.

10. 1 2 3 4 5

EXERCISE 10

DIRECTIONS: Each group below consists of four sentences. In the answer column, blacken the space under the number that corresponds to the number of the incorrect sentence. If there are no errors, blacken the fifth space.

ANSWERS AND EXPLANATIONS APPEAR AT THE END OF THE CHAPTER

1. (1) The roast smelled so good that my mouth began to water.
    (2) Los Angeles is larger than any other city in California.
    (3) If I were in Hawaii now, I'd be lying on the beach.
    (4) I like this kind of apple better than the other.

2. (1) The question of whom we should elect was raised .
    (2) The question whom should be elected was raised.
    (3) The questions of who should be elected were raised.
    (4) We raised the question of who should be elected.

3. (1) It is for neither you nor me to decide.
    (2) The telegram for Mark and I arrived just as we were leaving.
    (3) I'm not so sure that he is as tall as I.
    (4) My friends and I have finally reached a decision.

4. (1) A carton of used parts is lying in the garage.
    (2) There seems to be no doubt about his guilt.
    (3) There seem to be no doubts about him going.
    (4) Neither the boys nor the girls were in favor of our going.

5. (1) Most of the men have left the building.
    (2) Most of the work has been completed.
    (3) As each boy left, we bid them a happy holiday.
    (4) Mary, together with Tom and Sue, is overjoyed at the possibility of spending the Christmas holidays in Vermont.

6. (1) Each one of our workers have been thoroughly screened.
    (2) I, who am only a lowly shipping clerk, am prepared to give my advice to the president of the company.
    (3) His remarks were neither innocuous nor unintentional.
    (4) His having done this kind of work will be a substantial asset to us.

7. (1) The messenger rode as quick as possible to the enemy camp.
    (2) I don't know whether he's coming today or tomorrow.
    (3) Carefully, he laid the mink stole back in the package.
    (4) Can we count on your being there this evening?

8. (1) He was one of those people who never seem content in their work.
    (2) Be sure that the man to whom you speak is listening to all you say.
    (3) To whom did you give my gift?
    (4) I was there for about three hours before I realized I was lost.

9. (1) If no one does their share, how can we get the job finished?
    (2) We wanted to know if Johnson had come yet.
    (3) Had Maurice been there before you called?
    (4) There seem to be at least three good reasons for his scoring as high as I on the exam.

10. (1) Mr. Tompkins, a man of many sides, was called upon to speak.
    (2) To whom, do you suppose, will the principal give the trophy?
    (3) Why have we not thought of this before?
    (4) Nobody knows the trouble I seen.

ANSWERS AND EXPLANATIONS: TEN GRAMMAR AND USAGE EXERCISES

EXERCISE 1

1. **(5)** *Am* is correct because the subjects are joined by *or* and the verb must agree with the one that is closer. *She* is also correct because it is the beginning of a new clause: "... than she IS."

2. **(2)** *Everyone* is a singular word and must agree with the *pronoun* that replaces it later in the sentence: *his* instead of *their.*

3. **(1)** The subjects (*Mary, Tom,* and *I*) are joined by *and,* which makes them plural. Since the verb must agree with the subject, the verb should be *are.*

4. **(1)** Since the subject of the sentence is *One* (*of the girls* is merely a modifier), the verb must agree with it. Thus the verb should be *was.*

5. **(5)** There is a tendency for people to say *There seems.* Remember that in a sentence beginning with *There* or *Here,* the subject is usually found later in the sentence. The subject here is *factors* (*factors* **seem**).

6. **(3)** Use the past perfect tense when speaking of the earlier of two past actions. Since the suspect left the building before the witnesses agreed, use *had left* instead of *left.*

7. **(4)** Use the possessive (*his*) before a gerund (*going*), not the objective (*him*). Note the pattern of this sentence which talks about two actions in the past: *had been—could have.* Don't use *could have—could have* or the alternative forms: *may, should, might,* or *have* more than once in the same sentence.

8. **(3)** *Went* is past tense; the present perfect, *have* **gone** is required here.

9. **(4)** *They,* not *them;* the word *than* is used to introduce another clause— *than they* (**are**)—so the nominative case is needed.

10. **(5)** *is* is the correct verb because the subjects (*boys* and *Sally*) are joined by *or* and the verb must agree with the subject that is closer (*Sally*).

EXERCISE 2

1. **(5)** *Has* is used instead of *have* because it must agree with the subject *Each. Were* is correct (rather than *was*) because it must agree with *who* which, in turn, replaces the plural word *people.*

2. **(5)** *Is* rather than *are* is correct because the subject is singular. Intervening phrases such as *together with* and *as well as* have no effect on the verb. If the connection had been made with *and, are* would be correct.

3. **(1)** Should be *whom* because objective case is required for the object of a preposition (*to*).

4. **(1)** Should be *was;* see the explanation for sentence 2.

5. (5) In (1) *who* is correct. Use the substitution: "Did you say *HE* called?" In (2) and (3) the tenses are correct, since the calling preceded the coming; therefore, *had called* (the past perfect) and *came* (the simple past.) In (4) *lie* rather than *lay* because it describes an act of resting or reclining rather than putting something down.

6. (2) *Many a* works like *each,* and is singular. (2) should be *he* so that it agrees with its antecedent. Had the sentence begun with *Many men,* all the underlined sections would have been plural: *have, they, were, themselves.*

7. (1) *As soon as* implies that the dismissing and the finding happened almost simultaneously; the tenses, therefore, must agree: *had been* should be *was.* Since the forgetting came before either the dismissal or the finding, the past perfect *had* is used. Note that *his,* not *their,* is used to agree with the singular *someone.*

8. (5) The reporting and the becoming clear occurred at the same time; past tense is used in both cases. *He* rather than *him* is used because the nominative case is required for the word following a *being* verb.

9. (4) While we usually think of *laying* a package down, once it has *been laid* down, it is resting or reclining: hense, *lying* is correct. Remember: lie-lay-lain; lay-laid-laid. Notice that (1) is past perfect and (2) is simple past because one precedes the other in time.

10. (5) *Class,* a collective noun, may be singular or plural depending on its use in the sentence. Here that request is made to individuals rather than to one unit.

EXERCISE 3

1. (5) Note the use of tense in this sentence to indicate differences in time.

2. (1) The verb should be singular *was* in order to agree with the subject *it.* Notice that *we* (not *us*) is used after a being verb.

3. (2) *Together with three of his friends* is a prepositional phrase. It is not part of the subject. *Is the one* should be used to agree with *Dick.* Had *and* been substituted for the phrase, the sentence would have been correct.

4. (4) Use *be* instead of *have been.* Note that while *everyone* is singular and would normally take *was, were* is used to express a condition or wish contrary to fact.

5. (2) Use *have* not *has. Who* is the subject of the clause and the word with which the verb must agree. And since the antecedent of *who* is *girls,* which is plural, the verb must be plural.

6. (1) *Seen* cannot be used alone. Use *saw* or *had seen.*

7. (4) Use *nor* with *neither;* or with *either.*

8. (3) Possessive case (*John's*) is required before a gerund (*running*).

9. (5)

10. (3) The subject of the sentence is the singular *credit* which must take a singular verb, *belongs*.

EXERCISE 4

1. (1) *Felt* is used here as a being rather than an action verb. For this reason, it takes the adjective form *bad* rather than the adverb *badly*. **Never** say *I feel badly*.

2. (4) *Suspicious* should be used instead of *suspiciously* because the adjective form is used after a being verb. The principle is the same as in the preceding sentence. Some verbs depend upon their use in the sentence for their classification:

> They *sounded* the trumpet (action) *loudly*. (adverb)
> The noise *sounded* (being) *loud*. (adjective)

3. (5) Note the *had . . . would have* pattern when two past actions, one of which happened before the other, are described.

4. (4) The use of *when* indicates that the crashing and the injuring happened simultaneously; hence, the past tense (*crashed*) should be used.

5. (1) *Allan and him* replaces *two seniors* which is the subject of the sentence. (This is called *apposition*. Subjects take the nominative case (*he*, not *him*). Note the use of the past (*were*) and the past perfect (*had finished*) to denote a difference in the time sequence.

6. (5)

7. (1) Use the possessive (*school's*) before a gerund.

8. (1) Use *I* instead of *myself* as the subject of a sentence. *Decided* does not need its own helping verb since it is part of the compound construction *have planned* and *have decided*.

9. (3) Use the *who-whom* substitute (*they-them* here instead of *he-him*). Fame and fortune have not made **them** proud. The answer is *whom*.

10. (3) There are three actions in this sentence: winning, counting, and knowing. The winning occurred before either the counting or the knowing, which happened at about the same time. Use the past perfect tense for the first action: *had won*.

EXERCISE 5

1. (1) Since the sentence is a question, it is reversed for grammatical analysis: "Either of the men have told you what happened . . ." *Either* is the subject, and because it is singular takes a singular verb: **has**.

2. **(1)** *Would have liked* and *have been* are the same tense. Never use *have* + a verb twice in the same sentence. If you are describing your feeling *now,* the sentence should read: **"I would like** *to have been* there ..." If you are describing your feeling *then,* it should read: **"I would have liked** *to be ..."*

3. **(1)** Remember the *had ... would have* pattern. Use the past perfect for the earlier of the two verbs (to have): "If I *had had* more time, I *would have been ..."*

4. **(3)** *You* should be *your*; possessive case needed before the gerund.

5. **(4)** A pronoun must agree with its antecedent. *Their* should be *his* so that it agrees with its antecedent *everyone*, which is singular.

6. **(5)** Note the use of *was* to agree with the subject *captain. Along with ... men* is a prepositional phrase and does not influence the subject; however, if *along with* were *and* there would be a compound subject requiring a plural verb *were.*

7. **(5)** Note the pattern carefully, and re-read the explanation for sentence 2.

8. **(2)** Should be *what* **seems.**

9. **(2)** "... three inches taller than *I* (am)."

10. **(3)** **Never say "use to"; always say "used to."**

EXERCISE 6

1. **(2)** *Me* should be *my*, since *smoking* (a gerund) really works like a noun. Substitute the word *hat*: Do you object to (me, my) hat? The choice is **easy.**

2. **(3)** *Sweet* required after the being verb *tastes.*

3. **(1)** Use *his* to agree with the singular *someone.*

4. **(4)** *Tom* and *me* needed. Objective case required for the object of the preposition. (Would you say *Wait for I* or *Wait for me*?)

5. **(1)** Use the substitution: "I am sure *he* will tell you ..." The answer, therefore, is *who.*

6. **(4)** Another who-whom substitution: "... if they had elected *him.*" Correct form, then, is *whom.*

7. **(3)** *I*, not *myself*, used for subject.

8. **(5)**

9. **(5)**

10. **(1)** *His brother and* **he** needed for the subject.

EXERCISE 7

1. **(5)**

2. **(2)** *Neither-nor* subjects take a verb that agrees with the part of the subject that is closer; *ones . . . were.*

3. **(3)** *There* is never a subject. The subject here is *arguments*; in order to agree, the verb must be *seem.*

4. **(5)**

5. **(2)** *Between* is a preposition and requires the objective case for its object. Always use *me, him, her,* and *them* after *between.*

6. **(3)** Subject is *fruit*; pattern must be *fruit looks*; *on the stands* is a prepositional phrase.

7. **(3)** *That* refers to *pens*, which is plural. Its verb must agree; hence, *write* rather than *writes.*

8. **(2)** *One . . . makes*; subject and predicate must agree.

9. **(4)** Someone **whom** *we can trust.* Substitute *he-him* for *who-whom* choice: We can trust **him.**

10. **(2)** *Much longer* instead of *much more longer.*

EXERCISE 8

1. **(3)** The water *had frozen.*

2. **(1)** The students *have* or *had* drunk; *drunk* cannot be used without a helping verb (*has-have-had*).

3. **(4)** The cable was *laid. Lie-lay-lain:* to rest or recline; *Lay-laid-laid:* to put or place.

4. **(4)** Use the substitution: "Do you suppose **he** will be elected?" Remember *he* goes with *who; him* goes with *whom.*

5. **(3)** Avoid the tendency to say *these kind* or *these type*. Kind is singular and the modifier must agree. Study the pattern below.

Singular	*Plural*
this, that BOY	these, those BOYS
this, that KIND	these, those KINDS

6. **(3)** *How* does he act? Adverb form (*differently*) is required. This applies to (1) and (2) as well.

7. **(1)** *Our team* is also in the league. It could not have scored more points than itself; therefore, *any other team* must be used.

8. **(2)** *Which* replaces one of the subjects in an *either-or* construction. Both of the subjects are singular. *Was* (the singular) rather than *were* (the plural) should be used.

9. (1) *Good-better-best:* Use the comparative form (*better*) when speaking of two; the superlative (*best*) when speaking of more than two.

10. (2) Mary cannot be older than herself; therefore, say "... any *other* girl ..."

EXERCISE 9

1. (2) *A box ...* **was**.

2. (2) *Laid* should be *lay*.

3. (1) *Hamlet ...* **is** *a favorite ....*

4. (1) *Not* **one** *...* **spots**.

5. (3) A *neither-nor* construction takes a verb that agrees with the closer of the two subjects: Answer is **was**.

6. (1) About *your* having.

7. (1) *Whoever* should be *whomever*.

8. (1) *Are the ones* should be *is the one*.

9. (2) These sentences all involve collective nouns, which are singular or plural depending upon the way they are used in the sentence. (2) speaks of the committee as a single unit rather than a group of individuals; therefore, it should read: "The committee has come to **its** decision."

10. (2) Questions are reversed for grammatical analysis. *He does think he is* (*who, whom*). *Who* (nominative case) is used after the being verb *is*.

EXERCISE 10

1. (5)

2. (2) Use a *he-him* substitution: "The question (whether) **he** should be elected was raised." Change *whom* to *who*.

3. (2) *For* takes the objective case: *for Mark and* **me**; note that the others are correct.

4. (3) Use possessive case (*his*) before the gerund (*going*).

5. (3) Change *them* to *him* to agree with the antecedent *each boy*, which is singular. *Bid* should be *bade*.

6. (1) Same principle as preceding sentence. *Have* should be *has* so that the subject and predicate agree.

7. (1) Use adverbial form (*quickly*) after a verb of action.

8. (4) Use the past perfect to describe the earlier of two past events. "I *had been* there for about three hours. ..."

9. (1) *Their* should be *his* to agree with the singular antecedent *no one*.

10. (4) *See-saw-seen; seen* cannot be used alone; hence, "Nobody knows the trouble **I have seen**."

STYLE AND CLARITY

Style and clarity refer to the accurate and effective use of language. Most errors in this area do not really violate a rule of grammar or usage. However, they do leave the reader with the sense that somehow the sentence could have been phrased more effectively. The study materials that follow are designed to give you some general guidelines which may be useful in dealing with items of this type on the test. You will notice that some concepts from the preceding chapter are repeated here. This is because sentence structure and general style frequently overlap.

UNCLEAR REFERENCE

Many errors in style can be avoided by making sure that the antecedent of a given pronoun is clearly defined. You will recall that a pronoun is a word that replaces a noun or another pronoun. The word it replaces is called the *antecedent*. In the sentence, "Father took us to the show which we really enjoyed," the antecedent of *which* is unclear. Does the sentence mean that we enjoyed the show? Or does it mean we enjoyed the fact that Father took us? Note how these revisions clear up this problem:

> We enjoyed Father's taking us to the show.
> We enjoyed the show that Father took us to see.

AWKWARD CONSTRUCTIONS

Consider the following sentence: "What I wanted was to see him as soon as possible." Notice how the sentence is made clumsy by the inclusion of extra words. This and other awkward constructions may be remedied by making them more concise through the elimination of needless words and phrases: "I wanted to see him as soon as possible."

INTERRUPTION AND SEPARATION

This category embraces those errors that result from placing modifying words or phrases in ineffective places, usually in the middle of a sentence instead of at the beginning or end.

> *Weak:* John watched the program, *which he enjoyed immensely*, last night.
> *Better:* John watched a program last night *which he enjoyed immensely*.
> *Still Better:* Last night, John watched a program *which he enjoyed immensely*.

SUBORDINATION

Related thoughts which really are complete sentences can be expressed in one of three ways:

1. As separate sentences:

    John wanted to go. He had to stay home.

2. As one sentence with a connecting word that emphasizes the relationship.

    John wanted to go, but he had to stay home. Or:
    John wanted to go, so he went.

3. As one sentence where one of the ideas becomes dependent upon the other.

    Although he wanted to go, John stayed home.

Test items of this type involve deciding how the thoughts may be most effectively stated and, in the case of combinations, which connecting word or words will be best.

SENTENCE SHIFTS

A sentence should be grammatically consistent. If it begins in the first person (*I, we*), it should not shift to the second or third (*you, he, she, it, they*).

Weak: I was freezing last night; *you* could see *your* breath in the moonlight.

Better: It was so cold last night that *I* could see *my* breath in the moonlight.

And the time sequence should be consistent, too. Avoid making unnecessary changes in tense.

Weak: First he came into the room. Then he says, "What's
(past) (present)
going on?"

Better: As soon as he came into the room, he said, "What's
(past) (past)
going on?"

OTHER COMMON ERRORS

These kinds of errors usually result from misuse of words or phrases and do not violate any specific grammatical rules.

1. In general, avoid the use of *due to* when *because of* can be used:

    Because of (not *due to*) the heavy rains, all the schools were closed.

2. Never say *is when* or *was when;* substitute *occurs when* or reword the sentence to clarify what happened.

    Weak: The climactic moment in *Hamlet is when* Hamlet confronts Claudius.

    Better: The climactic moment in *Hamlet occurs when* Hamlet confronts Claudius.

    Still Better: The climactic moment in *Hamlet is the confrontation between Hamlet and Claudius.*

3. *Note:* Things are picked *off* the ground, **not** *off of* the ground.

4. Never say *is because.*

    Weak: The reason for his silence *is because* he is shy.

    Better: The reason for his silence *is that* he is shy.

    Still Better: His silence *results from* his shyness.

5. Use *different from* instead of *different than.*

    Wrong: My scarf is *different than* yours.

    Right: My scarf is *different from* yours.

6. Avoid double negatives.

    Wrong: I *don't* have *none* of those hats.

    Right: I *don't* have *any* of those hats.

    Wrong: I *haven't* seen *nobody.*

    Right: I *haven't* seen *anybody.*

Although the preceding explanations are not exhaustive, they do cover most of the points you will need to pass the examination. Now turn to the following practice exercises. They have been specifically designed to test your ability to handle those questions on style and diction that are most likely to appear on the test.

EXERCISE 1

DIRECTIONS: Each sentence below is followed by four possible revisions. In the answer column, blacken the space under the number that corresponds to the number of the most acceptable revision. If none of the revisions is acceptable, or if the sentence is correct as it is, blacken the fifth space.

ANSWERS AND EXPLANATIONS APPEAR AT THE END OF THE CHAPTER

1. 1 2 3 4 5

1. Usually the water is quite calm and today it seems rather choppy.
    (1) Usually the water is quite calm, and today it seems rather choppy.
    (2) Usually the water is quite calm, so today it seems rather choppy.
    (3) Usually the water is quite calm, today it seems rather choppy.
    (4) Usually the water is quite calm, but today it seems rather choppy.

2. 1 2 3 4 5

2. Mark decided to do the job himself which was difficult.
    (1) Mark decided to do the job himself and it was difficult.
    (2) The difficult job was decided to be done by Mark.
    (3) Mark decided to do the difficult job himself.
    (4) Mark himself decided to do the job. It was difficult.

3. 1 2 3 4 5

3. We have decided, after considering the alternatives, to accept the offer.
    (1) We have decided to consider the alternatives after accepting the offer.
    (2) After accepting the offer, we have decided to consider the alternatives.
    (3) After considering the alternatives, we have decided to accept the offer.
    (4) We have considered the alternatives. We accept the offer.

4. 1 2 3 4 5

4. Being that it's Wednesday, my mother will be making spaghetti.
    (1) My mother will be making spaghetti being that it's Wednesday.
    (2) My mother is making spaghetti. It must be Wednesday.
    (3) Because it's Wednesday, my mother will be making spaghetti.
    (4) Although it's Wednesday, my mother will make spaghetti.

5. 1 2 3 4 5

5. Has there been, in your opinion, any improvement in his work?
    (1) Do you opinion any improvement in his work?
    (2) In your opinion, has his work improved?
    (3) Has his work in your opinion improved?
    (4) Has there been any improvement in your opinion of his work?

6. 1 2 3 4 5

6. The best part of the novel was when the hero fought the villain.
    (1) When the hero fought the villain, it was the best part of the novel.
    (2) The best part of the novel is when the hero fights the villain.
    (3) The fight between the hero and the villain is the best part of the novel.
    (4) The hero and the villain are the best parts of the novel.

7. 1 2 3 4 5

7. The reason that the classes are so large this year is because the school is over-crowded.
    (1) The reason that the classes are so large this year is: because the school is overcrowded.
    (2) The reason that the classes are so large this year results from the school is overcrowded.
    (3) The reason that the classes are so large this year may be attributed to the school is overcrowded.
    (4) The reason that the classes are so large this year is that the school is overcrowded.

8. 1 2 3 4 5

8. He was unsatisfactory with his hotel suite.
    (1) He was dissatisfied with his hotel suite.
    (2) He was not satisfactory with his hotel suite.
    (3) He was unsatisfied about his hotel suite.
    (4) He was not very satisfied concerning his hotel suite.

9. What I wanted to do was find out whether he knew the answer.

 (1) Whether he knew the answer, that's what I wanted to know.

 (2) I wanted to find out whether he knew the answer.

 (3) What I wanted to do involved finding out whether he knew the answer.

 (4) I wanted to know if he had found out the answer.

  9.   1   2   3   4   5

10. What I believe is that every man should do his best.

 (1) In my opinion, I think every man should do his best.

 (2) I believe that every man should do his best.

 (3) What I believe is: every man should do their best.

 (4) That every man should do his best is what I believe.

  10.   1   2   3   4   5

EXERCISE 2

DIRECTIONS: Each sentence below is followed by four possible revisions. In the answer column, blacken the space under the number that corresponds to the number of the most acceptable revision. If none of the revisions is acceptable, or if the sentence is correct as it is, blacken the fifth space.

ANSWERS AND EXPLANATIONS APPEAR AT THE END OF THE CHAPTER

1. He tried to find out the teacher's name that he was going to have for math.

 (1) He tried to find out the teacher that he was going to have for math's name.

 (2) To find out the math teacher's name was what he tried to do.

 (3) He tried to find out the name of the teacher whom he was going to have for math.

 (4) He tried to find out the math teacher's name that he was going to have.

  1.   1   2   3   4   5

2. Because it had a flat tire, the car was pushed by us to the garage.

 (1) We pushed the car to the garage. Because it had a flat tire.

 (2) The car had a flat tire, and we pushed it to the garage.

 (3) Because it was flat, we pushed the car to the garage.

 (4) The car had a flat tire, so we pushed it to the garage.

  2.   1   2   3   4   5

3. There are some comments in the book which anyone who reads them will be interested in.

 (1) There are some comments in the book which anyone who reads them will find interesting.

 (2) There are some comments in the book which will interest every reader.

 (3) There are some comments in the book which will be found interesting to all.

 (4) There are some comments in the book that everyone will like.

  3.   1   2   3   4   5

4. Research indicates that children's art work is more imaginative than adults.

 (1) Research indicates that children's art work is more imaginative than adults are.

  4.   1   2   3   4   5

(2) Research indicates that children's art work is more imaginative than those of adults.

(3) Research indicates that children's art work is more imaginative than that of adults.

(4) Research indicates that children's art work is more imaginative than adult work.

5. Opening a curtain, a full house was revealed.

(1) A full house was revealed, opening the curtain.

(2) Opening a curtain revealed a full house.

(3) The open curtain revealed a full house.

(4) The full house was revealed by the opening of the curtain.

6. Yesterday we finally got to see the movie which was wonderful.

(1) Yesterday we saw the movie. It was wonderful.

(2) Yesterday we finally got to see the movie, and it was wonderful.

(3) We finally got to see the wonderful movie yesterday.

(4) Yesterday we finally got to see the movie. Which was wonderful.

7. Sixteen inches of snow had fallen during the night and we were late getting to school.

(1) Sixteen inches of snow had fallen during the night, we were late getting to school.

(2) Sixteen inches of snow had fallen during the night so we were late getting to school.

(3) Sixteen inches of snow had fallen during the night; and we were late getting to school.

(4) Sixteen inches of snow had fallen during the night, therefore, we were late getting to school.

8. The guests had enjoyed the meal. They thanked their host.

(1) The guests had enjoyed the meal, and they thanked their host.

(2) The guests, who had enjoyed the meal, thanked their host.

(3) The guests thanked their host for enjoying the meal.

(4) They thanked their host for the meal they had enjoyed.

9. The movie was over, and we stopped for some coffee.

(1) The movie was over, but we stopped for some coffee.

(2) We stopped for coffee because the movie was over.

(3) When the movie was over; we stopped for coffee.

(4) After the movie, we stopped for coffee.

10. I know everyone, even the best of students, have an off day now and then.

(1) I know that everyone, even the best of students, has an off day now and then.

(2) Everyone has an off day now and then. Even the best of students.

(3) I know that everyone, even the best of students, have an off day now and then.

(4) I know even the best of students have an off day occasionally.

EXERCISE 3

DIRECTIONS: Each sentence below is followed by four possible revisions. In the answer column, blacken the space under the number that corresponds to the number of the most acceptable revision. If none of the revisions is acceptable, or if the sentence is correct as it is, blacken the fifth space.

ANSWERS AND EXPLANATIONS APPEAR AT THE END OF THE CHAPTER

1. It was late and we were tired and so we went home.

    (1)   We went home because it was late and tired.
    (2)   We went home because we were tired and late.
    (3)   We were tired and it was late, so we went home.
    (4)   We were tired and it was late, we went home.

2. Do all the men know when the whistle blows it's time for lunch?

    (1)   When the whistle blows, do all the men know that it is time for lunch?
    (2)   Are all the workers cognizant of the significance of the whistle as it relates to their partaking of some midday nourishment?
    (3)   Do all the men know that when the whistle blows, it's time for lunch?
    (4)   Do all the men blow their whistles when it's lunch time?

3. They had lost the first game, they were determined to win the second.

    (1)   They lost the first game, and were determined to win the second.
    (2)   They had lost the first game but were determined to win the second.
    (3)   They had lost the first game; so were determined to win the second.
    (4)   Although they were determined to win the second game, they lost.

4. This is a meal of which anyone who tries it will be satisfied.

    (1)   This is a meal of which all who eat will be satisfied.
    (2)   This meal will satisfied anyone who tries it.
    (3)   This meal will satisfy anyone who tries it.
    (4)   This is a satisfying meal for everybody.

5. Joan was asked by Mary to arrive early.

    (1)   Mary was asked by Joan to arrive early.
    (2)   Mary asked Joan to arrive early.
    (3)   Joan asked Mary to arrive early.
    (4)   Mary asked Joan if she could come early.

6. I had heard many good things about the movie but I went to see it.

    (1)   I went to see the movie hearing many good things.
    (2)   I went to see the movie; because I had heard many good things about it.
    (3)   Because I had heard many good things about it, I went to see the movie.
    (4)   Because I had heard many good things about the movie, I went to see it.

7. 1 2 3 4 5

7. Telegrams were sent by the people to their congressmen.

    (1)   The people sent telegrams to their congressmen.
    (2)   The congressman received telegrams from the people.
    (3)   The people sent telegrams to their congressmen.
    (4)   The congressmen received telegrams from their people.

8. 1 2 3 4 5

8. He had neither respect nor pride about his work.

    (1)   He had neither respect in or pride for his work.
    (2)   He had neither respect nor pride for his work.
    (3)   He had neither respect for nor pride in his work.
    (4)   He has either respect for or pride in his work.

9. 1 2 3 4 5

9. Have you heard the program was postponed?

    (1)   Have you heard the program? It was postponed.
    (2)   Have you heard the program that was postponed?
    (3)   Have you heard that the program was postponed?
    (4)   Have you heard a program was postponed?

10. 1 2 3 4 5

10. Being that it had snowed, the school was closed.

    (1)   The school was closed due to the snow.
    (2)   Because it had snowed, the school was closed.
    (3)   Being that the snow was heavy, the school was closed.
    (4)   The accumulation of icy precipitation necessitated an unscheduled educational hiatus.

EXERCISE 4

DIRECTIONS: Each sentence below is followed by four possible revisions. In the answer column, blacken the space under the number that corresponds to the number of the most acceptable revision. If none of the revisions is satisfactory, or if the sentence is correct as it stands, blacken the fifth space.

ANSWERS AND EXPLANATIONS APPEAR AT THE END OF THE CHAPTER

1. 1 2 3 4 5

1. We were told they were coming in large numbers to see the game.

    (1)   They told us they were coming to the game in large numbers.
    (2)   We were told that they were coming to the game in large numbers.
    (3)   We were told of their coming to the game in large numbers.
    (4)   We were coming to their game in large numbers.

2. 1 2 3 4 5

2. Looking up the bright stars can be seen.

    (1)   Look up, you can see the bright stars.
    (2)   If you look up, you can see the bright stars.
    (3)   When looking up, you can see the bright stars.
    (4)   The bright stars can be seen upon looking up.

3. All the people cannot get tickets.

    (1) Tickets cannot be gotten by all of the people.

    (2) All of the people cannot get tickets.

    (3) Not all of the people can get tickets.

    (4) Tickets are hard to get.

4. Arrangements by the bride and groom for the wedding had been made.

    (1) Arrangements for the bride and groom's wedding had been made.

    (2) Arrangements for the wedding had been made by the bride and the groom.

    (3) The bride and groom had made the wedding arrangements.

    (4) The groom had arranged for the bride's wedding.

5. Standing by the railroad tracks a whistle could be heard.

    (1) A whistle could be heard standing by the railroad tracks.

    (2) By standing by the railroad tracks, a whistle could be heard.

    (3) We could hear a whistle standing by the railroad tracks.

    (4) As we stood by the tracks, we could hear a whistle.

6. The police questioned the teller and the safe was examined.

    (1) The police who examined the safe questioned the teller.

    (2) The police questioned the teller who examined the safe.

    (3) The police questioned the safe and examined the teller.

    (4) The police questioned the teller and examined the safe.

7. When one comes to bat in this situation, you can either bunt or swing away.

    (1) When you come to bat in this situation, you can either bunt or swing away.

    (2) When one bats in this situation, one should bunt and swing away.

    (3) Upon coming to bat in this situation, either bunting or swinging away may be done.

    (4) Bunt and swing away in this situation.

8. Senator Byrnes, after his defeat, never plans to run again.

    (1) Having been defeated, Senator Byrnes never plans to run again.

    (2) Having been defeated, Senator Byrnes plans to never run again.

    (3) Having been defeated, Senator Byrnes plans never to run again.

    (4) Having been defeated, Senator Byrnes plans to run again never.

9. When hot, your ice cream will melt.

    (1) When hot ice cream melts.

    (2) Ice cream melts when hot.

    (3) Heat melts ice cream.

    (4) It's hot, you're ice cream is melting.

10. Yours is different than mine.

    (1) Yours is different than mine is.

    (2) You and I are different.

    (3) Yours differs from mine.

    (4) Mine is different than yours.

ANSWERS AND EXPLANATIONS: STYLE AND CLARITY EXERCISES

EXERCISE 1

1. **(4)** *But* show the relationship best; note the comma.
2. **(3)** Most economical language; does not change the meaning.
3. **(3)** Brings the thoughts together; does not change the meaning.
4. **(3)** *Because* should be substituted for *being that*.
5. **(2)** Modifier now placed in clearer position.
6. **(3)** Eliminates *was when* without changing the meaning.
7. **(4)** Eliminates *is because* without changing the meaning; properly punctuated.
8. **(1)** Replaces wrong word, *unsatisfactory*.
9. **(2)** Smooths out an awkward construction without changing the meaning.
10. **(2)** Most economical language. Note the repetition occurring in "In my opinion, I think."

EXERCISE 2

1. **(3)** Choices (1), (2) and (4) are all awkward.
2. **(4)** Choice (1) is a fragment; choice (2) has the flat being pushed; choice (3) has a flat car.
3. **(2)** Choice (1) is awkward; choice (3) is too long and clumsy; choice (4), *liking* is not the same.
4. **(3)** Choice (1) compares art to people; choice (2) *those* is wrong; choice (4) *work* is too general.
5. **(3)** Choice (1) has a dangling modifier; choices (2) and (4) are awkward.
6. **(3)** Expresses the thought in the most concise language.
7. **(2)** Choice (1), run on; choices (3) and (4), faulty punctuation.
8. **(2)** Choice (1) *and* should be *so;* choice (3) changes the meaning; choice (4) who are *they?*
9. **(4)** Choices (1) and (2) change the meaning; choice (3) incorrect punctuation.
10. **(1)** Choice (2) is a fragment; choices (3) and (4) have errors in agreement (*have*).

EXERCISE 3

1. **(3)** Choices (1) and (2) change meaning; choice (4) is a run-on.
2. **(3)** Choices (1) and (4) change the meaning; choice (2) is too fancified.
3. **(2)** Choices (1) and (3) are improperly punctuated; choice (4) changes the meaning.
4. **(3)** Choice (2) has a tense error; choice (1) is too fancy; choice (4), too vague.
5. **(2)** The other choices change the meaning.
6. **(4)** Choice (3) is less clear because *it* comes before *movie*.

7. **(3)** Choice (4) has the congressmen "owning" the people; choices (1) and (2) refer to *one* congressman.
8. **(3)** *Neither* goes with *nor;* note the word usage: respect **for**; pride **in**.
9. **(3)** The others change the meaning.
10. **(2)** Never use *being that; because of* is preferable to *due to;* choice (4) is too fancy.

EXERCISE 4

1. **(2)** The others change the meaning.
2. **(2)** Uses the most concise language.
3. **(3)** The others either change the meaning or are clumsy.
4. **(3)** Concise and clear.
5. **(4)** Good, clear reference; meaning unchanged.
6. **(4)** Creates parallel structure without changing the meaning.
7. **(1)** Others tend to be awkward.
8. **(3)** Modifier *never* is most clearly placed.
9. **(3)** Simplest language and clearest meaning.
10. **(3)** Meaning clear and unchanged.

CHOOSING THE RIGHT WORD

Many of our errors in writing arise from our wrong use of words. For instance, we often use the word *except* when we really mean *accept*. Another common mistake is writing *principle* when we really intended to write *principal*. On the official test, you will be asked to spot these and similar errors. To prepare you for this part of the examination, we have provided you with a list of the most common word-choice "demons" you will be likely to face. Study it carefully. It has been especially designed to increase your chances of passing. However, before you begin, take the diagnostic test below.

WORD-CHOICE DIAGNOSTIC TEST

DIRECTIONS: For each sentence, indicate the word that is more appropriate.

ANSWERS AND EXPLANATIONS APPEAR AT THE END OF THE TEST

1. John and Martha are (angry at, angry with) Tom.

2. Are you familiar with the (principal, principle) parts of a sentence?

3. Will this test have any (affect, effect) on our final grade?

4. The pants had to be taken in at the (waste, waist).

5. (Who's, Whose) coat is this?

6. Fred is bigger (then, than) Tommy.

7. Brian wrote a letter on the new (stationery, stationary) he had bought.

8. Her pink hat (complemented, complimented) her new dress.

9. The show was intended to raise the (moral, morale) of the troops.

10. It's (alright, all right) with me.

11. After dinner we had ice cream for (desert, dessert).

12. Harry decided to seek additional (advice, advise).

13. Next term we will take the second part of the (coarse, course).

14. Overconfidence has frequently (lead, led) to defeat.

15. The meeting was conducted rather (formally, formerly).

16. (It's, Its) difficult to predict the results of the new drug.

17. (They're, Their) always very sure of themselves.

18. John is two years older (then, than) his brother.

19. Be careful not to (lose, loose) the ten dollar bill.

20. We're (already, all ready) to start.

ANSWERS AND EXPLANATIONS: DIAGNOSTIC TEST

1. angry with   *You are *angry at* things, but *angry with* people.
2. principal   *A *principle* is a rule or law. A principal is the head of a school. *Principal* also means "chief" or "major."
3. effect   *Affect* is a verb meaning to "change." *Effect* is a noun meaning "result."
4. waist   *Waste is what is left over.
5. Whose   *Who's* is a contraction of *who is.*
6. than*   *Than* is used in making comparisons, while *then* expresses time.
7. stationery   *Stationary* means "not moving."
8. complemented   *Complement* means to "complete," while *compliment* means to "praise."
9. morale   *Moral* refers to ethical teachings. *Morale* is a person's state of mind.
10. all right   *There is no such word as *alright.*
11. dessert   *A *desert* is arid, barren land.
12. advice   *Advise* is a verb.
13. course   *Coarse* means "rough."
14. led   *Lead* is a verb meaning "to go before or proceed," and *led* is the past tense of this verb.
15. formally   *Formerly* describes a past condition.
16. It's   *It's* is the contraction of *it is,* while *its* is the possessive form of *it.*
17. They're   *They're* is the contraction of *they are,* while *their* is a possessive adjective.
18. than   *Use *than* for comparison; use *then* to express time.
19. lose   *Lose* is a verb meaning "to part with by accident," while *loose* is an adjective meaning "not fastened securely."
20. all ready   *All ready* means "everyone is ready," while *already* means "previously."

WORD-CHOICE "DEMONS"

accept, except   *Accept* means to receive, usually willingly. (He *accepted* our invitation. If I'm not home, my neighbor will *accept* the package.) *Except* means "but." (Everyone went *except* me.)

adapt, adopt   *Adapt* means "to change." (We will *adapt* the plan to suit our needs.) *Adopt* means "to accept." (We decided to *adopt* the proposal. The Smiths have *adopted* their third child.)

advice, advise   *Advice* is a noun meaning "a suggestion." *Advise* is a verb meaning "to recommend or give advice to." (Although I tried to *advise* him on the matter, he refused to take my *advice*.)

already, all ready; altogether, all together; all right   *Already* means "previously." (He has *already* done it.) *All ready* refers to everyone being ready. (Are they *all ready?*) *Altogether* may be used synonymously with "completely." (His answer is *altogether* wrong.) *All together,* like *all* *ready*, refers to people. (We are *all together* in this noble struggle.) *All right* implies satisfaction or correctness. (I got the questions *all right*. It's *all right* with me.) *Note: Alright* is NEVER ACCEPTABLE.

allusion, illusion *Allusion* means "reference." (His work consisted of one literary *allusion* after another.) *Illusion* refers to a mistaken idea or vision. (We were sure it had been an optical *illusion*.)

altar, alter *Altar* indicates a table usually found in a church. (The priest stood at the *altar*.) *Alter* means "to change." (The tailor will have to *alter* this new suit of mine.)

amount, number Do not use these words interchangeably. *Amount* refers to "quantity." (The *amount* of effort that has been put into this job is enormous.) *Number* refers to persons or things that can be counted. (There are a *number* of problems associated with this proposal.)

angry at, angry with *Angry at* refers to things. *Angry with* refers to people. The same principle may be appiled to *agree to* (some**thing**) and *agree with* (some**one**). (I became *angry at* the sight of such disorder. I was *angry with* John.)

anywheres, nowheres Both are incorrect. Use *anywhere* and *nowhere*.

beside, besides *Beside* means "next to." (Come stand *beside* me.) *Besides* means "in addition to." (Who went to the movie *besides* Paul and Barbara?)

between, among; each other, one another Use *between* and *each other* to refer to two people or things. (Divide it *between* him and me. Tom and I spoke to *each other*.) Use *among* and *one another* for more than two. (The prize money was split up *among* Tom, George, and Fred. If people would learn to communicate more effectively with *one another*, much tension would be reduced.)

born, borne *Born* has to do with birth. (What time was the baby *born?*) *Borne* means "to bear" or "to carry." (He has *borne* his burden well for many years.)

brake, break *Brake* is a device used for stopping. (The *brake* on my car is defective.) *Break* means "to shatter." (If you leave, you'll *break* my heart.)

capitol, capital The word *capitol* has only one meaning: the building in which a state legislature meets. However, when the *c* is capitalized, it refers to the building housing the United States Congress in Washington, D.C. The word *capital*, on the other hand, has several meanings, one of which is "the city in which the seat of government is located." (Sacramento is the *capital* of California. Paris is the *capital* of France.)

coarse, course   *Coarse* means "rough, crude." (He broke into a rash from wearing the *coarse* sweater.) *Course* means a route or an organized sequence of studies. (I simply don't know what *course* to take. Next term, we'll take the second half of the history *course*.)

complement, compliment   *Complement* means "to complete." (Her hat *complemented* her dress.) *Compliment* is used to mean "praise." (He paid his wife a lovely *compliment*.)

continual, continuous   *Continual* implies an action that stops occasionally. (He was *continually* asking questions.) *Continuous* describes an action that progresses without pause. (My alarm clock rings *continuously* for an hour before it shuts itself off.

council, counsel   *Council* describes a group of men, usually gathered for some legislative purpose. (Who do you think will be running for the city *council* next year?) *Counsel* means "advice" or "to advise." (He came to me seeking guidance and *counsel*.)

credible, creditable, credulous   *Credible* means "believable" (the opposite of *incredible*), and is used to refer to things. (He told us a *credible* story.) *Credulous* refers to people and describes the quality of believing too readily. (Tom is a most *credulous* individual.) *Creditable* means "worthy of credit, deserving praise." (He has done a *creditable* job.)

desert, dessert   *Desert* describes arid, barren land. It also refers to the act of abandoning something. (We read about the Sahara *Desert*. Three soldiers were prepared to *desert* the company.) *Dessert* is the final course of a meal. (Hey Mom, what's for *dessert?*)

discover, invent   When you find out about something for the first time, you *discover* it. You *invent* something when you bring it into being. (Franklin *discovered* electricity, but it took Edison to *invent* the light bulb.)

die, dye   *Die* has to do with death. (The sergeant was *dying* and he knew it.) You *dye* things by changing their color. (Is she still *dyeing* her hair?)

draw, drawer   *Draw* is what an artist does, and a *drawer* is where he keeps his brushes.

eager, anxious   *Eager* expresses a sense of anticipation. (I am *eager* to see the new movie.) *Anxious* implies a sense of worry or concern. (I'm a bit *anxious* about my test.)

effect, affect   *Effect* as a noun means "result"; as a verb, it means "to bring into being." (What will the *effect* of his speech be? We intend to *effect* a few changes here.) *Affect* is a verb, meaning "to cause a change in." (His remarks didn't *affect* me in the least.)

emigration, immigration *Emigration* is the act of people leaving a country. *Immigration* is the act of people entering a country.

famous, infamous (notorious) A person who is widely known for generally favorable reasons is *famous*. An individual whose faults make him well known is *infamous* (or *notorious*). (Although Pete Thomson was a *famous* lawyer, his brother was an *infamous* confidence man.)

farther, further *Farther* refers to physical distance. (I've already walked ten miles and can't go any *farther*.) *Further* means "more" or "additional." (I don't wish to pursue this argument any *further*.)

formally, formerly *Formally* means "in a formal or established manner." *Formerly* describes a past state or condition. (The press knew what the president would say before his speech was formally delivered. Antoine's Hair Stylists was *formerly* known as Tony's Barber Shop.)

imply, infer *Imply* has to do with giving a hint. *Infer* is associated with drawing a conclusion. (I did not intend to *imply* that he was not working. I could only *infer* from his remarks that he was dissatisfied.)

in, into *In* describes something being within or inside of something else. (Guess what I have *in* my pocket.) *Into* denotes movement from the outside to the inside. (Just then, John came *into* the room.)

it's, its *It's* is a contraction of *it is*, while *its* is the possessive form of *it*. (*It's* my book; don't mark up *its* pages.)

kind, sort, type These words may be followed by *of* but not *of a*. (This *kind of* [**not** *of a*] book is worth reading.)

lead, led *Lead* as verb means "to precede or go before." As a noun, it refers to a metal. *Led* is the past tense of the verb *lead*. (I bought a *lead* pencil. Every general wants to *lead* his men to victory. Harry has been *led* astray by his friends.)

like, as *Like* is a preposition used to introduce a phrase. *As* is used to introduce a clause. (He looks *like* his brother. He works *as* quickly as he can.) *Note:* Use *as if* or *as though* instead of *like* whenever possible. (He looks *like* he's tired **should be** He looks *as if* he's tired.)

loose, lose *Loose* is an adjective meaning "not fastened securely"; *lose* is a verb meaning "to part with by accident." Just remember that if your button is *loose*, you might *lose* it.

miner, minor A *miner* is a person who works in a mine. A *minor* is someone who is young. (Are *minors* allowed to become *miners?*)

moral, morale *Moral* is related to ethics or personal standards. (He was a man of high *moral* qualities.) *Morale* refers to a state of mind and spirit. (Every year Bob Hope attempts to build up the *morale* of American troops by visiting military bases.)

nauseated, nauseous   These words do not mean the same thing. *Nauseated* means "sick." *Nauseous* means "sickening." (The *nauseous* odor of the dead fish made us *nauseated*.)

off, from   Do not confuse these words. We borrow money *from* someone, not *off* someone.

passed, past   *Passed* is the past tense of the verb *to pass*. (We *passed* his house yesterday.) *Past* refers to something that is over. (In the *past*, we always did it this way.)

peace, piece   *Peace* is related to the absence of war; quiet, and contentment. *Piece* is synonymous with *slice*. (In order to restore *peace*, I gave them both a *piece* of cake.)

persecute, prosecute   When you treat someone cruelly because of his race, religion, or beliefs, you are *persecuting* him. (The Nazis *persecuted* the Jews in Europe.) When a district attorney attempts to prove in court that you are a burglar, he is *prosecuting* you. (Mr. Cohen is a witness for the *prosecution*.)

personal, personnel   *Personal* relates to you or to another as individuals. (He is a *personal* friend of mine. My reason is too *personal* to talk about.) *Personnel* has to do with employees. (We decided to have a Christmas party for all of the office *personnel*.)

plain, plane   *Plain* means "simple, unadorned." (Please try to speak in *plain* English.) *Plane* has to do with a flat surface or an airplane. (Ahead of us stretched a vast, grassy *plane*. All *planes* have been grounded because of the poor weather.)

precede, proceed   *Precede* means to "go in front of." *Proceed* means "to go ahead." (When the group *proceeds* down the hall, Jane will *precede* Agatha.)

principal, principle   *Principal* has two meanings: (1) "the executive officer in a school," and (2) "chief or main." *Principle* is synonymous with *law* or *rule*. (The *principal* congratulated the graduating class. What was his *principal* reason for going? In order to understand why the machine is valuable, you must understand the *principle* behind it.)

quiet, quite   *Quiet* refers to the absence of noise. (It's certainly *quiet* in here tonight.) *Quite* is synonymous with *rather*. (I was *quite* tired after my hard day's work.)

shall, will   For all practical purposes, and in particular for the High

School Equivalency Examination, no distinction need be made between these two words.

stationary, stationery *Stationary* means "fixed, not movable." (Walls are usually stationary, while chairs are not.) *Stationery* means paper and envelopes. *Hint:* Think of the *er* at the end of *paper*. (Did you see Maureen's new pink *stationery?*)

than, then Use *than* for comparisons. (Harry is taller *than* I am.) Use *then* to express a sense of time. (What did you do *then?*)

their, there, they're *Their* indicates possession. *There* indicates place or direction. *They're* is a contraction of *they are*. (*They're* going *there* in *their* car.)

to, too, two *To* is a preposition used to introduce a phrase. (She is going *to* the store. He went *to* bed.) *Too* means "also" or "an excess." (I have *too* many. I am going *too*.) *Two* is the number 2. (I have *two* bats.)

waist, waste Your *waist* is what you put your belt around. *Waste* as a verb deals with improper use of something. (Don't *waste* water.) As a noun, *waste* is what is left over. (Getting rid of garbage and other *waste* is a problem.)

who's, whose *Who's* is a contraction for *who is*. *Whose* is a possessive form. (I don't know *who's* going. *Whose* book is this?)

write, right When you *write* your answers on the test, let's hope you get them all *right*.

EXERCISE 1

DIRECTIONS: In each of the following sentences, there are four underlined words. In the answer column, blacken the space under the number that corresponds to the number of the incorrect word. If all the words are correct, blacken the fifth space.

ANSWERS APPEAR AT THE END OF THE CHAPTER

1. Of course I'll accept their invitation; I consider it quite a complement.

2. The principle reason for my not going any further may be inferred from the attitude of the personnel when they come to the bargaining table.

3. Their morale might have been effected when six of the men decided to desert.

4. The district attorney was not <u>anxious</u> to <u>prosecute</u> the man who had <u>led</u>
                                 1   2   3

   the <u>miners</u> in the two-week strike.
        4

4. 1 2 3 4 5

5. Before the resolution was <u>passed</u>, the <u>council</u> recommended a week of
<u>further</u> investigation and more discussion <u>between</u> the three committees.

5. 1 2 3 4 5

6. I was <u>eager</u> to leave the <u>capital</u> early since the great <u>number</u> of tourists were
<u>liable</u> to cause a traffic jam.

6. 1 2 3 4 5

7. The <u>principal's</u> <u>counsel</u> <u>led</u> me to believe that everything would soon be
<u>alright</u>.

7. 1 2 3 4 5

8. Because <u>there</u> had been an increasing <u>amount</u> of accidents, the company
instructed all <u>personnel</u> to double check the <u>brake</u> cylinders.

8. 1 2 3 4 5

9. His <u>allusions</u> to Shakespeare may have been <u>apt</u>, but they seemed <u>all together</u>
<u>incredible</u> to me.

9. 1 2 3 4 5

10. The <u>principle</u> of limited <u>immigration</u> quotas is beginning to <u>loose</u> favor in
the nation's <u>capital</u>.

10. 1 2 3 4 5

EXERCISE 2

DIRECTIONS: In each of the following sentences, there are four underlined words. In the answer column, blacken the space under the number that corresponds to the number of the incorrect word. Blacken the fifth space if they are all correct.

ANSWERS APPEAR AT THE END OF THE CHAPTER

1. The <u>principle</u> <u>effects</u> of the bill are <u>likely</u> to <u>lead</u> to a need for even more
legislation.

1. 1 2 3 4 5

2. Of <u>course</u>, a <u>personal</u> <u>complement</u> can be <u>quite</u> effective in some cases.

2. 1 2 3 4 5

3. 1 2 3 4 5

3. The two <u>men</u> <u>who's</u> <u>illusions</u> had been shattered were more <u>than</u> eager to
       1   2   3   4
   find the right explanation.

4. 1 2 3 4 5

4. A few minutes <u>later</u>, he took some kind of <u>an</u> object <u>from</u> his coat pocket
   and put it <u>in</u> the drawer.
   4

5. 1 2 3 4 5

5. The <u>famous</u> criminal stated that the <u>implications</u> of the investigator
   1   2
   amounted to <u>moral</u> <u>persecution</u>.
   3   4

6. 1 2 3 4 5

6. <u>Continual</u> discussion, with only occasional <u>breaks</u> for meals, <u>led</u> to a new
   1   2   3
   <u>coarse</u> of action.
   4

7. 1 2 3 4 5

7. We have decided to <u>altar</u> the bill slightly and then <u>adopt</u> it rather <u>than</u> to
   1   2   3
   postpone the vote as had been <u>formerly</u> suggested.
   4

8. 1 2 3 4 5

8. Any alteration at the <u>waist</u> is <u>apt</u> to make this dress <u>too</u> <u>loose</u>.
   1   2   3   4

9. 1 2 3 4 5

9. We had <u>discovered</u> that the <u>affects</u> of the gas were a factor in making the
   1   2
   <u>miners</u> become <u>nauseated</u>.
   3   4

10. 1 2 3 4 5

10. In a <u>week</u>, we should be able to judge <u>quite</u> <u>plainly</u> <u>who's</u> prediction is
    1   2   3   4
    more accurate.

EXERCISE 3

DIRECTIONS: In each of the following sentences, there are four underlined words. In the answer column, blacken the space
under the number that corresponds to the number of
the incorrect word. Blacken the fifth space if they are all
correct.

ANSWERS APPEAR AT THE END OF THE CHAPTER

1. 1 2 3 4 5

1. His remarks <u>led</u> us to believe that even if we were to <u>loose</u>, <u>everything</u> would
   1   2   3
   be <u>all right</u>.
   4

2. 1 2 3 4 5

2. Of <u>coarse</u>, not everyone knows how to <u>accept</u> a <u>personal</u> <u>compliment</u>.
   1   2   3   4

3. In his address, the <u>principal</u> made an <u>allusion</u> to the <u>amount</u> of people who

                               1   2   3

    had been <u>born</u> in January.

               4

3. 1 2 3 4 5

4. We decided to make an <u>adaptation</u> in the program so that <u>its</u> likely <u>effects</u>

                                  1   2   3

    would be more <u>exceptable</u>.

                       4

4. 1 2 3 4 5

5. Are our lawmakers so <u>anxious</u> about <u>immigration</u> that they will agree <u>with</u>

                                   1   2   3

    a bill that is not <u>altogether</u> fair?

                        4

5. 1 2 3 4 5

6. The man <u>who's</u> place <u>you're</u> taking should, of <u>course</u>, be <u>complimented</u>.

                1   2   3   4

6. 1 2 3 4 5

7. <u>You're</u> <u>liable</u> to find some <u>stationery</u> in this <u>drawer</u> if you look.

      1   2   3   4

7. 1 2 3 4 5

8. The <u>famous</u> statesman is <u>liable</u> to appear in the <u>capital</u> a bit <u>later</u> this year.

         1   2   3   4

8. 1 2 3 4 5

9. The <u>continual</u> <u>allusions</u> to our fighting men <u>implied</u> that the speaker had

         1   2   3

    great confidence in their <u>moral</u>.

                             4

9. 1 2 3 4 5

10. <u>There</u> bound to <u>know</u> <u>who's</u> <u>right</u>.

       1   2   3   4

10. 1 2 3 4 5

EXERCISE 4

DIRECTIONS: In each of the following sentences, there are four underlined words. In the answer column, blacken the space under the number that corresponds to the number of the incorrect word. If all the words are correct, blacken the fifth space.

ANSWERS APPEAR AT THE END OF THE CHAPTER

1. They were <u>eager</u> to <u>proceed</u> <u>like</u> they had been <u>told</u>.

                1   2   3   4

1. 1 2 3 4 5

2. He <u>led</u> us <u>passed</u> a place that looked <u>like</u> some kind of <u>desert</u>.

      1   2   3   4

2. 1 2 3 4 5

3. In <u>two</u> <u>weeks</u> we were <u>eager</u> to <u>proceed</u> on our journey.

      1   2   3   4

3. 1 2 3 4 5

4. Joe <u>implied</u> that he would be <u>likely</u> <u>to</u> agree to our proposal that he <u>accept</u>

        1   2   3   4

    the money.

4. 1 2 3 4 5

5. 1 2 3 4 5

5. The members of the city <u>council</u> have decided not to <u>waste</u> any more
   ₁   ₂

   <u>stationery</u> <u>then</u> they usually do.
   ₃   ₄

6. 1 2 3 4 5

6. <u>Besides</u> Tom, Mary, Ellen, and Joyce were <u>formally</u> inducted <u>in</u> the club
   ₁   ₂   ₃

   at the initiation ceremony held at the school this <u>past</u> Tuesday.
   ₄

7. 1 2 3 4 5

7. The <u>apt</u> pupil is <u>likely</u> to have his <u>moral</u> improved if, after studying
   ₁   ₂   ₃

   diligently, he finds out that he's <u>passed</u> the test.
   ₄

8. 1 2 3 4 5

8. Don't <u>waste</u> time trying to decide <u>who's</u> <u>right</u> and <u>whose</u> wrong in this case.
   ₁   ₂ ₃   ₄

9. 1 2 3 4 5

9. I think that in his speech the senator attempted to <u>infer</u> that <u>minors</u> were
   ₁   ₂

   not <u>quite</u> sophisticated enough to be granted any <u>further</u> privileges.
   ₃   ₄

10. 1 2 3 4 5

10. His story seemed <u>credible</u> enough at first, but as he went a bit <u>farther</u> into
    ₁   ₂

    the matter, I found some of his statements <u>quite</u> diffcult to <u>accept</u> as the
    ₃   ₄

    honest truth.

EXERCISE 5

DIRECTIONS: In each of the following groups, there are four sentences. In each sentence, a word is underlined. In the answer column, blacken the space under the number that corresponds to the number of the sentence having an incorrect underlined word. If none of the sentences in a group have an incorrect word, blacken the fifth space.

ANSWERS APPEAR AT THE END OF THE CHAPTER

1. 1 2 3 4 5

1. (1) Everyone went <u>except</u> John.

   (2) We would like to <u>adopt</u> a child.

   (3) Are they <u>all ready</u>?

   (4) It's <u>alright</u> with me.

2. 1 2 3 4 5

2. (1) Personally, I agree <u>with</u> John.

   (2) It was an optical <u>illusion</u>.

(3) The <u>alter</u> was decorated for Christmas.

(4) There were a large <u>number</u> of people gathered in the street.

3. (1) Divide it <u>between</u> Mary, Helen, and Jane.

   (2) Who went <u>besides</u> John?

   (3) The defendant was held <u>liable</u> for damages.

   (4) When were you <u>born</u>?

4. (1) The <u>break</u> on the car was worn out.

   (2) Do you know the <u>capital</u> of Alabama?

   (3) What <u>courses</u> are you taking next term?

   (4) A <u>complement</u> follows a linking verb.

5. (1) We sought advice and <u>counsel</u>.

   (2) His story seemed <u>credulous</u> enough.

   (3) Don't <u>desert</u> me now.

   (4) Did Marconi <u>invent</u> the wireless?

6. (1) He can <u>draw</u> well.

   (2) She <u>dyed</u> her hair blonde.

   (3) I <u>shall</u> go there tomorrow.

   (4) The Bronsons owned a <u>stationary</u> store.

7. (1) He's taller <u>then</u> his brother.

   (2) Oh, that's much <u>too</u> much!

   (3) He tied the rope around his <u>waist</u>.

   (4) I felt <u>weak</u> after the accident.

8. (1) We were <u>eager</u> to go.

   (2) They were <u>anxious</u> about the results.

   (3) Nothing seems to <u>effect</u> Robert.

   (4) He told us he had <u>emigrated</u> from Puerto Rico.

9. (1) The tavern is only three miles <u>further</u>.

   (2) The <u>notorious</u> criminal was finally brought to justice.

   (3) Be careful or you'll <u>lose</u> your wallet.

   (4) I didn't mean to <u>imply</u> that he was lazy.

10. (1) This notice is intended for all <u>personnel</u>.

3. 1 2 3 4 5

4. 1 2 3 4 5

5. 1 2 3 4 5

6. 1 2 3 4 5

7. 1 2 3 4 5

8. 1 2 3 4 5

9. 1 2 3 4 5

10. 1 2 3 4 5

(2) May I have another <u>peace</u> of pie?

(3) Please try to speak more <u>plainly</u>.

(4) I tried to do it <u>as</u> John would have.

ANSWERS: WORD-CHOICE EXERCISES

(Explanations are provided in the "Word-Choice Demons" list under the appropriate word.)

EXERCISE 1

1. (4) compliment
2. (1) principal
3. (3) affected
4. (1) eager
5. (4) among
6. (4) likely
7. (4) all right
8. (2) number
9. (3) altogether
10. (3) lose

EXERCISE 2

1. (1) principal
2. (3) compliment
3. (2) whose
4. (2) **Never** use *kind of an;* use *kind of.*
5. (1) infamous, notorious
6. (4) course
7. (1) alter
8. (2) likely
9. (2) effects
10. (4) whose

EXERCISE 3

1. (2) lose
2. (1) course
3. (3) number
4. (4) acceptable
5. (3) to
6. (1) whose
7. (2) likely
8. (2) likely
9. (4) morale
10. (1) They're

EXERCISE 4

1. (3) as
2. (2) past
3. (5)
4. (5)
5. (4) than
6. (3) into
7. (3) morale
8. (4) who's
9. (1) imply
10. (2) further

EXERCISE 5

1. (4) all right
2. (3) altar
3. (1) among
4. (1) brake
5. (2) credible
6. (4) stationery
7. (1) than
8. (3) affect
9. (1) farther
10. (2) piece

PUNCTUATION

The word *punctuation* describes the period, comma, exclamation point, and other marks used in writing to separate words, phrases, and sentences. Punctuation marks have one important function: to help you better understand a writer's thoughts. On the official test, you will come across a number of questions designed to test your ability to recognize faulty punctuation. To help you do well on these questions, we have prepared a concise guide to the common rules of punctuation. Before you begin to study it, however, take the diagnostic test below.

PUNCTUATION DIAGNOSTIC TEST

DIRECTIONS: Each sentence below contains four underlined sections. Each section contains either a punctuation mark or nothing. In the answer column, blacken the space under the number that corresponds to the number of the section that is NOT correctly punctuated. If there are no errors, blacken the fifth space.

ANSWERS AND EXPLANATIONS APPEAR AT THE END OF THE TEST

1. "The full moon" said Tom, "seems to have a strange effect on people and animals."
   1   2   3
   4

   1. 1 2 3 4 5

2. John Debbs, a man we've known for years is back in town with his wife and children.
   1   2   3   4

   2. 1 2 3 4 5

3. Lincoln was a great president, as a matter of fact, he may have been the greatest.
   1   2   3
   4

   3. 1 2 3 4 5

4. During the depression many men, women, and children went hungry for days and days.
   1   2   3
   4

   4. 1 2 3 4 5

5. When June, 28 finally came around, we were all happy about the prospect of summer vacation.
   1   2   3
   4

   5. 1 2 3 4 5

6. 1 2 3 4 5

6. We knew about the sale on ladies' coats, but we hadn't heard about the
$\qquad$ <u> </u>   1   2

special on mens hats.
         3   4

7. 1 2 3 4 5

7. When Joe said goodbye to me, I was almost in tears.
            1   2   3   4

8. 1 2 3 4 5

8. The sign over the door read, "Wallace McNulty, Pediatrician.
       1   2   3   4

9. 1 2 3 4 5

9. Miss Hopkins said, "Remember to dot your i's and cross your t's."
    1   2   3   4

10. 1 2 3 4 5

10. "Come here Mary," called Mother.
   1   2 3   4

ANSWERS AND EXPLANATIONS: DIAGNOSTIC TEST

1. **(1)** moon,"   *See Rule 20.
2. **(2)** years,   *See Rule 9.
3. **(1)** president; as *or* president. As   *See Rule 1 and Rule 12.
4. **(1)** depression,   *See Rule 8.
5. **(1)** June 28   *Do not use a comma between the month and day. See Rule 10.
6. **(3)** men's   *See Rule 18.
7. **(5)**
8. **(4)** Pediatrician."   *See Rule 20.
9. **(5)**
10. **(2)** here, Mary   *See Rule 9.

RULES OF PUNCTUATION

END PUNCTUATION

There are three punctuation marks that are used at the end of a sentence. They are: the *period* (.), the *exclamation point* (!), and the *question mark* (?).

The Period (.)

RULE 1: **Use a period at the end of most sentences.**

A period signifies a full stop—a red light. It is always used at the end of a sentence when the sentence is a statement, a command delivered in a normal tone of voice, or a polite request.

      Statement: The cow jumped over the moon.
     Command: Hand me those scissors in the second drawer. Stand up straight.
Polite request: Please shut the door as you leave.

RULE 2:   Use three periods to show that words have been left out.

Several periods are used when a passage or sentence is quoted only in part, some of the words being omitted. If the omission you wish to represent occurs at the end of your sentence, there will be four periods. If the omission is elsewhere in your sentence, three periods are used.

> It begins, "I do solemnly swear. . . ."
> The rule that applies here is, "There shall be no kicking with . . . the ball of the foot."

In the second example, there is evidently more to the rule, but the writer wants to call his reader's attention only to the part having to do with the ball of the foot.

RULE 3:   Use a period after abbreviations and initials.

> *Abbreviations:*
> Avenue: *Ave.*
> Mister: *Mr.*
> Connecticut: *Conn.*
> *Initials:*
> William Joseph Jones: *W. J.* Jones
> Bachelor of Arts: *B.A.*

Sometimes, though, as when a business firm uses the initials of its company name as a trade name, the periods are omitted.

> International Business Machines: *IBM*
> General Motors: *GM*

The Exclamation Point (!)

RULE 4:   Use an exclamation point to indicate strong emotion.

The only other mark, besides the period, for making a final stop in a statement is the exclamation point (!). It is used instead of the period to indicate strong emotion, as of surprise, anger, or horror. Don't overdo use of the exclamation point. If a period will suffice, use the period.

> Help! I'm drowning!
> Stop! Stop, thief!

The Question Mark (?)

RULE 5:   Use a question mark for direct questions. Do not use a question mark for indirect questions.

The question mark is used only for a direct question. Normally, a direct question is one that requires an answer.

> Is that you, Mary?
> What time are you coming home?
> Has the paper come yet?

Sometimes, though, the question is asked only for rhetorical effect; it is akin to an exclamation and no answer is expected or desired.

> O Muse, whither hast thou fled?
> John, will you never grow up?

If the question is indirect—that is, if it is a part of a sentence that is really a statement—the sentence ends with a period.

> I asked you if you are coming home.

For this example to be a direct question, it would be worded: "Are you coming home?"

Sometimes, what appears to be a question is really a request or a command. In such cases, though the question mark is technically the correct marking to use, the period is permissible.

> Will you please leave the door open.
> Won't you have a seat.

EXERCISE 1

DIRECTIONS: The end of each sentence below is missing a punctuation mark. Indicate the mark that is missing.

ANSWERS APPEAR AT THE END OF THE CHAPTER

1. Do you think you can come with us on Friday

2. Take this outside and put it in the trash can

3. Mother asked whether we wanted dinner early on Thursday

4. Would you be good enough to see me at your earliest convenience

5. Run for your lives

INTERNAL PUNCTUATION

The other punctuation marks are used within a sentence. These consist of the following: the *comma* (,), the *semicolon* (;), the *colon* (:), *parentheses* (( )), *brackets* ([]), the *dash* (—), the *hyphen* (-), the *apostrophe* ('), and *quotation marks* (" ").

The Comma (,)

RULE 6: **Use a comma to separate three or more items in a series.**

The items in the series may be words, phrases, or clauses. (A clause is any group of words containing a subject and a verb.) While not necessary, it is good practice to place the comma before *and* or *or* at the end of the series.

He ordered a hamburger, french fries, onion rings, a pizza with pepper and sausage, and a Coke.

Now look at the example without a final comma:

He ordered a hamburger, french fries, onion rings, a pizza with pepper and sausage and a Coke.

It is still understandable, of course, but the comma makes clearer the fact that the Coke is a separate item and not part of the pizza.

RULE 7:   Use a comma before certain conjunctions when you have a sentence with two complete thoughts.

I will study hard for the exam, *for* I intend to pass it.
Each morning the sun rises, *and* each evening it sets.

RULE 8:   Use a comma after an introductory group of words.

When you have a sentence with two complete thoughts and the first thought will not stand alone, you use a comma to separate the two thoughts.

When I am ready, I will do it.
If you will not go, Mary will take your place.

Some sentences begin with prepositional phrases. When necessary, put a comma after the introductory phrase to insure clarity.

After the party, we stopped for coffee. (necessary)
Through the woods came a patrol of soldiers. (unnecessary)

RULE 9:   Use a comma before and after a word or phrase that interrupts the smooth flow of a sentence.

Mrs. Jones, *John's mother*, was walking along the street.
That boy, *the one in the gray hat*, is no friend of mine.

RULE 10:   Use a comma between the day and the year in a date.

I was born on April 9, 1940.

RULE 11:   Use a comma after a person's name when it is followed by a title.

William Vanson, Esq.
Paul Robinson, Attorney

EXERCISE 2

DIRECTIONS: Each sentence below contains four underlined sections. Each section may contain an error in the use of the comma. In the answer column, blacken the space under the number that corresponds to the number of the section that is NOT correctly punctuated. If there are no errors, blacken the fifth space.

ANSWERS AND EXPLANATIONS APPEAR AT THE END OF THE CHAPTER

1. ¹ ² ³ ⁴ ⁵
   1. After church last Sunday, Tom, and Milton decided to walk downtown.
      1   2   3

2. ¹ ² ³ ⁴ ⁵
   2. When you come home please make sure to hang up your coat and fold
      1   2   3   4
      your trousers.

3. ¹ ² ³ ⁴ ⁵
   3. John McCarthy, the tall boy, with the red hair, is my brother's best friend.
      1   2   3   4

4. ¹ ² ³ ⁴ ⁵
   4. Tom Simpson, a lawyer and James Quinn, his friend, arranged to meet.
      1   2   3   4

5. ¹ ² ³ ⁴ ⁵
   5. We had bacon and eggs, toast with butter and two cups of coffee for
      1   2   3   4
      breakfast.

6. ¹ ² ³ ⁴ ⁵
   6. Joe and I wanted to go camping that weekend but the rain dampened
      1   2   3
      our plans.
      4

7. ¹ ² ³ ⁴ ⁵
   7. Mary, Sue, and Alice had tickets for the concert, however they were
      1   2   3   4
      unable to go.

8. ¹ ² ³ ⁴ ⁵
   8. John and I were both born on December 31, 1946.
      1   2   3 4

9. ¹ ² ³ ⁴ ⁵
   9. Tom Smith, an old friend of mine was down on his luck and out of work.
      1   2   3   4

10. ¹ ² ³ ⁴ ⁵
   10. John is the boy, who is the best qualified to become captain of the team and
       1   2   3   4
       president of the class.

The Semicolon (;)

RULE 12: Use a semicolon to separate two or more complete thoughts that would otherwise be separated by AND, BUT, OR, NOR, SO, or FOR.

The semicolon is like a blinking red traffic light; it says, "Stop; then go."

> The cat kept after the mouse, and he finally caught it.
> The cat kept after the mouse; he finally caught it.

RULE 13: Use a semicolon before long conjunctions and connecting phrases (THEREFORE, HOWEVER, CONSEQUENTLY, MORE-OVER, NEVERTHELESS, AS A MATTER OF FACT, AS A RESULT).

> The situation had become intolerable; *therefore*, a general strike was called.

> John won the medal last week; *as a matter of fact*, he should have won it last year.

EXERCISE 3

DIRECTIONS: In the following sentences, place a comma, a period, or a semicolon wherever necessary.

ANSWERS AND EXPLANATIONS APPEAR AT THE END OF THE CHAPTER

1. My name is Marvin L Hanks.

2. I was born November 17 1934.

3. I live at 3224 Edgewood Ave in Richmond.

4. The police tracked the thief they finally caught him.

5. When your name reads A S Hempstead M D you can legally practice medicine.

6. When I became sleepy I walked around when my legs became numb I tried to jump but when I fell I knew there was no hope for me unless help came soon.

The Colon (:)

RULE 14: Use a colon before a list.

The colon always tells you that something is to follow.

> There were four items missing: shoes, an umbrella, a wallet, and a fountain pen.

The Hyphen (-)

RULE 15: Use a hyphen for dividing and joining words.

The hyphen is used in two main ways. First, it is used to divide a word that would extend beyond the margin of your paper.

> I want to make a deliber-
> ate effort.

Second, it is used to join two words into a compound word.

> three-masted schooner
> bright-eyed child

The Dash (—)

RULE 16: Use the dash to interrupt a sentence when you want to emphasize the interruption.

The dash is used (usually in pairs), as is the comma, to set off a word or words that interrupt the flow of thought in the sentence. The major difference between the dash and the comma is that the dash places a stronger emphasis on the separation of the words it sets off. Dashes also are used when commas might be confusing.

> Let's get together tomorrow night—early—so we'll have plenty of time to plan the party.

This method of writing the sentence places a greater emphasis on the earliness of the meeting than would have been the case if the sentence has been written in a more normal way: "Let's get together early tomorrow night, so we'll have plenty of time to plan the party."

Parentheses (( )) and Brackets ([ ])

RULE 17: Use parentheses and brackets for side remarks and explanations.

Parentheses and brackets are used, always in pairs, for side remarks and explanations. Brackets, used much less frequently than parentheses, are for personal remarks or explanations within quoted material and for parenthetical remarks within parenthetical remarks.

> If you had known what I knew (and I'm glad you didn't), you would have been discouraged in your efforts.

> I know very little (thank goodness) about it.

> The quotation reads: "I will stay until Sue [Susan Detweiler, Jackson's first cousin] comes."

> They studied some of the Germanic languages, the Romance languages (including French, Italian and Spanish [Castilian]), and Russian.

The Apostrophe (')

RULE 18: Use the apostrophe for possessives and contractions.

The apostrophe is used mainly to form possessives of nouns and to indicate a letter or letters omitted when two words (or a compound word, such as *cannot*) are made into a contraction.

Possessives of nouns:	Contractions:
Mary's coat	can't (cannot)
lady's (singular) coat	I'd (I should, I would, I had)
ladies' (plural) coats	didn't (did not)
woman's (singular) coat	don't (do not)
women's (plural) coats	I'll (I shall, I will)
	I've (I have)

Note: Do not use the apostrophe with possessive pronouns (its, yours, ours, theirs, etc.).

> *Wrong:* Is that my book or *her's?*
> *Right:* Is that my book or *hers?*

RULE 19: Use the apostrophe for plurals of letters, numbers, and words.

> *b's*
> *5's*
> *+'s*
> *pro's* and *con's*
> *why's* and *wherefore's*

Quotation Marks (" ")

RULE 20: Use quotation marks to set off words and phrases that are repeated exactly as said by another person or in another source.

> Mother asked, "When did you come home last night?"

A comma is used to separate the quotation from the rest of the sentence. The comma always comes *before* the quotation marks.

> John said, "Come here or I'll hit you."
> "Come here," said John, "or I'll hit you."

Notice that at the end of a sentence the period always comes *before* the closing quotation marks.

> "Well," said Tom, "I haven't seen you for a while."

Semicolons and colons always *follow* the closing quotation marks:

> They said, "Drop in and see us"; so I dropped in to see them.

Finally, remember that there should never be more than one end punctuation mark at the end of a sentence. When a quotation comes at the end of a sentence, you are frequently faced with the choice of punctuating the sentence or the quotation. NEVER DO BOTH. Instead, use the end punctuation which seems more important.

> *Wrong:* Do you know who said, "A man's home is his castle."?
> *Right:* Do you know who said, "A man's home is his castle"?
> *Wrong:* At the end of the play, the audience shouted, "Bravo!".
> *Right:* At the end of the play, the audience shouted, "Bravo!"

RULE 21: Use quotation marks for slang and for words used in unusual senses.

> Do you think Frank is losing his "cool"?
> He told me Joe was making more than fifty "thou" a year.

It is sometimes difficult to determine what is slang and what is standard usage. Generally speaking, it is better to use words that do not need to be set off by quotation marks. Overuse of quotation marks is a sign of amateurishness.

RULE 22: Use single quotation marks (' ') for quotations within quotations.

If there is a quotation within a quotation, the inside quotation is marked with single quotation marks (' ') and the overall quotation is marked double marks (" ").

> Mary said, "I tell you I heard the baby say, 'stick up, bang, bang.' "
> And I said to her, "Anytime you need me, just holler 'help' down the air vent."

Before going on to the exercises that follow, review what you've studied by looking over the summary style sheet below.

PUNCTUATION STYLE SHEET

1. My name is John.
2. It begins, "I do solemnly swear...."
3. J. T. Sloan lives at 22-35 76th St.
4. Help! A mouse!
5. Is that you, Mary?
6. I like wine, women, and song. I like wine and women.
7. I saw John, and he saw me. I saw John and went home.
8. When you are finished, tell me.
9. Mr. Sims, the butcher, lives across the street.

10. Pearl Harbor was bombed on December 7, 1941.

11. Charles Crump, Optometrist.

12. John was persistent; he finally won.

13. We were warned against going; nevertheless, we went. John was, nevertheless, determined to go.

14. Among the items ordered were the following: books, pencils, erasers, and chalk.

15. bright-eyed child

16. If you are coming—and we hope you do—please bring Frank.

17. I knew very little (thank goodness) about it.

18. That lady's dress is blue.

19. b's, 5's, and's

20. She said, "I saw you."

21. That music has a "heavy" sound to it.

22. I turned to her and said, "I would love to read 'The Outcasts of Poker Flat' again, wouldn't you?"

EXERCISE 4

DIRECTIONS: Each sentence below contains four underlined sections. Each section contains either a punctuation mark or nothing. In the answer column, blacken the space under the number that corresponds to the number of the section that is NOT correctly punctuated. If there are no errors, blacken the fifth space.

ANSWERS AND EXPLANATIONS APPEAR AT THE END OF THE CHAPTER

1. There were three boys in attendance; John, whom we had known for
    years; Karl, who had arrived from South America some eight months
    before; and Tom, a relative newcomer to the group.

    1. 1 2 3 4 5

2. After all the girls had gone home, Mother called "It's time for bed," and
    we trudged upstairs.

    2. 1 2 3 4 5

3. "I am sorry about the delay," said the clerk, "I can assure you; however,
    that it won't happen again."

    3. 1 2 3 4 5

4. 1 2 3 4 5

4. "But <u>Mr</u> Jones<u>," said</u> Harry, <u>"that's</u> what <u>I've</u> been trying to tell you."
    1   2   3   4

5. 1 2 3 4 5

5. "Sam Baker<u>," said</u> the manager, <u>"is a man,</u> <u>who</u> has given many years of
    1   2   3

fine service to the <u>firm."</u>
                4

6. 1 2 3 4 5

6. You may think this is a fine <u>job,</u> <u>but,</u> I have read the book and <u>don't</u>
                   1   2   3

think <u>it's</u> very good.
    4

7. 1 2 3 4 5

7. We have <u>decided,</u> <u>therefore,</u> <u>that</u> what he really said <u>was,</u> "Maybe I'll
         1   2   3

<u>come."</u>
 4

8. 1 2 3 4 5

8. They wanted to <u>know if</u> we had been there <u>before</u> and <u>if,</u> we intended to
              1   2   3 4

come again.

9. 1 2 3 4 5

9. The three boys who came <u>were:</u> <u>Tom,</u> <u>Dick,</u> and <u>Jerry.</u>
                      1   2   3   4

10. 1 2 3 4 5

10. It was over two weeks <u>ago</u> that I ordered the following <u>items;</u> three sets
                  1   2

of <u>glassware,</u> two <u>cushions,</u> and eight yards of red linen.
    3   4

EXERCISE 5

DIRECTIONS: Each sentence below contains four underlined sections. Each section contains either a punctuation mark or nothing. In the answer column, blacken the space under the number that corresponds to the number of the section that is NOT correctly punctuated. If there are no errors, blacken the fifth space.

ANSWERS AND EXPLANATIONS APPEAR AT THE END OF THE CHAPTER

1. 1 2 3 4 5

1. Although they had been in the United States but a short <u>time—three</u> months
                                             1

<u>perhaps,</u> <u>Juan</u> and his <u>brother,</u> <u>Jose,</u> were speaking English fluently.
    2   3   4

2. 1 2 3 4 5

2. "Wine, <u>women</u> and <u>song,"</u> said <u>Tom,</u> <u>"are</u> three of my favorite things."
           1   2   3   4

3. 1 2 3 4 5

3. I do not know who wrote <u>"The Raven;"</u> <u>however,</u> <u>it</u> <u>won't</u> be too difficult
                     1   2   3   4

to find out.

4. 1 2 3 4 5

4. "If you expect us to pick you <u>up,"</u> said Mother, <u>"you'd</u> better <u>call,</u> and
                        1   2   3

tell us what time you'll be <u>leaving."</u>
                     4

5. Who was it who said, "Give me liberty or . . . death?
   $\underline{}$ $\underline{}$ $\underline{}$ $\underline{}$
   1   2   3   4

5. 1   2   3   4   5

6. "Who, in your opinion, was the greatest American president?" asked Mrs.
   $\underline{}$ $\underline{}$ $\underline{}$
   1   2   3

   Jones?
   $\underline{}$
   4

6. 1   2   3   4   5

7. I couldnt believe that John and his father were involved in the scandal that
   $\underline{}$ $\underline{}$
   1   2

   had been reported in the paper; the facts, however, spoke for themselves.
   $\underline{}$ $\underline{}$
   3   4

7. 1   2   3   4   5

8. The stranger, a man in a black hat, walked across the street and into, the
   $\underline{}$ $\underline{}$ $\underline{}$ $\underline{}$
   1   2   3   4

   store.

8. 1   2   3   4   5

9. If you are prompt in returning your order, we can guarantee delivery by
   $\underline{}$
   1

   Christmas—which, by the way, is only a week away.
   $\underline{}$ $\underline{}$ $\underline{}$
   2   3   4

9. 1   2   3   4   5

10. The final act, a combination of humor and pathos, had the audience
    $\underline{}$ $\underline{}$ $\underline{}$
    1   2   3

    standing on its feet, and applauding.
    $\underline{}$
    4

10. 1   2   3   4   5

EXERCISE 6

DIRECTIONS: Each sentence below contains four underlined sections. Each section contains either a punctuation mark or nothing. In the answer column, blacken the space under the number that corresponds to the number of the section that is NOT correctly punctuated. If there are no errors, blacken the fifth space.

ANSWERS AND EXPLANATIONS APPEAR AT THE END OF THE CHAPTER

1. John and Mary said they would take a trip to: Spain, Italy, and Portugal.
   $\underline{}$ $\underline{}$ $\underline{}$ $\underline{}$
   1   2   3   4

1. 1   2   3   4   5

2. He's finally come home (thank goodness) and we won't have to worry
   $\underline{}$ $\underline{}$ $\underline{}$ $\underline{}$
   1   2   3   4

   any longer.

2. 1   2   3   4   5

3. When I say, "Move," I want you to move—and move quickly.
   $\underline{}$ $\underline{}$ $\underline{}$ $\underline{}$
   1   2   3   4

3. 1   2   3   4   5

4. I can't believe that Mr. Smith said "that he would retire at the end of
   $\underline{}$ $\underline{}$ $\underline{}$
   1   2   3

   the year.
   $\underline{}$
   4

4. 1   2   3   4   5

5. "When you have finished dinner; be sure to wash the dishes," called
   $\underline{}$ $\underline{}$
   1   2

   Mother from the kitchen.
   $\underline{}$ $\underline{}$
   3   4

5. 1   2   3   4   5

6.   1 2 3 4 5

6. It has been two years, three months, two, and a half weeks since I joined
the army.
1   2   3   4

7.   1 2 3 4 5

7. There were twenty people in the room, most of them had been waiting for
hours .
1   2   3   4

8.   1 2 3 4 5

8. "I've just read Arthur Millers new play," said the young man.
1   2   3   4

9.   1 2 3 4 5

9. When you go to the store, please buy some bread, milk butter, and eggs.
1   2   3   4

10.   1 2 3 4 5

10. For breakfast, I usually have either pancakes, oatmeal, or bacon, and eggs.
1   2   3   4

EXERCISE 7

DIRECTIONS: Each sentence below contains four underlined sections. Each section contains either a punctuation mark or nothing. In the answer column, blacken the space under the number that corresponds to the number of the section that is NOT correctly punctuated. If there are no errors, blacken the fifth space.

ANSWERS AND EXPLANATIONS APPEAR AT THE END OF THE CHAPTER

1.   1 2 3 4 5

1. Will you be good enough to take a seat, Mr. Brown.
1   2   3   4

2.   1 2 3 4 5

2. Because I had been working hard all day, I decided to lie down before
1   2
dinner, and take a nap.
3   4

3.   1 2 3 4 5

3. Texas, which is located in the southern part of our country is well known
1   2
for its cotton, its oil, and its cattle.
3   4

4.   1 2 3 4 5

4. When the leaves begin to turn color we know that summer is gone and
1   2   3
fall will soon be here.
4

5.   1 2 3 4 5

5. There were three kinds of sandwiches on the menu—ham and Swiss,
1   2
roast beef, and peanut butter, and jelly.
3   4

6.   1 2 3 4 5

6. "Thousands of dollars have already been spent on research," said the
1
doctor, "and thousands more will be spent next year."
2   3   4

7. "Why," she asked, "wasn't I informed when the date was changed?".
      1   2   3   4

                                                                                  7. 1 2 3 4 5

8. The boys were excited about the game, they had been preparing for it for weeks.
             1   2   3

                        8. 1 2 3 4 5

9. This may not be the best way to do it, there are, however, alternative methods.
            1   2   3   4

                        9. 1 2 3 4 5

10. Among the survivors of the plane crash were: two doctors, a nurse, and an army chaplain.
                                         1   2   3

                        10. 1 2 3 4 5

EXERCISE 8

DIRECTIONS: Each sentene below contains four underlined sections. Each section contains either a punctuation mark or nothing. In the answer column, blacken the space under the number that corresponds to the number of the section that is NOT correctly punctuated. If there are no errors, blacken the fifth space.

ANSWERS AND EXPLANATIONS APPEAR AT THE END OF THE CHAPTER

1. When I was in Pittsburgh: I visited the museum, the art gallery, and Forbes Field.
                      1   2   3 4

                        1. 1 2 3 4 5

2. John, who had been out in the snow all morning, came home wet and cold, his spirits were undaunted, and he announced that, after lunch, he planned to go out again.
         1
      2   3   4

                        2. 1 2 3 4 5

3. "Can you tell me, sir," asked the elderly woman, "how I can get to Penn Station."
                   1 2   3
    4

                        3. 1 2 3 4 5

4. Everyone but Mr. Rogers has reported already and I'm sure he'll be in before long.
          1   2   3   4

                        4. 1 2 3 4 5

5. The office building, which was erected in 1916, will be torn down, and replaced by a municipal parking lot.
                 1   2   3
    4

                        5. 1 2 3 4 5

6. 1 2 3 4 5

6. The mayor, together with three assistants was on his way to the scene
1   2   3
of a fire that had been raging for hours.
4

7. 1 2 3 4 5

7. I have mentioned your fine work in my latest report, I am sure the manager
1   2
will take my advice and give you a promotion.
3   4

8. 1 2 3 4 5

8. Tired and hungry, the patrol of men filed into the barracks, and sat down.
1   2   3   4

9. 1 2 3 4 5

9. The man asked for my name and address, my telephone number, and my
1   2   3
date of birth.
4

10. 1 2 3 4 5

10. "The first English word I learned," said Ramon, "was 'hello'".
1   2   3   4

ANSWERS AND EXPLANATIONS: PUNCTUATION EXERCISES

EXERCISE 1

1. question mark
2. period
3. period
4. period
5. exclamation point

EXERCISE 2

1. **(2)** No comma between subjects joined by *and* or *or*
2. **(1)** Comma needed. *See Rule 8.
3. **(3)** No comma needed.
4. **(2)** Comma needed. See Rule 9.
5. **(3)** Comma needed. *See Rule 6.
6. **(3)** Comma needed. *See Rule 7.
7. **(4)** Replace comma with semicolon. *See Rule 13.
8. **(5)**
9. **(2)** Comma needed. *See Rule 9.
10. **(1)** No comma needed. *Do not use a comma to set off a clause that is necessary to the meaning of the sentence.

EXERCISE 3

1. My name is Marvin L. Hanks. *See Rule 3.
2. I was born November 17, 1934. *See Rule 10.
3. I live at 3224 Edgewood Ave. in Richmond. *See Rule 3.
4. The police tracked the thief; they finally caught him. *See Rule 12.

5. When your name reads A. S. Hempstead, M.D., you can legally practice medicine.   *See Rule 3.

6. When I became sleepy, I walked around; when my legs became numb, I tried to jump; but when I fell, I knew there was no hope for me unless help came soon.   *See Rules 8 and 12.

EXERCISE 4

1. (1) attendance: *See Rule 14.
2. (2) called, "It's   *See Rule 8.
3. (2) , however,   *See Rule 9.
4. (1) Mr.   *See Rule 3.
5. (3) man who   *Don't use a comma to set off a clause that is necessary to the meaning of the sentence.
6. (2) but I   *Don't use a comma between *but* and the subject of an independent clause.
7. (5)
8. (4) if we   *Don't use a comma between a subordinating conjunction and the subject of the clause.
9. (1) were Tom   *Don't use a colon when the list is preceded by a verb.
10. (2) items: *See Rule 14.

EXERCISE 5

1. (2) perhaps—Juan   *See Rule 16.
2. (1) women, and   *See Rule 6.
3. (2) Raven";   *See Rule 20.
4. (3) call and   *This comma interrupts the smooth flow of the sentence.
5. (4) death"?   *See Rule 20.
6. (4) Jones.   *The question mark belongs to the direct quotation only.
7. (1) couldn't   *See Rule 18.
8. (4) into the   *This comma interrupts a prepositional phrase.
9. (5)
10. (4) feet and   *This comma is not needed.

EXERCISE 6

1. (2) to Spain   *Don't use a colon when the list is preceded by *to*.
2. (3) goodness), and   *See Rules 7 and 17.
3. (5)
4. (3) said that   *Don't use a comma to set off an indirect quotation.
5. (1) dinner, be   *See Rule 8.
6. (3) two and   *This comma breaks up a distinct item *two and a half weeks*.
7. (2) room; most *or* room. Most   *See Rules 12 and 1.
8. (2) Miller's   *See Rule 18.
9. (3) milk, butter   *See Rule 6.
10. (4) bacon and eggs.   *This comma breaks up a distinct item *bacon and eggs*.

EXERCISE 7

1. **(5)**
2. **(3)** dinner and *This comma interrupts the smooth flow of the sentence.
3. **(2)** country, is *See Rule 9.
4. **(1)** color, we *See Rule 8.
5. **(4)** butter and *This comma breaks up a distinct item *peanut butter and jelly.*
6. **(5)**
7. **(4)** changed?" *See Rule 20.
8. **(3)** game; they *or* game. They *See Rules 1 and 12.
9. **(2)** it; there *or* it. There *See Rules 1 and 12.
10. **(1)** were two *Don't use a colon when the list is preceded by a verb.

EXERCISE 8

1. **(1)** Pittsburgh, I *See Rule 8.
2. **(2)** cold; his *See Rule 12.
3. **(4)** Station?" *See Rule 20.
4. **(2)** already, and *See Rule 7.
5. **(3)** down and *This comma interrupts the smooth flow of the sentence.
6. **(2)** assistants, was *See Rule 9.
7. **(1)** report; I *or* report. I *See Rules 1 and 12.
8. **(3)** barracks and *This comma interrupts the smooth flow of the sentence.
9. **(5)**
10. **(4)** hello.' " *See Rule 22.

CAPITALIZATION

Just as a spotlight is used on a stage to help you focus on the important action, so a capital letter is used in writing to help you locate important names, places, and ideas. A capital letter is thus a visual mark telling the reader: "Here's a word worthy of your attention!" On the official test, you will be asked to spot errors caused by misusing—or not using—capitals. To help you do well on these questions, we have provided you with a number of capitalization rules. They have been carefully prepared to cover all the situations you are likely to face on examination day. However, before you study them, take the diagnostic test below.

CAPITALIZATION DIAGNOSTIC TEST

DIRECTIONS: In each of the following sentences, there are four underlined words. In the answer column, blacken the space under the number corresponding to the number of the word that has been incorrectly capitalized. (A word is also incorrect when it should be capitalized—and is not.) Blacken the fifth space if there are no errors in capitalization.

ANSWERS AND EXPLANATIONS APPEAR AT THE END OF THE TEST

1. Christopher Columbus discovered America for spain.
   1   2   3   4

2. "come to my house," said Joe, "and see my slides of Delaware."
    1   2   3   4

3. Argentina, Puerto Rico, and Chile are Spanish-Speaking countries.
   1   2   3   4

4. Last summer, we saw the Rocky Mountains and the Mississippi River.
      1   2   3   4

5. The bridge to Brooklyn is in the lower part of Manhattan.
        1   2   3   4

6. Did Bob really try to swim The English Channel?
       1   2   3   4

7. The Civil War left some southern plantations in ruins.
       1   2   3   4

8. There are many people in this city who are Irish.
         1   2   3   4

9. The professor made a study of Hinduism when he was in India.
       1   3   4

1. 1 2 3 4 5
2. 1 2 3 4 5
3. 1 2 3 4 5
4. 1 2 3 4 5
5. 1 2 3 4 5
6. 1 2 3 4 5
7. 1 2 3 4 5
8. 1 2 3 4 5
9. 1 2 3 4 5

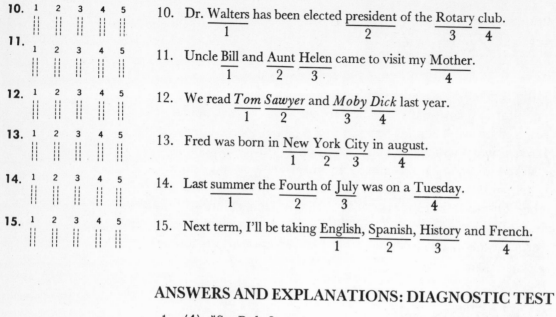

10. Dr. <u>Walters</u> has been elected <u>president</u> of the <u>Rotary</u> <u>club</u>.
       1   2   3 4

11. Uncle <u>Bill</u> and <u>Aunt</u> <u>Helen</u> came to visit my <u>Mother</u>.
      1   2   3   4

12. We read *Tom Sawyer* and *Moby Dick* last year.
           1   2   3   4

13. Fred was born in <u>New</u> <u>York</u> <u>City</u> in <u>august</u>.
              1   2   3   4

14. Last <u>summer</u> the <u>Fourth</u> of <u>July</u> was on a <u>Tuesday</u>.
      1   2   3   4

15. Next term, I'll be taking <u>English</u>, <u>Spanish</u>, <u>History</u> and <u>French</u>.
                        1   2   3   4

ANSWERS AND EXPLANATIONS: DIAGNOSTIC TEST

1. (4) *See Rule 2.
2. (1) *See Rule 1.
3. (4) *See Rule 2.
4. (5)
5. (5)
6. (2) *See Rule 3.
7. (5)
8. (5)

9. (5)
10. (4) *See Rule 8.
11. (4) *See Rule 10.
12. (5)
13. (4) *See Rule 13.
14. (5)
15. (3) *See Rule 15.

RULES OF CAPITALIZATION

RULE 1: **Capitalize the first word of a sentence and the first word of a direct quotation if it begins a sentence.**

> *T*he evening was beautiful.
> *W*hen did he call?
> Patrick Henry said, "*G*ive me liberty or give me death."

Note: The second part of a divided question does not take a capital letter unless it begins a sentence.

> "*I* am here," said John, "*t*o see the new manager."
> "*P*lease come," said John. "*W*e'd like to see you."

RULE 2: **Capitalize proper nouns and adjectives. Do not capitalize common nouns.**

A proper noun is the name of a particular person, place or thing.
A proper adjective is a word made from a proper noun.
A common noun names a whole class of persons, places, or things.

Proper Noun	Proper Adjective	Common Noun
England	English	country
Texas	Texan	state
Paris	Parisian	city

Actually, this is the most important rule. Most of those which follow may be regarded as subsections of this rule.

Do not capitalize prefixes, suffixes, or other words that are attached to proper nouns (*pro, un, anti, speaking*).

    un-American   *pro*-French   Spanish-*speaking*

RULE 3: **Capitalize the first letter of each word, except prepositions, in a geographical name.** *The* is not part of the name and is not capitalized.)

    Australia, the United States of America, the Atlantic Ocean the Rocky Mountains, the City of New York, The Department of Commerce, Fifth Avenue, Seventy-third Street.

RULE 4: **Common nouns that are part of proper nouns are capitalized.**

Part of Noun	Not Part of Noun
the Brooklyn *Bridge*	the *bridge* in Brooklyn
New York *State*	He lives in the *state* of New York
Mississippi River	a *river* in *Mississippi*

RULE 5: **Words modified by proper adjectives are not capitalized unless they are part of a geographical name.**

the Indian *Ocean*	the Indian *language*
British *Columbia*	the British *army*
the *Irish* Sea	Irish *whiskey*

EXERCISE 1

DIRECTIONS: In each of the following sentences, there are four underlined words. In the answer column, blacken the space under the number corresponding to the number of the word that has been incorrectly capitalized. (A word is also incorrect when it should be capitalized—and is not.) Blacken the fifth space if there are no errors in capitalization.

ANSWERS AND EXPLANATIONS APPEAR AT THE END OF THE CHAPTER

1.
  1 2 3 4 5

1. The <u>Romans</u> ruled <u>britain</u> from <u>A.D.</u> 43 until <u>A.D.</u> 410.
     1   2   3   4

2. At the <u>mouth</u> of the <u>Nile</u> lies the great <u>City</u> of <u>Cairo</u>.
       1   2   3   4

3. <u>Mary's</u> <u>European</u> tour included a trip down <u>the</u> <u>Seine</u>.
   1   2   3   4

4. How would <u>you</u> define "<u>anti-american</u> <u>practices</u>"?
          1   2   3   4

5. I bought some <u>Irish</u> <u>Whiskey</u> when I landed in the <u>city</u> of <u>Dublin</u>.
          1   2   3   4

6. Thousands of people of <u>Italian</u> <u>descent</u> marched in the Columbus <u>Day</u> <u>parade</u>.
                     1   2   3 / 4

7. The <u>Greek</u> <u>Poet</u> <u>Homer</u> wrote the <u>Iliad</u> in 1100 B.C.
    1   2   3   4

8. <u>We</u> live in the <u>valley</u> of the <u>Hudson</u> <u>river</u>.
  1   2   3   4

9. The teacher asked if anyone knew the location of <u>the</u> <u>Bay</u> <u>Of</u> <u>Biscayne</u>.
                                   1 2 3   4

10. We then sang the <u>national</u> <u>Anthem</u> of <u>Costa</u> <u>Rica</u>.
            1   2   3   4

RULE 6: Capitalize words that refer to sections of the country. Do not capitalize words that refer to directions of the compass.

> The *S*outh will rise again.
> We drove *s*outh for an hour.
> He decided to seek his fortune in the *M*idwest.
> People from Ohio have a *m*idwestern accent.

RULE 7: Capitalize the names of languages, races, nationalities, and religions. Capitalize words formed from them.

> the *N*egro people   a *J*ewish service
> a *D*utch trading ship   a *S*panish dictionary
> a *C*atholic priest   a *B*uddhist monk

RULE 8: Capitalize important words in the names of organizations, buildings, firms, schools, and churches. (Capitalize *the* only when it is part of the name.)

> the *K*nights of *C*olumbus   *L*ong *I*sland *R*ailroad
> the *C*hrysler *B*uilding   *B*ryant *H*igh *S*chool
> the *B*oard of *E*ducation   *J*ones and *B*rown, *L*td.

RULE 9:   Always capitalize the titles of high official positions. Capitalize less important positions only when a person's name appears with
them.

the *President* of the United States	the *president* of a club
the *Secretary* of *State*	Mr. Smith's *secretary*
Judge Benson	the *judge*
the *Pope*	a *priest*
	a *minister*

EXERCISE 2

DIRECTIONS: In each of the following sentences, there are four underlined words. In the answer column, blacken the space
under the number corresponding to the number of the
word that has been incorrectly capitalized. (A word is
also incorrect when it should be capitalized—and is
not.) Blacken the fifth space if there are no errors in
capitalization.

ANSWERS AND EXPLANATIONS APPEAR AT THE END OF THE CHAPTER

1. I applied for membership in the Book of the Month club.
                               1 2   3 4

2. Harry decided to attend the University of southern California.
                                1   2 3   4

3. The students at Lynbrook high School were required to buy English history
                        1   2   3   4

    books.

4. Rabbi Stern invited two priests and a Minister to lunch.
       1   2   3   4

5. The president of the student council planned to become a Teacher.
         1   2   3   4

6. Many of the people in the northern part of the country have come from the
                                1   2

    eastern part of Europe.
      3   4

7. Mr. Sims is listed as chairman of the board of sloan and Tuttle.
                    1   2   3   4

8. Because he had been born in the South, Tom found the Midwest a little
         1   2   3   4

    strange at first.

9. The Knights of Pythias held a convention in the city of Memphis.
        1   2   3   4

10. If you drive north for an hour, you will come to a small Canadian Trading
           1   2   3

    post.
    4

Answer columns (each item, options 1 2 3 4 5):

1. 1 2 3 4 5
2. 1 2 3 4 5
3. 1 2 3 4 5
4. 1 2 3 4 5
5. 1 2 3 4 5
6. 1 2 3 4 5
7. 1 2 3 4 5
8. 1 2 3 4 5
9. 1 2 3 4 5
10. 1 2 3 4 5

RULE 10:   Capitalize the title of a relative only when it is followed by the relative's name.

> I saw *U*ncle Harry talking to *A*unt Rose.
> I saw my *u*ncle talking to my *a*unt.

RULE 11:   Capitalize the important words in titles of books, magazines, movies, and works of art. (Capitalize *the* if it is the first word in the title.)

> They read *The Old Man and the Sea.*
> We saw *All's Well That Ends Well.*
> *True Grit* was a fine movie.
> Did you read "*How to Stop Smoking*" in the *Reader's Digest?*

RULE 12:   Capitalize words referring to God and the Bible.

> God will answer if you ask *H*im.
> The tale of Samson is found in the *B*ible.

RULE 13:   Capitalize the names of days of the week, months of the year, and holidays. Do not capitalize seasons.

> *M*onday, *T*uesday, and *W*ednesday are three days of the week.
> *J*une, *J*uly, and *A*ugust are the hottest months of the year.
> I think *s*pring is much more beautiful than *f*all.

RULE 14:   Capitalize the names of historical events, documents, and historical periods.

> the *C*onstitution of the *U*nited *S*tates
> the *D*eclaration of *I*ndependence
> the *E*ra of *G*ood *F*eeling
> the *I*ce *A*ge

RULE 15:   Capitalize school subjects when they name specific courses, not just general areas. Always capitalize languages.

> Next year, I'll take *S*panish and *h*istory.
> Herman didn't do too well in *T*yping *I*.
> Harriet's favorite subject is *t*yping.

EXERCISE 3

DIRECTIONS: In each of the following sentences, there are four underlined words. In the answer column, blacken the space under the number corresponding to the number of the word that has been incorrectly capitalized. (A word is also incorrect when it should be capitalized—and is not.) Blacken the fifth space if there are no errors in capitalization.

ANSWERS AND EXPLANATIONS APPEAR AT THE END OF THE CHAPTER

1. In Maine and Massachusetts, the <u>nineteenth</u> of <u>April</u>, <u>Patriots</u> <u>day</u>, is a
                                         1   2   3   4

holiday.

2. After <u>World</u> <u>War</u> II, the <u>Marshall</u> <u>Plan</u> brought relief to Europe.
            1   2   3   4

3. Tell <u>Cousin</u> <u>Ed</u> I'll visit him in <u>March</u>.
        1   2 3   4

4. Some of the <u>battles</u> of the <u>Revolution</u> were fought in the <u>dead</u> of <u>Winter</u>.
               1   2   3   4

5. The <u>period</u> following the <u>Civil</u> <u>War</u> is known as <u>reconstruction</u>.
       1   2 3   4

6. I had hoped that my <u>Mother</u> and <u>father</u> would go along with <u>my</u> <u>uncle</u>.
                  1   2   3   4

7. In the <u>temple</u> were statues of the <u>ancient</u> <u>gods</u> of <u>Egypt</u>.
       1   2   3   4

8. I have always liked commercial subjects such as <u>stenography</u> and <u>typing</u>,
                                          1   2

but my favorite course was one in <u>American</u> <u>History</u> 1.2.
                               3   4

9. I told my <u>father</u> that I expected to do well in <u>mathematics</u>, <u>science</u>, and
         1   2   3

<u>french</u>.
4

10. The movie, *The Ten Commandments,* was based on the <u>Bible</u>.
          1 2   3   4

Answer columns (for items 1–10):

	1	2	3	4	5
1.	‖	‖	‖	‖	‖
2.	‖	‖	‖	‖	‖
3.	‖	‖	‖	‖	‖
4.	‖	‖	‖	‖	‖
5.	‖	‖	‖	‖	‖
6.	‖	‖	‖	‖	‖
7.	‖	‖	‖	‖	‖
8.	‖	‖	‖	‖	‖
9.	‖	‖	‖	‖	‖
10.	‖	‖	‖	‖	‖

Now that you have studied the rules and done the exercises, review what you have learned by studying the capitalization style sheet below.

CAPITALIZATION STYLE SHEET

Mexico *C*ity	a *c*ity in Mexico
*Y*ellowstone *N*ational *P*ark	our *n*ational *p*arks
*T*wenty-ninth *S*treet	across the *s*treet
Silver *L*ake	a shallow *l*ake
the *E*ast	a mile to the *e*ast
*N*orth America	*n*orthern Wisconsin
the *E*xplorers *C*lub	a *c*lub for explorers
Ford Motor *C*ompany	an automobile *c*ompany
Central *H*igh *S*chool	a new *h*igh *s*chool
Iona *C*ollege	going to *c*ollege
French *R*evolution	a successful *r*evolution
The Wrigley *B*uilding	a Chicago *b*uilding

CAPITALIZATION STYLE SHEET (Cont.)

the *F*ourth of July   the *f*ifth of July
the *S*enior *P*rom   a *p*rom dress
the *S*enior *C*lass   *s*eniors in the *c*lass
*E*nglish, *S*panish   *s*teno and *t*yping
*H*istory II   class in world *h*istory
*D*ean Baker   a college *d*ean
*S*enator Jones   a *s*enator's duties
*S*on of *G*od   tribal *g*ods
tell *M*other   tell my *m*other
*C*ousin Sara   my *c*ousin
the *D*emocratic party   the *d*emocratic way of life
The Last of the Mohicans
the *Reader's Digest*

The tests which follow are based on *all* the rules you have studied so far.

EXERCISE 4

DIRECTIONS: In each of the following sentences, there are four underlined words. In the answer column, blacken the space
under the number corresponding to the number of the
word that has been incorrectly capitalized. (A word is
also incorrect when it should be capitalized—and is
not.) Blacken the fifth space if there are no errors in
capitalization.

ANSWERS AND EXPLANATIONS APPEAR AT THE END OF THE CHAPTER

1. 1   2   3   4   5
    ‖   ‖   ‖   ‖   ‖

1. Last <u>summer</u>, on our trip to the <u>West</u> we visited <u>Yellowstone</u> <u>national</u> Park.
          1   2   3   4

2. 1   2   3   4   5
    ‖   ‖   ‖   ‖   ‖

2. Many of the <u>senators</u> who are now in <u>Washington</u> are members of the
               1   2

<u>Republican</u> <u>party</u>.
     3   4

3. 1   2   3   4   5
    ‖   ‖   ‖   ‖   ‖

3. When <u>Uncle</u> Joe saw the overturned table, he cried, "Oh, <u>Brother</u>, <u>what's</u>
          1   2   3   4

been going on here!"

4. 1   2   3   4   5
    ‖   ‖   ‖   ‖   ‖

4. "To be or not <u>to</u> be," said <u>Hamlet</u>. "<u>that</u> is the <u>question</u>."
                  1   2   3   4

5. 1   2   3   4   5
    ‖   ‖   ‖   ‖   ‖

5. Do you intend to go on to <u>College</u> when <u>you</u> graduate from our <u>high</u> <u>school</u>?
                              1   2   3   4

6. If <u>mother</u> says it's all right we can go to visit <u>Cousin</u> Len and <u>Aunt</u> Martha
       1   2   3

    for the <u>Fourth</u> of July.
              4

6. 1 2 3 4 5

7. "Tell me all you know," said <u>Inspector</u> <u>Bennett</u>, "<u>Or</u> <u>I'm</u> afraid things
                                   1   2   3 4

    will go rather hard for you."

7. 1 2 3 4 5

8. Edgar Allan Poe wrote a beautifully conceived <u>short</u> <u>story</u> called "<u>The</u>
                                                1   2   3

    Cask <u>of</u> Amontillado."
         4

8. 1 2 3 4 5

9. In the <u>olden</u> <u>days</u>, people worshiped many <u>gods</u> <u>whose</u> names are all but
             1   2   3   4

    forgotten now.

9. 1 2 3 4 5

10. On January <u>Fifteenth</u> we will have a <u>commencement</u> ceremony at which
               1   2

    Dr. Brown, who is <u>principal</u> of our <u>school</u>, will speak.
                      3   4

10. 1 2 3 4 5

EXERCISE 5

DIRECTIONS: In each of the following sentences, there are four under-lined words. In the answer column, blacken the space under the number corresponding to the number of the word that has been incorrectly capitalized. (A word is also incorrect when it should be capitalized—and is not.) Blacken the fifth space if there are no errors in capitalization.

ANSWERS AND EXPLANATIONS APPEAR AT THE END OF THE CHAPTER

1. <u>I</u> agree with Mr. <u>Smith's</u> remark that my <u>sister</u> is "<u>her</u> own worst enemy."
   1   2   3   4

1. 1 2 3 4 5

2. I received a <u>letter</u> which, according to the <u>postman</u>, probably came from
               1   2

    the <u>city</u> of <u>Toronto</u>.
        3   4

2. 1 2 3 4 5

3. "If you drive <u>south</u>," said the <u>Farmer</u>, "<u>you'll</u> be there by the time you're
               1   2   3

    ready for <u>dinner</u>."
            4

3. 1 2 3 4 5

4. The latter part of the <u>nineteenth</u> <u>century</u> is sometimes called the <u>age</u> of
                     1   2   3

    <u>Victoria</u>.
      4

4. 1 2 3 4 5

5. The <u>Grand</u> <u>canyon</u> is located in the <u>western</u> <u>part</u> of the United States.
     1   2   3   4

5. 1 2 3 4 5

6. 1 2 3 4 5

6. We found what appeared to be some old indian arrowheads at the foot of
                                                1   2
the high mountain.
     3   4

7. 1 2 3 4 5

7. The policeman saw a Dodge sedan speed along the boulevard and turn
                              1   2
into Seventy-Third Street.
             3   4

8. 1 2 3 4 5

8. The assemblymen from Queens County decided to hold a gigantic barbecue
        1   2   3
in the middle of Forest park.
                        4

9. 1 2 3 4 5

9. When you are in New York, be sure to visit the Chrysler building, which
                                                  1   2
is located in the midtown section of Manhattan.
                    3   4

10. 1 2 3 4 5

10. "The assembly program this morning will be sponsored by the English
         1
Department," said the principal as he addressed the students.
   2   3   4

EXERCISE 6

DIRECTIONS: In each of the following sentences, there are four underlined words. In the answer column, blacken the space
under the number corresponding to the number of the
word that has been incorrectly capitalized. (A word is
also incorrect when it should be capitalized—and is
not.) Blacken the fifth space if there are no errors in
capitalization.

ANSWERS AND EXPLANATIONS APPEAR AT THE END OF THE CHAPTER

1. 1 2 3. 4 5

1. The first people who came to the New World from europe found many
        1   2   3   4
strange sights.

2. 1 2 3 4 5

2. In the early days of this country, it is only too clear that the White man
           1   2   3
mistreated the Indians.
               4

3. 1 2 3 4 5

3. Mr. Thompson was appointed advisor to our club because he knows
                             1
every Senior in the high school.
      2   3   4

4. 1 2 3 4 5

4. The state Theater and the old Hathaway Hotel are to be torn down and
        1   2   3   4
be replaced by a large parking lot.

5. My <u>mother</u> says that all small children look as if they had been sent from
   $\overline{}$
   1

   <u>above</u>, <u>but</u> that as they get older, they stop behaving like <u>Angels</u>.
   2   3   4

   5. 1 2 3 4 5

6. John Clark was finally promoted to the <u>rank</u> of <u>Sergeant</u> in the United
   1   2

   <u>States</u> <u>Marines</u>.
   3   4

   6. 1 2 3 4 5

7. Does anyone in the <u>class</u> know the name of the Chief Justice of the <u>Supreme</u>
   1   2

   <u>Court</u> when Woodrow Wilson was the <u>president</u>?
   3   4

   7. 1 2 3 4 5

8. Last <u>summer</u>, we ate in a <u>Chinese</u> <u>Restaurant</u> on Mott <u>Street</u>.
   1   2   3   4

   8. 1 2 3 4 5

9. <u>Angie</u> decided to buy herself a new <u>Royal</u> <u>Typewriter</u> last <u>spring</u>.
   1   2   3   4

   9. 1 2 3 4 5

10. The <u>Panama</u> <u>canal</u> is one of the most important waterways in the <u>Western</u>
    1   2   3

    <u>Hemisphere</u>.
    4

    10. 1 2 3 4 5

ANSWERS AND EXPLANATIONS: CAPITALIZATION EXERCISES

EXERCISE 1

1. (2) *See Rule 2.
2. (3) *See Rules 2 and 4.
3. (5)
4. (3) *See Rule 2.
5. (2) *See Rule 5.
6. (5)
7. (2) *See Rule 2.
8. (4) *See Rule 4.
9. (3) *See Rule 3.
10. (2) *See Rule 2.

EXERCISE 2

1. (4) *See Rule 8.
2. (3) *See Rule 8.
3. (2) *See Rule 8.
4. (4) *See Rules 2 and 9.
5. (4) *See Rules 2 and 9.
6. (3) *See Rule 6.
7. (3) *See Rule 2.
8. (5)
9. (3) *See Rule 2.
10. (3) *See Rule 2.

EXERCISE 3

1. (4) *See Rule 13.
2. (5)
3. (5)
4. (4) *See Rule 13.
5. (4) *See Rule 14.
6. (1) *See Rule 10.
7. (5)
8. (4) *See Rule 15.
9. (4) *See Rule 15.
10. (5)

EXERCISE 4

1. **(4)** *See Rules 3 and 4.
2. **(4)** *See Rule 8.
3. **(3)** *See Rule 10.
4. **(3)** *See Rule 1.
5. **(1)** *See Rule 2.

6. **(1)** *See Rule 10.
7. **(3)** *See Rule 1.
8. **(5)**
9. **(5)**
10. **(1)** *See Rule 2.

EXERCISE 5

1. **(5)**
2. **(5)**
3. **(2)** *See Rule 2.
4. **(3)** *See Rule 14.
5. **(2)** *See Rule 4.

6. **(1)** *See Rule 2.
7. **(3)** *See Rule 3.
8. **(4)** *See Rule 4.
9. **(2)** *See Rule 4.
10. **(5)**

EXERCISE 6

1. **(4)** *See Rule 2.
2. **(3)** *See Rule 2.
3. **(2)** *See Rule 2.
4. **(1)** *See Rule 4.
5. **(4)** *See Rule 2.

6. **(2)** *See Rule 2.
7. **(4)** *See Rule 9.
8. **(3)** *See Rules 2 and 5.
9. **(3)** *See Rules 2 and 5.
10. **(2)** *See Rule 4.

PRONUNCIATION

On the official test, you may be given several questions on pronunciation. It is your job to identify the word that is pronounced incorrectly. A typical question of this kind might look like this:

97. (1) reduction—re-DUK-shun
    (2) friendly—FREND-lee
    (3) simple—SIMP-l
    (4) personal—per-SON-al

Note that each of the four choices above consists of two types of spelling. The first is the normal spelling of the word. The second is the *phonetic* spelling of the word. To write a word phonetically is to write the word the way it *sounds*.

In order to write a word the way it sounds, you must divide it into *syllables*. A syllable is a word or part of a word uttered in a single, unbroken breath. The word *me,* for example, has only one syllable (*me*). However, the word *paper* has two syllables (pa-per), *agitate* has three syllables (a-ji-tat), and *consequently* has four syllables (kon-se-kwent-lee).

EXERCISE 1

DIRECTIONS: Indicate the number of syllables in each of the following words.

ANSWERS APPEAR AT THE END OF THE CHAPTER

1. unfortunate	5. after	8. fantastic
2. recently	6. thoughtful	9. heaven
3. forget	7. unusual	10. wandering
4. returned		

In every word of more than one syllable, we place greater stress on one of the syllables than we do on the others. Say the words that appear below, emphasizing the capitalized syllables in each case:

because:	BEE-kaws	be-KAWS
fountain:	foun-TEN	FOUN-ten
slowly:	slo-Lee	SLO-lee

Note that the words in the left-hand column are being emphasized on the wrong syllable, while the words in the right-hand column are receiving the correct stress.

In some long words, more than one syllable is stressed:

penitentiary: PEN-i-TEN-cha-ree
destitution: DES-ti-TU-shun
recreation: REK-re-A-shun

To write a word phonetically all you do is break up the word into syllables, decide which syllable or syllables should be stressed, and write the stressed syllable or syllables in capital letters. Thus, *bayonet* becomes BAY-o-net and *demolition* becomes DEM-o-LISH-on.

EXERCISE 2

DIRECTIONS: Write the following words phonetically, indicating the stressed syllable in capital letters.

ANSWERS APPEAR AT THE END OF THE CHAPTER

1. me _____

2. paper _____

3. agitate _____

4. consequently _____

5. recently _____

6. formulate _____

7. wonderful _____

8. terminate _____

9. heavenly _____

10. discotheque _____

Don't be concerned (kun-SERND) if your answers are slightly different from those given. As long as you can recognize how many syllables there are in a word and which ones should be stressed (STREST), you've got most of the battle won (WUN).

Now let's return to the sample test item given at the beginning of the chapter:

(1)   reduction—re-DUK-shun
(2)   friendly—FRIEND-lee
(3)   simple—SIMP-l
(4)   personal—per-SON-al

Can you tell which one is pronounced incorrectly?

Reduction has three syllables, the second of which should be stressed. The word is pronounced correctly. If you try saying it by stressing another syllable, you'll "hear" your error: RE-duk-shun *or* re-duk-SHUN. Words 2 and 3 are also correct. However, look at number 4 (per-SON-al). It does have three syllables, but when we say *personal* we emphasize the first syllable (PER-son-al).

Now try the exercises that follow.

EXERCISE 3

DIRECTIONS: Each of the following groups consists of four words. Each word appears as it is normally spelled, followed by a phonetic spelling of the word (spelled as it is pronounced). In the answer column, blacken the space under the number corresponding to the number of the word that is pronounced (phonetically spelled) incorrectly. If all the words in a group are pronounced correctly, blacken the fifth space.

ANSWERS APPEAR AT THE END OF THE CHAPTER

1. (1) athletics—ATH-e-let-ix   (3) thirsty—THERST-ee
   (2) upset—up-SET   (4) quicken—KWIK-en

    1. 1 2 3 4 5

2. (1) bridge—BRIDJ   (3) tomorrow—too-MA-ro
   (2) rehearse—re-HERS   (4) mascot—mas-KOT

    2. 1 2 3 4 5

3. (1) consider—kun-SID-er   (3) school—SKOOL
   (2) bequest—be-KWEST   (4) radio—ra-DEE-o

    3. 1 2 3 4 5

4. (1) conquest—KON-kwest   (3) after—AF-ter
   (2) release—re-LEES   (4) often—of-TEN

    4. 1 2 3 4 5

5. (1) reverse—re-VERS   (3) typical—tip-i-KAL
   (2) thinking—THINK-ing   (4) trepidation—trep-i-DA-shun

    5. 1 2 3 4 5

6. (1) reverberate—re-VER-   (3) around—A-round
       bu-rat   (4) delightful—de-LIT-ful
   (2) echo—EK-o

    6. 1 2 3 4 5

7. (1) difficult—DIF-i-kult   (3) discotheque—dis-ko-TEK
   (2) theoretical—thee-o-RET-   (4) kingdom—king-DUM
       i-kal

    7. 1 2 3 4 5

8. (1) remember—re-mem-BER   (3) disturb—dis-TURB
   (2) awaken—a-WAKE-en   (4) enlighten—en-LIT-en

    8. 1 2 3 4 5

9. (1) volunteer—vol-un-TEER   (3) destiny—DES-tin-ee
   (2) thoughtful—THAWT-ful   (4) imagine—I-maj-in

    9. 1 2 3 4 5

10. (1) vitriolic—Vi-tree-O-lik   (3) welcome—wel-KOM
    (2) container—kun-TAN-er   (4) together—too-GETH-er

    10. 1 2 3 4 5

EXERCISE 4

DIRECTIONS: Each of the following groups consists of four words. Each word appears as it is normally spelled, followed by a phonetic spelling of the word (spelled as it is pronounced). In the answer column, blacken the space under the number corresponding to the number of the word that is pronounced (phonetically spelled) incorrectly. If all the words in a group are pronounced correctly, blacken the fifth space.

ANSWERS APPEAR AT THE END OF THE CHAPTER

1. (1) listen—lis-TEN
   (2) fender—FEN-der
   (3) remain—ree-MAN
   (4) history—HIS-tu-ree

2. (1) imagine—i-MAJ-in
   (2) surrender—sir-END-er
   (3) quickly—KWIK-lee
   (4) fortunate—fort-CHOO-net

3. (1) darken—DARK-en
   (2) poetry—PO-et-ree
   (3) beginning—BE-gin-ing
   (4) domino—DOM-in-o

4. (1) phonograph—FON-o-graf
   (2) delinquent—de-LING-kwent
   (3) awful—aw-FUL
   (4) destiny—DES-tin-ee

5. (1) broadcast—BRAWD-kast
   (2) brigade—BRI-gad
   (3) psychology—sy-KOL-o-jee
   (4) eclipse—e-KLIPS

6. (1) extinguish—eks-TING-gwish
   (2) extortion—ek-STOR-shun
   (3) express—eks-PRESS
   (4) exactly—eggs-AKT-lee

7. (1) operation—op-er-A-shun
   (2) interject—in-ter-JEKT
   (3) indicate—IN-di-kat
   (4) reduction—re-DUK-shun

8. (1) comprehension—kom-pre-HEN-shun
   (2) concave—kon-KAV
   (3) comrade—KOM-rad
   (4) compulsion—KOM-pul-shun

9. (1) reject—RE-jekt
   (2) antagonize—an-tag-o-NIZ
   (3) directly—di-REKT-lee
   (4) demonstrate—DEM-un-strat

10. (1) fluctuate—FLUK-choo-at
    (2) engagement—en-GAGE-ment
    (3) dissent—di-SENT
    (4) respectful—RE-spekt-ful

EXERCISE 5

DIRECTIONS: Each of the following groups consists of four words. Each word appears as it is normally spelled, followed by a phonetic spelling of the word (spelled as it is pronounced). In the answer column, blacken the space under the number corresponding to the number of the word that is pronounced (phonetically spelled) incorrectly. If all the words in a group are pronounced correctly, blacken the fifth space.

ANSWERS APPEAR AT THE END OF THE CHAPTER

1. (1) correction—ku-REK-shun   (3) machine—ma-SHEEN
   (2) multiply—MUL-ti-ply   (4) vagrancy—va-gran-SEE

2. (1) eager—EE-ger   (3) omission—o-MISH-un
   (2) procrastinate—pro-KRAS   (4) dainty—dan-TEE
       tin-at

3. (1) commence—kum-MENS   (3) artistic—ar-TIS-tik
   (2) ordinary—or-DIN-e-ree   (4) carbon—KAR-bun

4. (1) dangerous—DANJ-e-rus   (3) elastic—e-LAS-tik
   (2) flagrant—FLA-grent   (4) molten—mol-TEN

5. (1) courageous—ku-RA-jus   (3) quiver—kwi-VER
   (2) definite—DEF-i-nit   (4) pagination—PAJ-i-na-shun

6. (1) doubtful—DOWT-ful   (3) fluency—floo-EN-see
   (2) condensation—kon-den-   (4) illuminate—i-LOO-min-at
       SA-shun

7. (1) prediction—PRE-dik-shun   (3) recreation—REK-re-A-shun
   (2) heavenly—HEV-en-lee   (4) combine—kum-BIN

8. (1) character—KA-rak-   (3) outrage—OUT-raj
       ter   (4) mention—men-SHUN
   (2) determine—de-TER-min

9. (1) democracy—de-MOK-   (3) module—MOD-yool
       ra-see   (4) distress—DI-stress
   (2) addition—a-DISH-un

10. (1) redundant—re-DUN-dent   (3) candid—can-DID
    (2) accomplish—a-KOMP-   (4) overt—O-vert
        lish

Answer column:

	1	2	3	4	5
1.	‖	‖	‖	‖	‖
2.	‖	‖	‖	‖	‖
3.	‖	‖	‖	‖	‖
4.	‖	‖	‖	‖	‖
5.	‖	‖	‖	‖	‖
6.	‖	‖	‖	‖	‖
7.	‖	‖	‖	‖	‖
8.	‖	‖	‖	‖	‖
9.	‖	‖	‖	‖	‖
10.	‖	‖	‖	‖	‖

EXERCISE 6

DIRECTIONS: Each of the following groups consists of four words. Each word appears as it is normally spelled, followed by a phonetic spelling of the word (spelled as it is pronounced). In the answer column, blacken the space under the number corresponding to the number of the word that is pronounced (phonetically spelled) incorrectly. If all the words in a group are pronounced correctly, blacken the fifth space.

ANSWERS APPEAR AT THE END OF THE CHAPTER

1. (1) variety—va-RI-e-tee   (3) regret—re-GRET
   (2) divisible—di-VIZ-i-bl   (4) commander—kum-MAND-er

2. (1) manager—MAN-e-jer   (3) agreement—a-GREE-ment
   (2) identity—I-den-ti-tee   (4) judgment—JUDJ-ment

3. (1) drinking—drink-ING   (3) movie—MOO-vee
   (2) display—dis-PLAY   (4) judgment—JUDJ-ment

	1	2	3	4	5
1.	‖	‖	‖	‖	‖
2.	‖	‖	‖	‖	‖
3.	‖	‖	‖	‖	‖

4. | 1 | 2 | 3 | 4 | 5 |

4. (1) aggression—a-GRESH-un
   (2) dividing—di-VI-ding
   (3) movement—moov-MENT
   (4) delegate—DEL-e-gat

5. | 1 | 2 | 3 | 4 | 5 |

5. (1) generosity—jen-e-ROS-i-tee
   (2) flavor—FLA-ver
   (3) terminate—TER-min-at
   (4) diplomat—dip-lo-MAT

6. | 1 | 2 | 3 | 4 | 5 |

6. (1) construction—kun-STRUK-shun
   (2) conductor—kun-duk-TER
   (3) purchase—PER-chess
   (4) particle—PAR-tik-l

7. | 1 | 2 | 3 | 4 | 5 |

7. (1) government—guv-er-MENT
   (2) necessary—NES-e-se-ree
   (3) dominate—DOM-in-at
   (4) articulate—ar-TIK-u-lat

8. | 1 | 2 | 3 | 4 | 5 |

8. (1) often—OFF-en
   (2) operation—op-e-RA-shun
   (3) reason—REE-zun
   (4) electricity—e-LEK-tris-i-tee

9. | 1 | 2 | 3 | 4 | 5 |

9. (1) snowfall—SNO-fal
   (2) rapidly—rap-ID-lee
   (3) wardrobe—WAR-drob
   (4) automotive—AW-to-MO-tiv

10. | 1 | 2 | 3 | 4 | 5 |

10. (1) colorful—KUL-er-ful
    (2) separation—sep-A-ra-shun
    (3) community—kom-MEW-ni-tee
    (4) under—UN-der

EXERCISE 7

DIRECTIONS: Each of the following groups consists of four words. Each word appears as it is normally spelled, followed by a phonetic spelling of the word (spelled as it is pronounced). In the answer column, blacken the space under the number corresponding to the number of the word that is pronounced (phonetically spelled) incorrectly. If all the words in a group are pronounced correctly, blacken the fifth space.

ANSWERS APPEAR AT THE END OF THE CHAPTER

1. | 1 | 2 | 3 | 4 | 5 |

1. (1) legend—LEG-end
   (2) forgetful—for-GET-ful
   (3) sardine—sar-DEEN
   (4) sardonic—sar-DON-ik

2. | 1 | 2 | 3 | 4 | 5 |

2. (1) grapefruit—GRAP-froot
   (2) marine—ma-REEN
   (3) apple—AP-l
   (4) accurate—ak-yur-AT

3. | 1 | 2 | 3 | 4 | 5 |

3. (1) demand—de-MAND
   (2) margin—mar-JIN
   (3) success—SUK-sess
   (4) subtraction—sub-TRAK-shun

4. | 1 | 2 | 3 | 4 | 5 |

4. (1) grateful—GRAT-ful
   (2) victory—vik-TU-ree
   (3) hopeful—HOP-ful
   (4) element—EL-e-ment

5. | 1 | 2 | 3 | 4 | 5 |

5. (1) meaning—MEEN-ing
   (2) normal—nor-MAL
   (3) visit—VIZ-it
   (4) building—BILD-ing

6. | 1 | 2 | 3 | 4 | 5 |

6. (1) curious—KYUR-ee-us
   (2) Spanish—span-ISH
   (3) going—GO-ing
   (4) singing—SING-ing

7. (1) capable—KAP-a-bl   (3) vaccinate—VAKS-in-at

   (2) discuss—dis-KUSS   (4) passport—pass-PORT

7.	1	2	3	4	5
	‖	‖	‖	‖	‖

8. (1) perfectly—per-FEKT-lee   (3) occupation—OK-yoo-PA-shun

   (2) dismay—dis-MAY   (4) doctor—DOK-tor

8.	1	2	3	4	5
	‖	‖	‖	‖	‖

9. (1) permission—per-MISH-un   (3) destination—des-tin-A-shun

   (2) accomplish—a-KOM-plish   (4) mercy—MER-see

9.	1	2	3	4	5
	‖	‖	‖	‖	‖

10. (1) original—o-RIJ-i-nal   (3) housewife—HOWS-wif

    (2) gradual—grad-YOO-al   (4) husband—HUZ-bend

10.	1	2	3	4	5
	‖	‖	‖	‖	‖

ANSWERS: PRONUNCIATION EXERCISES

EXERCISE 1

1. (4) un-for-tu-nate   5. (2) af-ter   8. (3) fan-tas-tic
2. (3) re-cent-ly   6. (2) thought-ful   9. (2) heav-en
3. (2) for-get   7. (4) un-u-su-al   10. (3) wan-der-ing
4. (2) re-turned

EXERCISE 2

1. MEE   5. RE-sent-lee   8. TERM-i-nat
2. PA-per   6. FORM-u-lat   9. HEV-en-lee
3. A-ji-tat   7. WUN-der-ful   10. DIS-ko-tek
4. KON-se-kwent-lee

EXERCISE 3

1. (1) ath-LET-ix   5. (3) TIP-i-kal   8. (1) re-MEM-ber
2. (4) MAS-kot   6. (3) a-ROUND   9. (4) i-MAJ-in
3. (4) RA-dee-o   7. (4) KING-dum   10. (3) WEL-kom
4. (4) OFF-en

EXERCISE 4

1. (1) LIS-en   5. (2) bri-GAD   8. (4) kom-PUL-shun
2. (4) FOR-choo-net   6. (5)   9. (2) an-TAG-o-niz
3. (3) be-GIN-ing   7. (5)   10. (4) re-SPEKT-ful
4. (3) AW-ful

EXERCISE 5

1. (4) VA-gren-see   5. (3) KWI-ver   8. (4) MEN-shun
2. (4) DAN-tee   6. (3) FLOO-en-see   9. (4) di-STRESS
3. (2) OR-din-e-ree   7. (1) pre-DIK-shun   10. (3) KAN-did
4. (4) MOL-ten

EXERCISE 6

1. (5)
2. (2) i-DEN-ti-tee
3. (1) DRINK-ing
4. (3) MOOV-ment
5. (4) DIP-lo-mat
6. (2) kon-DUK-ter
7. (1) GUV-ern-ment
8. (4) e-lek-TRIS-i-tee
9. (2) RAP-id-lee
10. (2) sep-a-RA-shun

EXERCISE 7

1. (5)
2. (4) AK-yur-et
3. (2) MAR-jin
4. (2) VIK-tu-ree
5. (2) NOR-mal
6. (2) SPAN-ish
7. (4) PASS-port
8. (1) PER-fekt-lee
9. (5)
10. (2) GRAD-joo-el

REVIEW EXERCISES

The three review exercises which follow have two purposes: (1) to serve as a general review of all you have studied so far, and (2) to acquaint you with other ways of asking questions that are sometimes used on the examination. However, regardless of the way in which the questions are put to you, remember that the content is almost always the same.

Before you begin the three review exercises that follow, review briefly any of the trouble spots that you may have run into during your study program. After you take the review exercises and check your answers, you'll be ready to take the simulated "Correctness and Effectiveness of Expression" test.

EXERCISE 1

DIRECTIONS: In each of the following sentences, choose the correct grammatical form for the italicized section. Then blacken its number in the answer column. If the italicized section is correct as it stands (no change), blacken space 1 in the answer column. If neither the italicized section nor any of the alternatives is correct (none right), blacken space 5 in the answer column.

ANSWERS AND EXPLANATIONS APPEAR AT THE END OF THE CHAPTER

1. It takes study *to become* a lawyer.
   (1) no change
   (2) before you can become
   (3) in becoming
   (4) for becoming
   (5) none right

   1. 1 2 3 4 5

2. His letters never *concern old people who wish* to be young.
   (1) no change
   (2) concerned old people who wish
   (3) concerned old people who had wished
   (4) concern old people who wishing
   (5) none right

   2. 1 2 3 4 5

3. You people like *we boys as much as we* boys like you.
   (1) no change
   (2) we boys as much as us
   (3) us boys as much as us
   (4) us boys as much as we
   (5) none right

   3. 1 2 3 4 5

4. Jane and Mary are *more poised than he, but Bill is the brighter* of all three.
   (1) no change
   (2) more poised than he, but Bill is the brightest
   (3) more poised than him, but Bill is the brightest
   (4) more poised than him, but Bill is the brighter
   (5) none right

   4. 1 2 3 4 5

5. 1 2 3 4 5

5. It is a thing of joy, beauty, *and containing* terror.

(1)   no change
(2)   and abounding in
(3)   and of
(4)   and contains
(5)   none right

6. 1 2 3 4 5

6. If he *was able, he would demand that she return* home.

(1)   no change
(2)   were able, he would demand that she return
(3)   was able, he would demand that she returns
(4)   were able, he would demand that she returns
(5)   none right

7. 1 2 3 4 5

7. He *use to visit when he was supposed to.*

(1)   no change
(2)   use to visit when he was suppose to.
(3)   used to visit when he was suppose to.
(4)   used to visit when he was supposed to.
(5)   none right

8. 1 2 3 4 5

8. I saw the *seamstress and asked her for a needle, hook and eye,* and thimble.

(1)   no change
(2)   seamstress, and asked her, for a needle, hook and eye
(3)   seamstress and asked her for, a needle, hook and eye
(4)   seamstress, and asked her for a needle, hook and eye,
(5)   none right

9. 1 2 3 4 5

9. A tall, *young man threw the heavy, soggy,* ball.

(1)   no change
(2)   , young man threw the heavy, soggy
(3)   young man threw the heavy, soggy
(4)   , young man threw the heavy soggy
(5)   none right

10. 1 2 3 4 5

10. The week *before my sister, thinking of other matters,* thrust her hand into the fire.

(1)   no change
(2)   before, my sister thinking of other matters
(3)   before my sister thinking of other matters,
(4)   before my sister, thinking of other matters
(5)   none right

11. 1 2 3 4 5

11. We seldom eat a roast at our house. *My* wife being a vegetarian.

(1)   no change
(2)   my
(3)   , my
(4)   ; my
(5)   none right

12. 1 2 3 4 5

12. I have only one request. *That* you leave at once.

(1)   no change
(2)   that
(3)   ; that
(4)   : that
(5)   none right

13. I admire stimulating conversation and appreciative listening, *therefore* I talk to myself.

    (1)   no change   (4)   therefore,
    (2)   , therefore,   (5)   none right
    (3)   therefore

13.   1   2   3   4   5

14. The *battle-scarred veteran was as bald as a newlaid egg.*

    (1)   no change
    (2)   The battlescarred veteran was as bald as a new-laid egg.
    (3)   The battle-scarred veteran was as bald as a new-laid egg.
    (4)   The battle scarred veteran was as bald as a new laid egg.
    (5)   none right

14.   1   2   3   4   5

15. The President's proclamation opened with the following statement: *"The intention of the government is,* to make the people aware of one of the greatest dangers to the safety of the country."

    (1)   no change
    (2)   , "The intention of the government is
    (3)   : "The intention of the government is:
    (4)   : "The intention of the government is
    (5)   none right

15.   1   2   3   4   5

16. I get only a *week vacation after two years work.*

    (1)   no change
    (2)   week's vacation after two years work.
    (3)   week's vacation after two years' work.
    (4)   weeks vacation after two years work.
    (5)   none right

16.   1   2   3   4   5

17. *You first* wash your brush in turpentine. Then hang it up to dry.

    (1)   no change   (4)   First
    (2)   First you   (5)   none right
    (3)   First you should

17.   1   2   3   4   5

18. The teacher insisted that you and *he were responsible for the mistakes of Joe and me.*

    (1)   no change
    (2)   him were responsible for the mistakes of Joe and me.
    (3)   he were responsible for the mistakes of Joe and I.
    (4)   him were responsible for the mistakes of Joe and I.
    (5)   none right

18.   1   2   3   4   5

19. *He sometimes in a generous mood gave the flowers to others* that he had grown in his garden.

    (1)   no change
    (2)   He in a generous mood sometimes gave to others the flowers
    (3)   In a generous mood he sometimes gave the flowers to others
    (4)   Sometimes, in a generous mood, he gave to others the flowers
    (5)   none right

19.   1   2   3   4   5

20. 1 2 3 4 5

20. He *is attending* college since September.

(1) no change
(2) has attended
(3) was attending
(4) attended
(5) none right

EXERCISE 2

DIRECTIONS: The following paragraphs contain a number of errors in grammar, punctuation, and spelling. In each of the questions below, a sentence or phrase from the paragraphs is italicized. Five ways of writing the italicized passage are given. Find the BEST way. Then blacken the space under its number in the answer column.

ANSWERS AND EXPLANATIONS APPEAR AT THE END OF THE CHAPTER

The use of the machine produced up to the present time many outstanding changes in our modern world. One of the most significant of these changes have been the marked decreases in the length of the working day and the working week. The fourteen-hour day not only has been reduced to ten hours but also, in some lines of work, to one of eight or even six hours. The trend toward a decrease is further evidenced in the longer weekend already given to employees in many business establishments. There seems also to be a trend toward shorter working weeks and longer summer vacations. An important feature of this development is that leisure is no longer the privilege of the wealthy few,—it has become the common right of most people. Using it wisely, leisure promotes health, efficiency, and happiness, for there is time for each individual to live their own full life and having opportunities for needed recreation.

Recreation, like the name implies, is a process of revitalization. In giving expression to the play instincts of the human race, new vigor is afforded by recreation to the body and to the mind. Of course, not all forms of amusement, by no means, constitute recreation. Furthermore, an activity that provides recreation for one person may prove exhausting for another. Today, however, play among adults, as well as children, is regarded as a vital necessity of modern life. Play being recognized as an important factor in improving mental and physical health.

Among the most important forms of amusement available at the present time are the automobile, the moving picture, radio and television, and organized sports. The automobile, especially, has been a boon to the American people, since it has been the chief means of them getting out into the open. The motion picture and radio and television have tremendous opportunities to supply wholesome recreation and to promote cultural advancement. A criticism often leveled against organized sports as a means of recreation is because they make passive spectators of too many people. It has been said "that the American public is afflicted with "spectatoritis," but there is some recreational advantages to be gained even from being a spectator at organized games. Such sports afford a release from the monotony of daily toil, get people outdoors, and also provide an exhilaration that has a tonic effect.

The chief concern, of course, should be to eliminate those forms of amusement that are socially undesirable. There are, however far too many people whom do not use their leisure to the best advantage. Sometimes leisure leads to idleness, and idleness may lead to demoralization. The value of leisure both to the individual and to society will depend on the uses made of it.

1. The use of the machine *produced* up to the . . .

    (1) produced   (4) had produced
    (2) produces   (5) will have produced
    (3) has produced

1. 1 2 3 4 5

2. . . . present time many outstanding changes in our modern world. One of the most significant of these changes *have been* the marked . . .

    (1) have been   (4) has been
    (2) was   (5) will be
    (3) were

2. 1 2 3 4 5

3. . . . decreases in the length of the working day and the working week. *The fourteen-hour day not only has been reduced* to ten hours but also, in some lines of work, to eight or even six hours. . . .

    (1) The fourteen-hour day not only has been reduced
    (2) Not only the fourteen-hour day has been reduced
    (3) Not the fourteen-hour day only has been reduced
    (4) The fourteen-hour day has not only been reduced
    (5) The fourteen-hour day has been reduced not only

3. 1 2 3 4 5

4. . . . The trend toward a decrease is further evidenced in the longer weekend *already* given to employees in many business establishments. . . .

    (1) already (2) all ready (3) allready (4) ready (5) all in all

4. 1 2 3 4 5

5. . . . There seems also to be a trend toward shorter working weeks and longer summer vacations. An important feature of this development is that leisure is no longer the privilege of the wealthy few,—*it* has become the common right of most people. . . .

    (1) ,— it (2) : it (3) ; it (4) . . . it (5) omit punctuation

5. 1 2 3 4 5

6. . . . *Using it wisely,* leisure promotes health, efficiency, and happiness, . . .

    (1) Using it wisely   (4) Because of its wise use
    (2) Having used it wisely (5) Because of its usefulness
    (3) If used wisely,

6. 1 2 3 4 5

7. . . . for there is time for each individual to live *their* own . . .

    (1) their (2) his (3) its (4) our (5) your

7. 1 2 3 4 5

8. 1 2 3 4 5

8. ... full life and *having* opportunities for needed recreation. ...

(1) having   (4) to have had
(2) having had   (5) had
(3) to have

9. 1 2 3 4 5

9. ... Recreation, *like* the name implies, is a process of revitalization. ...

(1) like (2) since (3) through (4) for (5) as

10. 1 2 3 4 5

10. ... In giving expression to the play instincts of the human race, *new vigor is afforded by recreation to the body and to the mind.* ...

(1) new vigor is afforded by recreation to the body and to the mind.
(2) recreation affords new vigor to the body and to the mind.
(3) there is afforded new vigor to the body and to the mind.
(4) by recreation the body and mind are afforded new vigor.
(5) the body and the mind afford new vigor to themselves by recreation.

11. 1 2 3 4 5

11. ... Of course, not all forms of amusement, *by no means*, constitute recreation. Furthermore, an activity that provides recreation for one person ...

(1) by no means   (4) by every means
(2) by some means   (5) by any means,
(3) by those means

12. 1 2 3 4 5

12. ... may prove exhausting for another. Today, however, play among adults, as well as children, is regarded as a vital necessity of modern life. *Play being recognized* as an important factor in improving mental and physical health. ...

(1) , Play being recognized as   (3) . They recognizing play as
(2) , by their recognizing play   (4) . Recognition of it being
         as   (5) , for play is recognized

13. 1 2 3 4 5

13. ... Among the most important forms of amusement available at the present time are the automobile, the moving picture, radio and television, and organized sports. The automobile, especially, has been a boon to the American people, since it has been the chief means of *them* getting out into the open. The motion picture and radio and television have tremendous opportunities to supply wholesome recreation and to promote cultural advancement. A criticism often leveled against organized ...

(1) them (2) their (3) his (4) our (5) the people

14. 1 2 3 4 5

14. ... sports as a means of recreation is *because* they make passive spectators of too many people. ...

(1) because (2) since (3) as (4) that (5) why

15. 1 2 3 4 5

15. ... It has been said *"that* the American public is afflicted with "spectatoritis," ...

(1) "that (2) "that" (3) that" (4) 'that (5) that

16. 1 2 3 4 5

16. ... but there *is* some recreational advantages to be gained even from being a spectator at organized games. ...

(1) is (2) was (3) are (4) were (5) will be

EXERCISE 3

DIRECTIONS: The following paragraph contains a number of errors in grammar, punctuation, and spelling. In each of the questions below, a sentence or phrase from the paragraph is italicized. Five ways of writing the italicized passage are given. Find the BEST way. Then blacken its number in the answer column.

ANSWERS AND EXPLANATIONS APPEAR AT THE END OF THE CHAPTER

When this war is over, no nation will either be isolated in war or peace. Each will be within trading distance of all the others and will be able to strike them. Every nation will be most as dependent on the rest for the maintainance of peace as is any of our own American states on all the others. The world that we knew was a world made up of individual nations, each having the priviledge of doing as they pleased without being embarassed by outside interference. That world has dissolved before the impact of an invention, the airplane has done to our world what gunpowder did to the feudal world. Whether the coming century will be a period of further tragedy or one of peace and progress depend very largely on the wisdom and skill with which the present generation adjusts their thinking to the problems immediately at hand. Examining the principal movements sweeping through the world, it can be seen that they are being accelerated by the war. There is undoubtedly many of these movements whose courses will be affected for good or ill by the settlements that will follow the war. The United States will share the responsibility of these settlements with Russia, England, and China. The influence of the United States, however, will be great. This country is likely to emerge from the war stronger than any other nation. Having benefitted by the absence of actual hostilities on our own soil, we shall probably be less exhausted than our allies and better able than them to help restore the devastated areas. However many mistakes have been made in our past, the tradition of America, not only the champion of freedom but also fair play, still lives among millions who can see light and hope scarcely nowhere else.

1. When this war is over, no nation will *either be isolated in war or peace.* . . .

    (1)   either be isolated in war or peace.
    (2)   be either isolated in war or peace.
    (3)   be isolated in neither war nor peace.
    (4)   be isolated either in war or peace.
    (5)   be isolated neither in war or peace.

2. . . . *Each* will be . . .

    (1) Each   (2) It   (3) Some   (4) They   (5) A nation

3. . . . *within trading distance of all the others and will be able to strike them.* . . .

1.	1	2	3	4	5

2.	1	2	3	4	5

3.	1	2	3	4	5

(1) within trading distance of all the others and will be able to strike them.
(2) near enough to trade with and strike all the others.
(3) trading and striking the others.
(4) within trading and striking distance of all the others.
(5) able to strike and trade with all the others.

4. 1 2 3 4 5

4. ... Every nation will be *most* as dependent on ...
(1) most (2) wholly (3) much (4) mostly (5) almost

5. 1 2 3 4 5

5. ... the rest for the *maintainance* of peace as is any of our own American states on all the others.
(1) maintainance   (4) maintenance
(2) maintainence   (5) maintanence
(3) maintenence

6. 1 2 3 4 5

6. ... The world that we knew was a world made up of individual *nations, each* ...
(1) nations, each   (4) nations; each
(2) nations. Each   (5) nations each
(3) nations: each

7. 1 2 3 4 5

7. ... having the *priviledge* of doing as ...
(1) priviledge   (4) privalege
(2) privelege   (5) privilege
(3) priveledge

8. 1 2 3 4 5

8. ... *they* pleased without being ...
(1) they   (4) he
(2) it   (5) the nations
(3) they individually

9. 1 2 3 4 5

9. ... *embarassed* by outside interference. ...
(1) embarassed   (4) embarrased
(2) embarrassed   (5) embarressed
(3) embaressed

10. 1 2 3 4 5

10. ... That world was dissolved before the impact of an *invention, the* airplane has done to our world what gunpowder did to the feudal world.
(1) invention, the   (4) invention. The
(2) invention but the   (5) invention and the
(3) invention: the

11. 1 2 3 4 5

11. ... Whether the coming century will be a period of further tragedy or one of peace and progress *depend* very largely on the wisdom and skill with ...
(1) depend   (4) depended
(2) will have depended   (5) shall depend
(3) depends

12. 1 2 3 4 5

12. ... which the present generation *adjusts their* thinking to the problems immediately at hand.
(1) adjusts their   (4) adjust our
(2) adjusts there   (5) adjust it's
(3) adjusts its

13. . . . *Examining the principal movements sweeping through the world, it can be seen* . . .

13. 1 2 3 4 5

   (1) Examining the principal movements sweeping through the world, it can be seen

   (2) Having examined the principal movements sweeping through the world, it can be seen

   (3) Examining the principal movements sweeping through the world can be seen

   (4) Examining the principal movements sweeping through the world, we can see

   (5) It can be seen examining the principal movements sweeping through the world

14. . . . that they are being *accelerated* by the war. . . .

14. 1 2 3 4 5

   (1) accelerated   (4) acellerated

   (2) acelerated   (5) acelerrated

   (3) accelarated

15. . . . There *is* undoubtedly many of these movements whose courses will be affected for good or ill by the settlements that will follow the war. . . .

15. 1 2 3 4 5

   (1) is   (2) were   (3) was   (4) are   (5) might be

16. . . . The United States will share the responsibility of these settlements with Russia, England, and China. The influence of the United States, *however*, will be great. This country is likely to emerge from the war stronger than any other nation. . . .

16. 1 2 3 4 5

   (1) , however,   (4) however

   (2) however,   (5) ; however,

   (3) , however

17. . . . Having *benefitted* by the absence of actual hostilities on our own soil, we shall probably be less . . .

17. 1 2 3 4 5

   (1) benefitted   (3) benefited   (5) benafitted

   (2) benifitted   (4) benifited

18. . . . exhausted than our allies and better able than *them* to help restore the devastated areas.

18. 1 2 3 4 5

   (1) them   (2) themselves   (3) they   (4) the world
      (5) the nations

19. . . . However many mistakes have been made in our past, the tradition of America, *not only the champion of freedom but also fair play,* . . .

19. 1 2 3 4 5

   (1) not only the champion of freedom but also fair play,

   (2) the champion of not only freedom but also of fair play,

   (3) the champion not only of freedom but also of fair play,

   (4) not only the champion but also freedom and fair play,

   (5) not the champion of freedom only, but also fair play,

20. . . . still lives among millions who can see light and hope *scarcely nowhere else.*

20. 1 2 3 4 5

   (1) scarcely nowhere else.   (4) scarcely anywhere else.

   (2) elsewhere.   (5) anywhere.

   (3) nowheres.

ANSWERS AND EXPLANATIONS: REVIEW EXERCISES

EXERCISE 1

1. **(1)**
2. **(1)**
3. **(4)** Use direct object *us.*
4. **(2)** Use superlative adjective *brightest* when more than two things are being compared.
5. **(5)** It is a thing of joy, beauty, and terror.
6. **(1)**
7. **(4)** *Used to* means "habitually or customarily."
8. **(4)** Use a comma to separate two independent clauses.
9. **(3)** *Young* is not separated from *tall* by a comma because *tall* modifies the whole noun *young man.*
10. **(5)** *The week before, my sister, thinking of other matters, thrust her hand into the fire.*
11. **(3)** The second construction is a sentence fragment and must be connected to the first construction.
12. **(4)** Use a colon to mean "pay attention to what follows."
13. **(5)** *I admire stimulating conversation and appreciative listening; therefore, I talk to myself.*
14. **(3)** Note the hyphenated compound adjective.
15. **(4)** Do not use a comma between *is* and an infinitive (*to make*).
16. **(3)** Note the use of the apostrophe with singular and plural nouns.
17. **(4)** The subject *you* is understood and does not need to be written out.
18. **(1)**
19. **(4)** The original sentence is awkward and contains a modifier (*that he had grown in his garden*) that is separated from the noun (*flowers*) it is modifying.
20. **(2)** Use the present perfect tense (*has attended*) to express an action that occurred in the past and is still continuing.

EXERCISE 2

1. **(3)** Use the present perfect tense to express an action that started in the past and is still continuing in the present.
2. **(4)** The verb must agree in number with the subject. Since the subject *one* is singular, the verb must be singular.
3. **(5)** Sentences using the *not only . . . but also* construction must immediately precede parallel elements in a sentence.
4. **(1)**
5. **(3)** Use a semicolon to separate two closely related independent clauses.
6. **(3)** See "Faulty Modification" in COMMON ERRORS IN SENTENCE STRUCTURE.
7. **(2)** The pronoun must agree in number with its antecedent. Since the antecedent *individual* is singular, the pronoun must be singular (*his*). It is true that *its* is also singular, but *its* is only used to refer to things.

8. **(3)** See "Lack of Parallel Construction" in COMMON ERRORS IN SENTENCE STRUCTURE.
9. **(5)** Use *as* to introduce a dependent clause; use *like* to introduce a prepositional phrase (He talks *like* his brother.).
10. **(2)** Choice (2) is clearest and most direct.
11. **(5)** Avoid double negatives in one sentence.
12. **(5)** Choice (5) is the best way of correcting this sentence fragment.
13. **(2)** Use the possessive pronoun before a gerund (*getting out*).
14. **(4)** The relative pronoun (*that*) is the only possible choice in this construction.
15. **(5)** Do not use quotation marks to introduce an *indirect* quotation.
16. **(3)** The verb must be made plural to agree with the plural subject *advantages*.

EXERCISE 3

1. **(4)** *Either-or* constructions must immediately precede parallel elements in a sentence.
2. **(1)**
3. **(4)** See "Lack of Parallel Construction" in COMMON ERRORS IN SENTENCE STRUCTURE.
4. **(5)** The word *as* later in the sentence signals the use of *almost*.
5. **(4)** This is the correct spelling.
6. **(1)**
7. **(5)** This is the correct spelling.
8. **(2)** *It* agrees with its antecedent *each*.
9. **(2)** This is the correct spelling.
10. **(4)** Two distinct ideas should be separated by a period.
11. **(3)** The verb must be made to agree in number with its singular subject (*Whether the coming century will be a period of further tragedy or one of peace and progress*).
12. **(3)** The pronoun must agree in number with its singular antecedent *generation*.
13. **(4)** See "Faulty Modification" in COMMON ERRORS IN SENTENCE STRUCTURE.
14. **(1)**
15. **(4)** The verb must be made to agree in number with the plural subject *many*.
16. **(1)**
17. **(3)** This is the correct spelling.
18. **(3)** Remember that this can be read: "better able to than they ARE...."
19. **(3)** The *not only ... but also* construction must immediately precede parallel elements in a sentence.
20. **(4)** Avoid the conflict between *scarcely* and the negative *nowhere*.

THE SIMULATED TEST

It is a well-known fact that astronauts prepare themselves for space travel by training under conditions that *simulate,* or imitate, the environment of outer space. Astronauts do this in order to ensure success on a real mission. In a similar manner, you increase your chances of passing the official examination by taking a test which simulates the form and content of the real thing. The test which follows is just such a device. It is a simulated version of the "Correctness and Effectiveness of Expression" section of the High School Equivalency Examination.

First, this test has approximately the same number of questions as the official test. Furthermore, the form of the questions, the topics tested, and the proportions allotted to each topic are similar. And finally, the level of difficulty of the questions on the actual test has been maintained here.

Read the directions to the simulated test carefully before you start. Give yourself about two hours to finish. (Experience has shown that approximately two hours is adequate to complete the official examination, although additional time may be permitted.)

An important note: **Do not leave any questions unanswered. On the High School Equivalency Examination, blank answers are marked wrong. Guess rather than leave an answer blank.**

ANSWERS AND EXPLANATIONS APPEAR AT THE END OF THE TEST

DIRECTIONS: (1–88) Each of the following sentences has four underlined sections. Choose the number of the section that is incorrect. Then blacken the space under that number in the answer column. If there are no incorrect sections, blacken the fifth space.

Grammar and Usage

1. 1 2 3 4 5

1. Just between <u>we</u> two, I <u>would like</u> to <u>have seen</u> Mary's face when Tim

       1   2   3

   <u>proposed</u>.

  4

2. 1 2 3 4 5

2. The boys <u>had been standing</u> in the rain for an hour before the box office

          1

   finally <u>opened</u> and they <u>are</u> able <u>to buy</u> tickets.

       2   3   4

3. 1 2 3 4 5

3. Jean and Sid, two friends of <u>ours,</u> <u>were</u> <u>going</u> to the opera last night when

                       1   2   3

   we <u>met</u> them.

    4

4. There <u>were</u> two boys <u>standing</u> in the rain—two boys <u>who</u> we had <u>seen</u>
        1   2   3   4

before.

               4. 1 2 3 4 5

5. The man jumped <u>up</u> and <u>greets</u> <u>us</u> when we <u>entered</u> the room.
                 1   2   3   4

               5. 1 2 3 4 5

6. "I'm not <u>use</u> to the water," <u>said</u> Jane, "and <u>I'd</u> rather <u>stay</u> home anyway."
          1   2   3   4

               6. 1 2 3 4 5

7. Either the <u>foreman</u> or one of his helpers <u>have</u> <u>left</u> his <u>lunch</u> here.
             1   2   3   4

               7. 1 2 3 4 5

8. Mary Sloan, one of the <u>brightest</u> girls in the class, <u>were</u> <u>chosen</u> to <u>represent</u>
                           1   2   3   4

the school in the contest.

               8. 1 2 3 4 5

9. It's a shame <u>there</u> <u>isn't</u> more of us <u>here</u> today.
   1   2   3   4

               9. 1 2 3 4 5

10. <u>Whom</u> did you <u>say</u> <u>is</u> coming to our <u>house</u> this afternoon?
     1   2 3   4

              10. 1 2 3 4 5

11. He said that we <u>were</u> <u>suppose</u> to <u>have been</u> there an hour ago.
    1   2   3   4

              11. 1 2 3 4 5

12. <u>Was</u> it <u>they</u> <u>whom</u> you <u>seen</u> at the game last week?
    1   2   3   4

              12. 1 2 3 4 5

13. When John <u>came</u> home after working, he <u>was</u> so tired that he had to <u>set</u>
            1   2   3

right <u>down</u>.
     4

              13. 1 2 3 4 5

14. There, <u>laying</u> in the corner, <u>were</u> two packages <u>wrapped</u> in red and <u>gold</u>
         1   2   3   4

paper.

              14. 1 2 3 4 5

15. <u>Either</u> John or I <u>were</u> <u>supposed</u> <u>to</u> be there this morning.
    1   2   3   4

              15. 1 2 3 4 5

16. Mr. Jones <u>is</u> the man <u>which</u> <u>told</u> me about <u>your</u> accident.
           1   2   3   4

              16. 1 2 3 4 5

17. Yesterday, <u>they</u> <u>lay</u> <u>their</u> uniforms <u>aside</u> with great regret.
           1 2   3   4

              17. 1 2 3 4 5

18. Shakespeare's <u>sonnets</u>, <u>as well as</u> his plays, <u>is</u> <u>known</u> to readers throughout
               1   2   3 4

the world.

              18. 1 2 3 4 5

19. I am sure you would <u>have loved</u> the play if you <u>would have</u> <u>seen</u> <u>it</u> last
                    1   2   3 4

night.

              19. 1 2 3 4 5

20. 1 2 3 4 5

20. A box of brand new shirts <u>were</u> <u>lying</u> on the floor of the <u>men's</u> clothing
1 2 3
store when we <u>entered</u>.
4

21. 1 2 3 4 5

21. They <u>told</u> us that Texas <u>was</u> in the <u>southern</u> <u>part</u> of the country.
1 2 3 4

22. 1 2 3 4 5

22. Three <u>miles</u> <u>are</u> too far for <u>anyone</u> to <u>walk</u> on a night like this.
1 2 3 4

Sentence Structure

23. 1 2 3 4 5

23. I'll <u>see</u> you in <u>about an</u> <u>hour. When</u> the situation <u>has cleared</u> up a bit.
1 2 3 4

24. 1 2 3 4 5

24. Down the <u>road came</u> an old <u>man. His</u> coat <u>open and</u> <u>his hat</u> tilted to
1 2 3 4
one side.

25. 1 2 3 4 5

25. <u>Although only</u> five new girls <u>have entered</u> our <u>school this</u> <u>year</u>, I haven't
1 2 3 4
gotten to know them all yet.

26. 1 2 3 4 5

26. Although <u>Phil and Joe</u> did their <u>best. The</u> team <u>still lost</u> the city-wide
1 2 3
<u>championship</u>.
4

27. 1 2 3 4 5

27. Sinclair <u>Lewis'</u> books <u>have won</u> great <u>acclaim, almost</u> everyone <u>has read</u>
1 2 3 4
Babbit.

28. 1 2 3 4 5

28. When you are <u>filling out</u> the forms, <u>one should</u> <u>be sure</u> to complete <u>all the</u>
1 2 3 4
blank spaces.

29. 1 2 3 4 5

29. After <u>school</u>, we all ran <u>home quickly</u>—as quickly as <u>we could. And</u>
1 2 3
changed <u>into</u> our old clothes.
4

30. 1 2 3 4 5

30. When I <u>go to</u> New York I want <u>to do some</u> skating, <u>to go</u> to the Statue of
1 2 3
Liberty, and <u>seeing</u> some of the other sights.
4

31. 1 2 3 4 5

31. We waited <u>in line</u> for six hours, <u>however,</u> they were all <u>sold out</u> by the time
1 2 3 4
our turn came.

32. John Thompson was a man everyone liked because of his wit and
   $\underline{}$ 1 $\underline{}$ 2

   generosity. Which were only two of his virtues.
   $\underline{}$ 3 $\underline{}$ 4

   32. 1 2 3 4 5

33. In regard to your question. I really would like to take another day or two
   $\underline{}$ 1 $\underline{}$ 2

   to think it over—a kind of meditation period.
   $\underline{}$ 3 $\underline{}$ 4

   33. 1 2 3 4 5

34. After a vote, the membership should abide by the majority decision. Until
   $\underline{}$ 1 $\underline{}$ 2 $\underline{}$ 3

   such time as they can vote again.
   $\underline{}$ 4

   34. 1 2 3 4 5

Style and Clarity

35. "Why don't you try and do it," said Mary, "I'm sure you can make the
   $\underline{}$ 1 $\underline{}$ 2 $\underline{}$ 3

   grade if you try."
   $\underline{}$ 4

   35. 1 2 3 4 5

36. The boys had done their best, so it was to no avail because they lost the
   $\underline{}$ 1 $\underline{}$ 2 $\underline{}$ 3 $\underline{}$ 4

   game.

   36. 1 2 3 4 5

37. Millions know that cigarette smoking is not good for them, and they
   $\underline{}$ 1 $\underline{}$ 2 $\underline{}$ 3 $\underline{}$ 4

   continue to smoke.

   37. 1 2 3 4 5

38. Mary introduced us to her new boy friend, to whom we had been intro-
   $\underline{}$ 1 $\underline{}$ 2 $\underline{}$ 3

   duced to before.
   $\underline{}$ 4

   38. 1 2 3 4 5

39. On the trip to California by plane, they serve meals at no extra charge
   $\underline{}$ 1 $\underline{}$ 2 $\underline{}$ 3

   to the passenger.
   $\underline{}$ 4

   39. 1 2 3 4 5

40. In my opinion, I think the boys could have done a great deal better if they
   $\underline{}$ 1 $\underline{}$ 2 $\underline{}$ 3

   had tried a little bit harder.
   $\underline{}$ 4

   40. 1 2 3 4 5

41. Coming along the street, I saw my two good friends, Joe and Dave, so I
   $\underline{}$ 1 $\underline{}$ 2

   called out to them.
   $\underline{}$ 3 $\underline{}$ 4

   41. 1 2 3 4 5

42. 1 2 3 4 5

42. We <u>were playing</u> poker <u>with a deck</u> of <u>cards which</u>, in my opinion, <u>I think</u>
          1   2   3   4
had six aces.

43. 1 2 3 4 5

43. The little dog of <u>which</u> Maurice <u>had become</u> quite fond <u>of</u>, seemed to
                  1   2   3
<u>have run</u> away from home.
  4

44. 1 2 3 4 5

44. When <u>you</u> have a problem, <u>a person</u> should always <u>try to</u> find a friend who
        1   2   3
can help <u>you</u>.
     4

45. 1 2 3 4 5

45. In the summer, I enjoy <u>swimming</u>, <u>playing baseball</u>, and <u>just</u> to <u>lie</u> around
               1   2   3   4
doing nothing.

46. 1 2 3 4 5

46. The old man looked <u>so</u> comical <u>as</u> he came out of the door <u>but</u> we just <u>had</u>
                    1   2   3   4
to laugh.

Word Choice

47. 1 2 3 4 5

47. Don't <u>waste</u> time trying to decide <u>who's</u> <u>right</u> and <u>whose</u> wrong in this
       1   2   3   4
matter.

48. 1 2 3 4 5

48. Tom, Janet, and Helen <u>were</u> <u>seen</u> walking <u>besides</u> Rose <u>near</u> the park.
                      1   2   3   4

49. 1 2 3 4 5

49. I tried <u>to</u> borrow a dollar <u>from</u> my brother, but I soon found <u>out</u> that he
      1   2   3
was broke <u>to</u>.
     4

50. 1 2 3 4 5

50. <u>Their</u> story has <u>lead</u> us to believe that <u>there</u> <u>were</u> more than four people
  1   2   3   4
involved.

51. 1 2 3 4 5

51. He <u>led</u> us <u>past</u> a place <u>that</u> seemed to be some kind of <u>desert</u>.
   1   2   3   4

52. 1 2 3 4 5

52. The <u>famous</u> criminal testified <u>that</u> the district attorney was conducting
     1   2
what amounted to a <u>moral</u> <u>persecution</u>.
              3   4

53. We decided to have the pants <u>altered</u>, rather <u>then</u> return <u>them</u> and try <u>to</u>
                                1   2   3   4

get our money back.

54. <u>They're</u> <u>liable</u> to be <u>affected</u> by any change in <u>plans</u>.
     1   2   3   4

55. Now that the disagreement <u>between</u> <u>them</u> has been settled, I think <u>that</u>
                            1   2   3

everything will be <u>alright</u>.
                  4

56. <u>There</u> going to spend <u>the</u> summer <u>vacation</u> in some of the <u>capitals</u> of
    1   2   3   4

Europe.

57. In his <u>speech</u>, the President <u>inferred</u> that the competition <u>among</u> govern-
         1   2   3

ment agencies is <u>affecting</u> the national economy.
                  4

58. The <u>drawer</u> toppled to the <u>floor</u> and <u>lay</u> on <u>it's</u> side.
       1   2   3   4

Capitalization

59. Last <u>Winter</u>, we spent the <u>month</u> of <u>January</u> in <u>Florida</u>.
         1   2   3   4

60. One of the most enjoyable ways to cross <u>the</u> <u>Atlantic</u> <u>Ocean</u> is by <u>ocean</u>
                                     1   2   3   4

liner.

61. There are many people in the <u>city</u> of <u>Boston</u> who have come from <u>European</u>
                          1   2   3

<u>countries</u>.
  4

62. He didn't have a <u>Foreign</u> <u>accent</u>, so it was difficult to believe that he had
  1   2   3

come from <u>Georgia</u>.
         4

63. "I am here," said <u>Inspector</u> <u>Dolan</u>, "<u>To</u> ask a few <u>questions</u>."
                   1   2   3   4

64. My father was a <u>captain</u> in the <u>irish</u> <u>Republican</u> <u>Army</u>.
           1   2   3   4

Punctuation

65. 1 2 3 4 5

65. After a long wait Bob and Jane finally heard their names called out and
        1   2   3
went into the principal's office.
     4

66. 1 2 3 4 5

66. There were three girls living in the apartment; Mary, who had come from
                                                   1
Utah; Jane, from San Francisco; and Pat, a native New Yorker.
     2   3   4

67. 1 2 3 4 5

67. We knew that Uncle George was coming to see us; but we didn't know
                                                  1   2
that he intended to stay for three weeks.
                  3   4

68. 1 2 3 4 5

68. When the bell rang the teacher said, "It's time to begin now," and the
                     1   2   3
children took their seats.
                    4

69. 1 2 3 4 5

69. "But Mother," said Jerry, "that's what I've been trying to tell you all
        1   2   3
along".
     4

70. 1 2 3 4 5

70. Was it F. D. Roosevelt who said, "The only thing we have to fear is fear
                         1   2   3
itself"
     4

71. 1 2 3 4 5

71. Thomas Jefferson who was one of our great presidents, was also a secretary
                  1   2   3   4
of state.

72. 1 2 3 4 5

72. When Christmas Eve finally came, John, Fred, and Mary were really tired.
                                    1   2   3   4

73. 1 2 3 4 5

73. I would like to place an order for the following items, two lampshades, a
               1   2   3
red tablecloth, and a set of steak knives.
              4

74. 1 2 3 4 5

74. Mr. Alexander told us that he had been born on June, 30, 1920.
                       1   2   3   4

75. 1 2 3 4 5

75. Suddenly, we heard a man crying, "Look out"!
           1   2   3   4

76. 1 2 3 4 5

76. Who, in your opinion, was the greatest shortstop, in baseball history?
       1   2   3   4

77. At the end of the period, the only students left in the room were Harry, and
          1   2   3   4

Tom.

                                         77. 1 2 3 4 5

78. During the summer, Dad took us to see: the Empire State Building, the
                        1   2   3
Brooklyn Bridge, and the Radio City Music Hall.
        4

   78. 1 2 3 4 5

79. I entered the office, and the receptionist asked me if I would mind taking a
                      1   2   3
seat in the corner?
              4

   79. 1 2 3 4 5

80. The newspaper, television, and the radio—all these have affected our daily
              1   2   3   4
lives.

   80. 1 2 3 4 5

81. Did you know, that Tom was coming and that he was bringing two friends
              1   2   3
with him?
      4

   81. 1 2 3 4 5

82. Who would have guessed that Sam would take the test, and pass it?
                  1   2   3   4

   82. 1 2 3 4 5

83. Quickly and quietly, the man entered the room, closed the door, and struck
                    1   2   3
a match
    4

   83. 1 2 3 4 5

84. We were glad to see him, and to find out that everything had been going
          1   2   3   4
well.

   84. 1 2 3 4 5

85. Once upon a time, there lived a wealthy man, who had two daughters.
                1   2   3   4

   85. 1 2 3 4 5

86. It had been raining all day; and people were beginning to worry about the
                          1   2   3
concert in the park.
      4

   86. 1 2 3 4 5

87. We have warned them about going swimming so soon after dinner on many
                      1   2
occasions, however, nothing seems to make a difference.
      3   4

   87. 1 2 3 4 5

88. We're not sure that there's enough time if its got to be done by midnight
      1   2   3   4
tonight.

   88. 1 2 3 4 5

Spelling

DIRECTIONS: (89–110) In each of the following groups of words, there may be one misspelled word. In the answer column, blacken the space under the number that corresponds to the number of the misspelled word. If there are no misspellings, blacken the fifth space.

89. (1) atheletics (2) position (3) guarantee (4) thirty

90. (1) playwright (2) precios (3) permanent (4) phrenologist

91. (1) responsible (2) salaries (3) sucessor (4) similar

92. (1) squalor (2) systematic (3) signifecant (4) scrutiny

93. (1) thermometer (2) triumph (3) temperature (4) twins

94. (1) tantalizing (2) undecided (3) unecessary (4) undulate

95. (1) alcohol (2) anticipate (3) aknowledge (4) axle

96. (1) attach (2) amendment (3) allies (4) artifisial

97. (1) attempt (2) apreciation (3) border (4) beaker

98. (1) consuquently (2) crochet (3) conclusively (4) commenced

99. (1) conquer (2) campaign (3) cesse (4) chagrined

100. (1) dissatisfy (2) distributor (3) dyeing (4) digestable

101. (1) despair (2) exhibition (3) extravagant (4) emergency

102. (1) guardian (2) glimpse (3) hoseiry (4) holly

103. (1) indebtedness (2) I'd (3) inasmuch (4) insescent

104. (1) inginuity (2) judgment (3) legitimate (4) lovable

105. (1) larceny (2) lasceration (3) merely (4) misdemeanor

106. (1) museum (2) matrimony (3) mattress (4) massercre

107. (1) nowadays (2) ocassionally (3) odyssey (4) physician

108. (1) principleship (2) portiere (3) possession (4) prisoner

109. (1) postpone (2) possibilities (3) paresite (4) pervade

110. (1) rediculous (2) receipted (3) recommendation (4) rickety

Pronunciation

DIRECTIONS: (111–118) Each of the following groups consists of four words. Each word appears as it is normally spelled, followed by a phonetic spelling of the word (spelled as it is pronounced). In the answer column, blacken the space under the number corresponding to the number of the word that is pronounced (phonetically spelled) incorrectly. If all the words in a group are pronounced correctly, blacken the fifth space.

111. (1) salutation—SAL-u-TA-shun   (3) record—re-KORD
     (2) thoughtful—THAWT-full   (4) minstrel—min-STREL

112. (1) invent—in-VENT   (3) mercury—mer-KE-ree
     (2) million—MIL-yun   (4) mercy—MER-see

113. (1) meditate—MED-i-tat   (3) master—mas-TER
     (2) matron—MA-trun   (4) toaster—TOAST-er

114. (1) lonely—lone-LEE   (3) injection—in-JEK-shun
     (2) divide—di-VID   (4) tension—TEN-shun

115. (1) banker—BANK-er   (3) wrinkle—RINK-l
     (2) confess—kun-FESS   (4) exactly—EGGS-act-lee

116. (1) brunette—broo-NET   (3) banish—BAN-ish
     (2) handy—han-DEE   (4) banquet—BANG-kwet

117. (1) balcony—BAL-ku-nee   (3) arithmetic—a-RITH-me-tik
     (2) articulate—AR-tik-u-LAT   (4) stopping—STOP-ing

118. (1) wonderful—wun-DER-ful   (3) safety—SAF-tee
     (2) amusing—a-MEWS-ing   (4) gallop—GAL-up

Answer columns for 111–118, each with numbers 1 2 3 4 5.

ANSWERS AND EXPLANATIONS: THE SIMULATED TEST

GRAMMAR AND USAGE

1. **(1)** us   *Use the object form of the pronoun after the preposition *between*.
2. **(3)** were   *Use the past tense of the verb when referring to the more recent action of two past actions (the less recent takes the past perfect tense—*had been standing*).
3. **(5)**
4. **(3)** whom   *See Rule 5 under "Pronoun Usage" in USAGE.
5. **(2)** greeted   *Use the past tense when describing an action completed in the past.
6. **(1)** used   *used to* means "accustomed to." The phrase *use to* is never correct.

7. **(2)** has   *Subjects joined by *or* take a verb that agrees in number with the *last* subject. Since the last subject *one* is singular, the verb has to be made singular.

8. **(2)** was   *A singular subject (*Mary Sloan*) must take a singular verb (*was chosen*).

9. **(3)** aren't   *A plural subject (*more*) must take a plural verb (*aren't*).

10. **(1)** who   *See Rule 5 under "Pronoun Usage" in USAGE.

11. **(3)** supposed to   *The phrase *suppose to* is never correct.

12. **(4)** saw   *Use the past tense when describing an action completed in the past. As a past participle, *seen* must be preceded by *have*, *had*, or *has*.

13. **(3)** sit   *Set means "to place" (He *set* the TV in the corner.)

14. **(1)** lying   *Lying is the present participle of *lie*, which means to be situated in a horizontal or low position." *Laying* is the present participle of *lay*, which means "to place in a horizontal or low position." Thus, the difference between the two verbs is the difference between already being in a low position (*lie*) and being *placed* in such a position (*lay*). You *lie* in the sun, **but** you *lay* papers on a desk.

15. **(2)** was   *Subjects joined by *or* take a verb that agrees with the last subject (*I*).

16. **(2)** who   *Use *which* for things, not persons.

17. **(2)** laid   *This sentence calls for the past tense of *lay*.

18. **(3)** are   *The verb must be made plural to agree with the plural subject *sonnets*.

19. **(2)** had seen   *Use the past perfect tense for the earlier of two past actions.

20. **(1)** was   *The verb must agree in number with the singular subject *box*.

21. **(2)** is   *The act of *telling* you a fact can happen in the past, but the *fact* being explained (the location of Texas) should be in the present.

22. **(2)** is   *When a measure of distance is considered as a single unit, it takes a singular verb.

SENTENCE STRUCTURE

23. **(3)** hour, when   *The construction beginning with *When* is a sentence fragment and it must be joined to the independent clause beginning with *I'll*.

24. **(2)** man, his   *The construction beginning with *His* is a sentence fragment, and it must be joined to the independent clause beginning with *Down*.

25. **(5)**

26. **(2)** best, the   *See "Sentence Fragments" in COMMON ERRORS IN SENTENCE STRUCTURE.

27. **(3)** acclaim; almost *or* acclaim. Almost   *Two closely related thoughts can be connected by either using a semicolon or making them into two simple sentences.

28. **(2)** you   *The subject in this independent clause should be made parallel to the subject of the dependent clause (*you*).

29. (3) we could—and   *The dash is used to emphasize an interruption within a sentence.
30. (4) to see   *See "Lack of Parallel Construction" in COMMON ERRORS IN SENTENCE STRUCTURE.
31. (2) six hours; however,   *Use a semicolon to separate two closely related ideas.
32. (3) generosity, which   *See "Sentence Fragments" in COMMON ERRORS IN SENTENCE STRUCTURE.
33. (2) question, I   *Use a comma to separate an introductory phrase from the main part of the sentence.
34. (3) decision until   *See "Sentence Fragments" in COMMON ERRORS IN SENTENCE STRUCTURE.

STYLE AND CLARITY

35. (1) try to   *Use the infinitive after *try*: *try to* tell him, *try to* finish the job, etc.
36. (3) of   *Incorrect usage.
37. (3) but   *Use *but* to contrast the ideas in the two clauses.
38. (4) Omit *to*   *The word *to* has already been used (*to whom*).
39. (2) meals are served   *Whom does *they* refer to?
40. (1) Omit *I think*   *In my opinion* already covers the point.
41. (1) Change to: As I was coming along the street, *or* As they were coming along the street,   *WHO was coming along the street? *I*? or the *friends*? A modifying phrase must *clearly* modify a word in the sentence.
42. (4) Omit *I think*   *The phrase *in my opinion* is sufficient.
43. (3) Omit *of*   *The first *of* in the sentence does the job. The second one is redundant.
44. (2) you   *See "Sentence Shifts" in STYLE AND CLARITY.
45. (4) lying   *The infinitive *to lie* is not consistent (or parallel) with the previous gerunds *swimming* and *playing*. Keep verbs in a series *parallel* to one another.
46. (3) that   *But* is a conjunction used to signal a contrast with what has gone before. There is no contrast being made in this sentence.

WORD CHOICE

47. (4) who's   *Whose* is a possessive pronoun. *Who's* is the contraction of *who is*.
48. (1) Beside   *Beside* means "next to." *Besides* means "in addition to."
49. (4) too   *Too* means "also."
50. (2) led   *Led* is the past participle of *lead*.
51. (5)
52. (1) *notorious* or *infamous*   *A person who is widely known for *good deeds* is considered *famous*.
53. (2) than   *Then* is an adverb indicating *when* something happened.
54. (2) likely   *Liable* means "to be subject to": If you loiter here, you are

liable to arrest. *Likely* refers to probability: It is very *likely* that our plans won't change.

55. (4) all right   *Alright* is not a word.
56. (1) They're   *They're* is the contraction of *they are. There* is an adverb meaning "in or at that place."
57. (2) implied   *Imply* means "to suggest." *Infer* means "to get something from some remark or action": I *inferred* from her smile that she liked me.
58. (4) its   *Its* is the possessive form of the pronoun *it; it's* is the contraction of *it is.*

CAPITALIZATION

59. (1) *w*inter   *The seasons are not capitalized.
60. (3) *O*cean   *Capitalize common nouns that are part of proper nouns: the Brooklyn *B*ridge.
61. (5)
62. (2) *f*oreign   *Capitalize only proper adjectives: *E*nglish, *A*lgerian, etc.
63. (3) *to*   *Capitalize the first word of a quotation *only if it begins a sentence.*
64. (2) *I*rish   *Capitalize proper adjectives: *D*anish, *N*orwegian, etc.

PUNCTUATION

65. (1) wait, Bob   *Use a comma after an introductory phrase.
66. (1) apartment: *Use the colon before a list of items.
67. (1) us, but   *Use a comma before *but* when it separates two complete thoughts.
68. (1) rang, the   *Use a comma after a dependent clause.
69. (4) along."   *Place a period before closing quotation marks.
70. (4) itself"?   *Place the question mark outside the quotation marks when the question mark is *not* part of the quotation.
71. (1) Jefferson, who   *Use a comma to set off an expression that interrupts the smooth flow of the sentence.
72. (5)
73. (2) items: two   *Use a colon to introduce a list of things.
74. (3) Omit the comma   *Don't use a comma between the month and day of a date.
75. (4) out!"   *Place the exclamation mark before the closing quotation marks when the exclamation mark is part of the direct quotation.
76. (3) Omit the comma   *Don't use a comma between a noun and its modifying phrase.
77. (4) Omit the comma   *Don't use a comma to separate *two* nouns joined by *and* or *or.*
78. (2) Omit the colon   *Don't use a colon when a verb introduces a list of items.
79. (4) corner   *Don't use a question mark when the question is an *indirect*

quotation. *Note:* The receptionist asked me, "Would you mind taking a seat in the corner?"

80. (5)
81. (1) Omit the comma   *Don't use a comma to separate the verb from its object.
82. (3) Omit the comma   *Don't use a comma between two short clauses: He slapped him and kicked him.
83. (4) Add a period   *Use a period to end a sentence.
84. (2) Omit the comma   *Don't use a comma between two infinitive phrases (*to see him* and *to find out*) joined by *and*.
85. (2) Omit the comma   *Don't use a comma to separate the antecedent (*man*) from its pronoun (*who*) when the pronoun is *necessary* to an understanding of the antecedent.
86. (1) day, and   *Don't use a semicolon to separate two independent clauses when the two clauses are already separated by *and*.
87. (3) ; however,   *Use a semicolon before *however* when it introduces an independent clause.
88. (4) it's   *It's* is the contraction of *it has*. *Its* is the possessive form of *it*.

SPELLING

89. (1) athletics
90. (2) precious
91. (3) successor
92. (3) significant
93. (5)
94. (3) unnecessary
95. (3) acknowledge
96. (4) artificial
97. (2) appreciation
98. (1) consequently
99. (3) cease
100. (4) digestible
101. (5)
102. (3) hosiery
103. (4) incessant
104. (1) ingenuity
105. (2) laceration
106. (4) massacre
107. (2) occasionally
108. (1) principalship
109. (3) parasite
110. (1) ridiculous

PRONUNCIATION

111. (4) MIN-strel
112. (3) MER-kyer-ee
113. (3) MAS-ter
114. (1) LONE-lee
115. (4) eggs-ACT-lee
116. (2) HAND-ee
117. (2) ar-TIK-u-lat
118. (1) WUN-der-ful